Chambers Crossword Manual

CHAMBERS CROSSWORD MANUAL

A guide for the novice *and* the enthusiast

by

DON MANLEY

Guild Publishing London

W & R Chambers Ltd
43-45 Annandale Street
Edinburgh EH7 4AZ

This edition published 1987 by Book Club
Associates by arrangement with W & R
Chambers Ltd.

Reprinted with corrections 1987

Graphics by Micro Initiatives, Knebworth, Herts, United Kingdom
Typeset by Blackwood Pillans & Wilson Ltd, Edinburgh
Printed in Great Britain by Butler & Tanner Ltd, Frome and London

In loving memory of my father
Chave Manley
1904-1978

Contents

Sources and Acknowledgements

The source of each puzzle is given below along with the copyright holder who gave permission (where appropriate). Every effort has been made to contact all copyright holders, but if there are any omissions we shall be glad to make amends at the earliest opportunity. Some puzzles have been slightly amended/corrected. My own puzzles are asterisked.

Crossword No.	Source	Permission given by
1	New York World	St Louis Post-Dispatch
2	The Crossword Puzzle Book (First series)	Simon & Schuster
3–6	London Evening News*	London Express News and Features
7	Crossword	Crossword Club/ Carroll Mayers
8	Daily Telegraph	The Daily Telegraph
9–15	Specially set for this book*	—
16	Games and Puzzles*	—
17–22	Hamlyn Books of Crosswords*	—
23–27	Specially set for this book*	—
28–29	Games and Puzzles*	—
30	Specially set for this book*	—
31	The Spectator*	The Spectator
32	Crossword*	Crossword Club
33–35	Observer	The Observer
36	The Word Square Puzzle Book	Hamlyn Publishing
37	Observer	The Observer
38	Sunday Companion	—
39–40	Daily Telegraph	The Daily Telegraph
41	Radio Times*	Radio Times
42–43	The Times	The Times/Wm Collins
44	Guardian	The Guardian
45	Observer	The Observer
46	Financial Times	Financial Times
47	Guardian	The Guardian
48–49	Birmingham Evening Mail*	The Birmingham Post & Mail

Introduction

This book is dedicated to the memory of my father, who must take much of the blame for my obsession with crossword puzzles. Chave Manley solved six puzzles a day (two each in the *Daily Mail*, the *Daily Express* and the *Daily Telegraph*) and one a week—usually on a Sunday afternoon—in the *Radio Times*. Until, that is, his son (with elder sister Jean's help) began filling the odd word in the 'small puzzle' of the *Express* and the 'quick crossword' of the *Telegraph*. By my teens I was hooked and was pestering my father to explain how the cryptic puzzles worked. Soon the back page of the school common-room *Times* was being inked in, and not long after I left school I made my crossword setting debut with the *London Evening News*, followed within 18 months by *Radio Times*. Then a few years later a whole new world opened up with the discovery of the *Observer*'s Ximenes and *The Listener*.

Not everyone has a father—or even a close friend—to explain the mysteries of the cryptic crossword, but I know that there are many in the ranks of the would-be solvers. 'You need a twisted mind for crosswords,' they say wryly—or else they denounce crosswords as a 'waste of time' without sounding convincing about it. The fact is that you *do* need to twist your mind to solve any problem, but why not? 'Problem-solving' is very much the fashion at the moment in the school curriculum. And there are, I believe, some real benefits in struggling with a good crossword: mental discipline and an increased vocabulary are two. But the benefits must not be overstated. Crosswords are primarily for fun, but isn't the swimming pool more enjoyable once you can swim?

Curiously, there have been very few books actually *about* crosswords; those that I know of are listed in the bibliography at the back. There is of course an insatiable demand for actual puzzles, and those who want a good selection should not be disappointed by the offerings in this book. My priority, though, has been to tutor the reader in the basic essentials *and* the essentials at the more advanced level. *Chambers 20th Century Dictionary* has long been the basic 'word bible' for the advanced crossword solver, but there has been little written to explain the puzzles for which it is so necessary. I hope I am putting this right.

In this work I deal with the background to the crossword, followed by the basic cryptic puzzle (such as you would find in your daily newspaper), and finally the more advanced puzzle. The ways in which clues are constructed have been described in detail and so too has 'crossword language'; but this is in no sense a complete 'crib' for the lazy solver. My method, with its small tutorial puzzles, is essentially heuristic, and I want to encourage solvers to learn for themselves.

Dr Johnson may not have 'read books through' but my intention is that the complete novice should treat this particular book as a sequential course. Try the tutorial puzzles, and if you cannot finish them look up the answers and learn from the notes before moving on. Then by the time you get to Chapter 12 you should be ready to enjoy a cryptic each day in your daily paper. Many readers may reach that stage and settle there quite happily. To them I say: 'Buy a Chambers and try to stretch yourself a little further. There are further joys for you in store!'

I must thank all those who have made this book possible. Many fellow-setters and their crossword editors have been most generous in allowing me to reproduce their puzzles, and a list appears on pp.ix-x. My family allowed me to escape to the study for hours when domestic duties beckoned. Jonathan Crowther, Les May, Michael Holroyd and Alec Robins have all lent me interesting material; the Bodleian Library enabled me to track down some crosswords of yesteryear. Richard Palmer and Derek Arthur spotted numerous errors in the original script and made many useful suggestions for improvements. Micro Initiatives used the wonders of modern technology to computerise the diagrams and to word-process the MS. Catherine Schwarz of Chambers has been an encouraging and supportive editor. Making crosswords look good is no easy task when so many things can go wrong; I am grateful for the patient expertise shown by Jack Osborne, Production Director of Chambers. I can only hope that our efforts are not in vain. Whatever your current level of attainment I hope you will find something of benefit within these pages.

Don Manley
Oxford 1986

1

The Crossword Emerges

The Victorian age is commonly portrayed in terms of unmitigated gloom; and yet it was also an age of fun and invention, and certainly it was the age of the word puzzle. In 1892 you might have bought *Everybody's Illustrated Book of Puzzles* (selected by a certain Don Lemon) for 6d. That Don of yesteryear offered you 794 puzzles complete with answers, and if we look at a few we shall see hints of what was to come when the crossword emerged in the twentieth century:

No. 6—Anagrams.

For the benefit of very young readers we will explain that making an anagram consists in forming a new word or words from the letters of other words. An illustration is: Cheer sick lands—the anagram for Charles Dickens. We now invite you, with the permission of Good Housekeeping, to an anagrammatical Dickens party, the guests of which are prominent characters in Dickens' writing: Blame Crumple; We debtor to toys; Clever fop I did pad; Pair my ages; His by a linen clock; Toy lily blows; Canny Skyes; Mere Walls; O, feel my corn bed; We kill red vics; Over it wilts; Bug ran by dear.

No. 200.—Double Acrostic.

Two words are here to be found out,
Both you have heard of, I've no doubt;
One is a thing that gives its aid
To ships engaged in peaceful trade.
The other thing is often found
To war's chief weapon closely bound.
These stars replace with letters true,
And both the things will look at you.
In the first letters, downwards read,
Is that by which the vessel's sped;
And in the last, if downwards, spelt,
That which adorns the soldier's belt.

1

1st line— What a bull does, if he can.
2d line— What is the most beauteous span.
3d line— Hog in armor is my third.
4th line—Boy in barracks often heard.
5th line—What the street boys often run.
6th line—What gives light, not like the sun.
7th line—What makes doctors oft despair.
8th line—What is black, with curly hair.
9th line—What is very hard to bear.

```
    *       *       *       *

  *   *   *   *   *   *   *

*   *   *   *   *   *   *   *   *

  *   *   *   *   *   *   *

  *   *   *   *   *   *

  *       *       *       *

* * * * * * * * * * * *

  *       *       *       *

  *       *       *       *
```

The word square was such 'old hat' that it evidently didn't need a diagram to explain it, but just in case you don't know what one looks like, here is the puzzle followed by its answer:

No. 420.—Easy Squares.

(a) 1. Crippled. 2. Hot and dry. 3. A deposit of mineral. 4. Paradise.
(b) 1. An article of food that appears early on the bill of fare. 2. To glance sideways. 3. A Turkish soldier. 4. The plural of an article used in writing.

(a) L A M E	(b) S O U P
A R I D	O G L E
MI N E	U L A N
E D E N	P E N S

Some of the puzzles are even given titles like the one below, but this is not yet the true crossword:

No. 541.—Cross Word Enigma.

My first is in cotton, but not in silk;
My second in coffee, but not in milk;
My third is in wet, but not in dry;
My fourth is in scream, but not in cry;

My fifth is in lark, but not in sparrow;
My sixth is in wide, but not in narrow;
My seventh in pain, but not in sting;
My whole is a flower that blooms in spring.

Anagrams, acrostics and word squares had in fact been going for donkeys' years—from the times of the Greeks, the Romans, the Hebrews and the medieval monks. You may like to know, for example, that Psalm 119 was an acrostic based on the Hebrew alphabet. But the most remarkable word square from ancient times is the 'reversible' one found on a Roman site at Cirencester:

```
R  O  T  A  S
O  P  E  R  A
T  E  N  E  T
A  R  E  P  O
S  A  T  O  R
```

which is Latin for 'The sower Arepo controls the wheels with force' and which can be rearranged in 'crossword' form as:

```
                  A

                  P
                  A
                  T
                  E
                  R
A   P  A  T  E  R  N  O  S  T  E  R   O
                  O
                  S
                  T
                  E
                  R

                  O
```

Could this be an early Christian crossword with A for alpha and O for omega? some have asked.

But enough of ancient history, fascinating though it is. The fact remains that the Victorians (for all their ingenuity) remained 'stuck' at a certain level, and so it was that the crossword *per se* took longer to emerge than Einstein's theory of relativity!

It was in 1913 that a certain Arthur Wynne produced the puzzle below for the *New York World*.

CROSSWORD No. 1

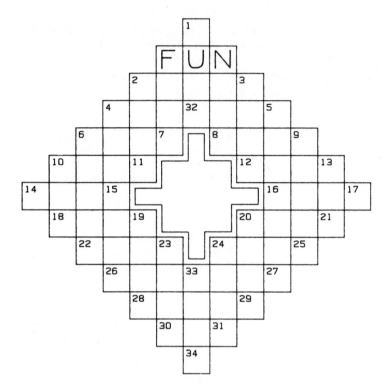

2-3	What bargain hunters enjoy
4-5	A written acknowledgment
6-7	Such and nothing more
10-11	A bird
14-15	Opposed to less
18-19	What this puzzle is
22-23	An animal of prey
26-27	The close of a day
28-29	To elude
30-31	The plural of is
8-9	To cultivate
12-13	A bar of wood or iron
16-17	What artists learn to do
20-21	Fastened
24-25	Found on the seashore
10-18	The fibre of the gomuti palm

6-22	What we all should be
4-26	A day dream
2-11	A talon
19-28	A pigeon
F-7	Part of your head
23-30	A river in Russia
1-32	To govern
33-34	An aromatic plant
N-8	A fist
24-31	To agree with
3-12	Part of a ship
20-29	One
5-27	Exchanging
9-25	To sink [Sunk?] in mud
13-21	A boy

Wynne, an immigrant from Liverpool remained a leading crossword setter for about ten years, and then (sad to say) he faded into obscurity.

It was in the 1920s that crosswords took off. Messrs Simon and Schuster launched an amazingly successful publishing company in America and their *Cross Word Puzzle Book* was published in England by Hodder and Stoughton (a copy of which I purchased second-hand in the 1960s for 6d!). The book begins with a detailed account of how to do a crossword. For the benefit of my one reader who has *never* seen any crossword and the entertainment of the others here is how the book started:

THE CROSS WORD PUZZLE BOOK
FIRST SERIES

Cross word puzzles are a great deal simpler to explain than to solve. And as the quickest and clearest way to explain any game is by demonstration, let us do a typical, if rather easy, example together.

Here is the puzzle:

CROSSWORD No. 2

HORIZONTAL
1 A pasty composition
6 Prefix, meaning new
7 Exist
9 Sixth note of the musical scale
10 A domestic animal
11 Affirmative particle
12 Indefinite article
14 In
15 Fuss
17 Went into

VERTICAL
1 Pacify
2 Indefinite article
3 Large body of water
4 Toward
5 Cooked before a fire
8 Male human being
9 Meadow
13 Short poem
15 Near
16 Alternative

All the puzzles are not the same square shape as this, but all have one thing in common: the black squares among the white make a symmetrical pattern, so that the whole looks like a piece of cross-stitch needlework, as for instance an old-fashioned 'sampler'.

What have we to do?

Each white square represents a single letter. The puzzle is—to find out what letter belongs in each white square. And you determine this by working out the words from the definitions, which you will see beside the puzzle. When you have completed the puzzle correctly you will find that it consists of a number of words *which read both horizontally and vertically*, interlocking round the pattern made by the black squares.

You will notice numbers in many of the white squares, corresponding to numbers in the lists of 'horizontals' and 'verticals'. These show the starting-points of words, sometimes a horizontal word (*e.g.* 6), sometimes a vertical word (*e.g.* 2), sometimes both horizontal and vertical words (*e.g.* 1). Each word starts in the first space to the *right* of a black square if it is a horizontal, and in the first space *below* a black square if it is a vertical. Some words of both kinds of course start on the outside squares, *i.e.*, we imagine a ring of black squares all round the puzzle.

We now know where the words begin. How long are they to be? Each will consist of just as many letters, one letter to a square, as it will take to reach the next black square (or the edge of the puzzle where no black square intervenes) in whichever direction we are going. For example, '1 horizontal' will be 7 letters long, and so will '1 vertical'. But '6 horizontal' will have only 3 letters; '2 vertical' will have only 2 letters; '7 horizontal' will have only 2 letters; and '13 vertical' will have 3: and so on.

Sometimes a letter will come between two blacks in the pattern. In this case it will only be used in making one word, either a horizontal or a vertical one: for instance, the last letter of '3 vertical' or the first of '13 vertical'. But generally a letter has got to fit into two words—one horizontal and one vertical. For instance, the second letter of '6 horizontal' must also be right for the second letter of '3 vertical'.

And then the fun begins.

Now let us work out this puzzle. (It's a very simple one; you won't have such an easy time again, I warn you!). Start with '1 horizontal'.

'A pasty composition'. How many letters? Seven—since there is no black square right the way across the top line. 'A pasty composition' of seven letters? Let us try PLASTER. (Write it in lightly. You'll soon find you need india-rubber at this game.)

Now is this the right word? We can soon find out; for if it is the right word, it has given us some splendid clues for no less than five of our 'verticals' (1-5).

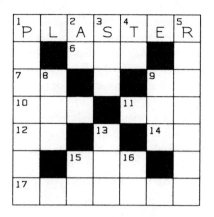

What about 'vertical 1'? 'Pacify', seven letters beginning (apparently) with 'P'. How about PLACATE? Yes, it fits. Write it in lightly. One check is not enough. But we can soon get proof positive that we are on the right track. For it looks as if '2 vertical', which as you see has two letters only (and therefore ought to be easy to guess), ought to begin with 'A'.

What is '2 vertical'? 'Indefinite article'. Obviously AN. It fits, and it begins with 'A'. Write it in. But we can check again. For '3 vertical' presumably begins with 'S'. It has three letters. It is a 'large body of water'. Exultantly, we write in SEA.

And so it goes on. You may like to note incidentally that the practice of putting the number of letters in brackets after a clue had not yet been introduced.

The newspapers also caught on in the 1920s, and by 1930 crosswords were commonplace. Indeed dictionaries were torn apart in libraries, worries were expressed about eyesight, and crosswords were increasingly regarded as an 'unsociable habit' (how little times have changed!). One of the developments in the twenties and thirties was the big-money puzzle with alternative answers. A clue might be offered as follows:

A yellow addition to your food (7)

with a corresponding answer in the diagram printed as

| | U | S | T | A | R | D |

Solvers were invited to use their skill to choose between MUSTARD and CUSTARD and see if they could reach the same set of answers as the panel of experts. Lotteries like this thrived in *Titbits* and other magazines until well after the Second World War, but they have little appeal for the true aficianado, so we can forget them without further mention.

The rest of crossword history belongs largely to the cryptic crossword, but before we look ahead you may like to have a go at four definition-type puzzles below. Crosswords 3, 4, 5 and 6 are all fairly typical English puzzles with simple vocabulary. They are puzzles I made up for the *London Evening News*; and contributors were exhorted to avoid proper nouns, foreign words, abbreviations, two-letter words. Though I have called these definition-type puzzles there is a hint of the cryptic in the clues to 34 across of No.3, 3 down of No.4 and 10 across of No.5. These are examples of the double definition clue which we shall be looking at in Chapter 3.

CROSSWORD No. 3

By D. F. Manley from the *London Evening News*

ACROSS
1 Wicket (5)
5 Fragrance (5)
9 Apartments (5)
10 Impel (4)
12 Fool (5)
13 Not total (7)
15 Quick look (4)
17 Retinue (4)
18 Den (4)
19 Machine (5)
22 Set (3)
23 Obliterate (5)
26 Love intensely (5)
28 Regulations (5)
31 Signify assent (3)
32 Mount (5)
34 Only a fish? (4)
35 Cask (4)
37 Warbled (4)
39 Settle (7)
41 Hair (5)
42 Detect (4)
43 Salute (5)
44 Music time? (5)
45 Tendency (5)

DOWN
1 Odd (8)
2 Fervidly hot (8)
3 Cringe (5)
4 Sharpener (4)
5 Snake (3)
6 Subdued grumbling (6)
7 Song (4)
8 Valley (4)
11 Wins (5)
14 Fitting (3)
16 Trudge (4)
20 Expiate (5)
21 Attention (4)
22 Hold out (4)
24 Annul (8)
25 Widened (8)
27 Poles (4)
29 Supplant (5)
30 Landed property (6)
33 Instigate (3)
34 Show contempt (5)
35 Sun-bathe (4)
36 Run (4)
38 Encourage (4)
40 Personality (3)

CROSSWORD No. 3

CROSSWORD No. 4

By D. F. Manley from the *London Evening News*

ACROSS
1 Prize vessels (4)
4 Posters (8)
10 Ratify (7)
11 Too (4)
12 Opening (8)
15 Spy on (4)
16 Tidier (6)
17 Image (4)
19 Unit of work (3)
20 Tended (6)
22 One of two (6)
26 Epoch (3)
27 Before (3)
28 Grease (6)
31 Traps (6)
33 Shed (3)
34 Speech impediment (4)
35 Fame (6)
38 Passage (4)
39 Temperature line on map (8)
41 Deserve (4)
42 Absconding (7)
43 Costs (8)
44 Cliques (4)

DOWN
1 Instrument (8)
2 Concerning shepherds (8)
3 Eating clubs? (6)
4 Blabbed (6)
5 Cut off (3)
6 Vindicate (6)
7 Cover with wax (4)
8 Disorderly flight (4)
9 Prophet (4)
13 Biting (4)
14 Venerates (7)
18 Clergymen (7)
21 Individuality (3)
23 Particle charged electrically (3)
24 Something transmitted from ancestors (8)
25 Answers (8)
29 Awkward boor (4)
30 Circular frames (6)
31 Tramples (6)
32 Foreigners (6)
35 Fully developed (4)
36 Ceremony (4)
37 Next (4)
40 Small deer (3)

CROSSWORD No. 4

12

CROSSWORD No. 5

By D. F. Manley from the *London Evening News*

ACROSS

1 Little scamps! (4)
3 Swellings (8)
10 A rope for the artist? (7)
11 Employer (4)
14 Came back (8)
15 Lowest point (5)
16 Stupid (5)
17 Apartments (4)
20 Estranged (9)
21 Dance (3)
23 Weights (4)
24 The truth (4)
25 Work unit (3)
26 Shopkeeper(9)
28 Arrive (4)
30 Performers (5)
33 Goods (5)
34 Lengthen (8)
36 Female (4)
37 Simpleton (7)
38 Sideboards (8)
39 Platform (4)

DOWN

1 Flood (8)
2 Depositing as security (8)
3 Room for a drink? (3)
4 Spoke falsely (4)
5 Pecuniary stakes (9)
6 Stupefy (4)
7 Smooth and concise (5)
8 Bird (4)
9 Flank (4)
12 Tars (7)
13 Ascents (5)
18 Grassland (9)
19 Flower-clusters (7)
21 Unbroken view (8)
22 Demands upon energy (8)
24 Pertaining to central point (5)
27 Extra payment (5)
29 Metal (4)
30 Cupola (4)
31 Incites (4)
32 Excitement (4)
35 Printer's measures (3)

CROSSWORD No. 5

CROSSWORD No. 6

By D. F. Manley from the *London Evening News*

ACROSS

1 Stake (4)
4 Refute (8)
10 Revert (5)
11 Material (3)
12 Asterisk (4)
14 Propose (8)
16 Great terror (5)
18 Gourd (5)
19 Put in (6)
21 Cutting instrument (3)
22 Sing (5)
23 Vehicle (3)
25 Way out (4)
27 Labyrinth (4)
28 Place (3)
29 Dig (5)
31 Lettuce (3)
32 Call for repetition (6)
35 Store (5)
38 Sand-hills (5)
39 Engraved design (8)
41 Disencumbers (4)
42 Single (3)
43 Counterfeits (5)
44 University course (8)
45 Pip (4)

DOWN

1 Patronage (8)
2 Send (8)
3 Weird (5)
4 Greyish-brown (3)
5 Metal (4)
6 First (6)
7 Renovate (5)
8 Precious stone (4)
9 Level (4)
13 Sunburn (3)
15 Gem (5)
17 Weep (3)
20 Volumes (5)
21 Minister (5)
23 Enrol as a Saint (8)
24 Retired (8)
26 Heavy gas (5)
29 Evades (6)
30 Conclude (3)
31 Bird (5)
33 Heals (5)
35 Sibilate (4)
34 Colour (3)
36 Particle (4)
37 Abounding (4)
40 Paddle (3)

CROSSWORD No. 6

1		2	3	■	4	5		6	7	8		9
	■	10				■	11			■		
12	13			■	14						15	
16			17	■		■	18					
19				20	■	21			■		■	
	■		■	22				■	23		24	
25	26		■	■		■		■	27			
28			■	29			30	■		■		
■		■	31			■	32	33		34		
35	36			■	37	■	38					
39					40	■	41					
	■	42		■	43				■			
44						■	45					

It is perhaps ironic that the crossword began in America but that the Americans have mostly got stuck with plain puzzles in the same way that the Victorians were stuck with their acrostics etc. Puzzle 7 is a fairly typical American puzzle.

CROSSWORD No. 7

By Amigo from *Crossword*

ACROSS
1 Coarse Algae
5 Mistake
10 Pardon me!
14 Situs
15 Scene
16 Unaspirated
17 Columbus, e g
19 Ionian Sea gulf
20 Unsound
21 Indonesian coin
22 The abomasum
23 Vehemence
25 Oppose
26 Stud
30 Scion
31 Washington State port city
34 Gracefully delicate
36 Sea duck
38 Healthy
39 US Foreign Policy goals: F D Roosevelt congressional message, 1941 (phrase)
42 Chief Babylonian god
43 Film actor and director: _____ Davis
44 Peepshow
45 Stoat
47 Anchor tackle
49 Tableland
50 Hindu mantras
51 Matrons
53 Corrupt
55 Entangle
56 Bruits
61 Baltic Sea gulf
62 Criticize
64 Hebrew month
65 Impassive
66 Gottfried's sister
67 Confined
68 Import
69 Arabian tribesman

DOWN
1 Moslem judge
2 Emerald Isle
3 Minus
4 South American rodent
5 Jewish ceremonial vessels
6 Surface measure
7 Prosopopeia
8 Grimace
9 Merit
10 Visigoth king
11 Previously
12 Grafted: Her.
13 Metheglin
18 Cape Horn native
24 Activists
25 Peeler
26 Immerse
27 Thomas Tryon novel: The _____
28 Calliope
29 Thor's wife
31 Finial
32 Classical dramatic farce
33 Bewildered
35 Nocturnal carnivores
37 Imagine
40 Custom
41 Weir
46 Disclose
48 Bridge hand
51 Italian poet
52 Divot
53 Swathe
54 Assistant
55 Assemble
57 Lawyers' patron saint
58 Vend
59 Irish Gaelic
60 Wound
63 Notes: Mus.

CROSSWORD No. 7

1	2	3	4	■	5	6	7	8	9	■	10	11	12	13
14				■	15					■	16			
17			18							■	19			
20					■	21			■	22				
■	■	■	23		24			■	25				■	■
26	27	28	29	■	30			■	31				32	33
34			35	■	36		37			■	38			
39				40						41				
42			■	43					■	44				
45			46			■	47		48	■	49			
■		50			■	51				52		■	■	■
53	54			■	55			■	56		57	58	59	60
61				■	62		63							
64				■	65				■	66				
67				■	68				■	69				

There is an immediate difference noticeable between this and the *plain* British puzzle: obscure words (including proper nouns), abbreviations and prefixes are all OK. In fact any combination of letters is turned into a clue if possible. Even A CAT would be allowed if given a clue of 'Room to swing_____'!

Before we leave the plain puzzle we ought to mention a type of clue which is neither a straight definition nor a cryptic clue. This example from the *Daily Telegraph* (25.5.67) will suffice:

[1.1] 'Has, having, and in quest to have, _____' (Shakespeare Sonnets) (7)

Did you know that the answer is EXTREME? If you didn't know, you might have worked it out from E-T-E-E.

[1.1] is a *quotation clue* which may perhaps be regarded as a particular type of *general knowledge* or *quiz clue*. Although the cryptic crossword solver will benefit from a good stock of general knowledge (and indeed may enhance general knowledge through solving!), the quiz clue is too much like a straight definition to be ranked as 'cryptic'. Nevertheless there is scope for puzzles containing clues like this:

[1.2] He wrote *Ode to a Grecian Urn* (4,5)

After all, one can fill in JOHN KEATS and feel like a connoisseur of literature! If you appreciate such puzzles, I recommend the weekly General Knowledge crossword in the *Sunday Express*.

2

A Digression on Diagrams

Although the clueless crossword above is very simple we can use it to define certain terms:

* The letters C, T, W and N are in squares that belong to both across and down answers. These are called *checked squares*.
* The letters A, O, E and I belong to only one answer each and these are in *unchecked squares* or *unches*.
* The words CAT, WIN, COW and TEN are of course the *answers*. When you come to solve a more difficult puzzle with its own instructions you may come across a word that denotes the answers as they appear on the diagram. That word is *lights*. Unfortunately this term is also used to refer to individual letters within words (as C,A,T,O,E,W,I,N, here). The particular meaning is usually obvious from the context, but I now avoid using 'lights' wherever possible.
* The central square is a blank and the whole crossword has a *blocked diagram*.

Now look at the puzzle below:

Here the checked squares contain C, T, O, E, W and N, and the unchecked squares contain A, R and I. Letters are kept apart by a bar rather than a block and this is known as a *barred diagram*.

Most crosswords are in fact blocked puzzles, but the most advanced ones are more often barred puzzles - the reasons for this will become clearer later in the book. For the moment look at Crossword 2 on p.5: You can see that there are very few unches and a lot of 'checking'. Crossword 7 on p.17 is even more extreme and has no unches. This means that in theory you could complete the puzzle by solving only one set of clues Across or Down. In practice though you will need to solve from both sets, since a lot of the clues seem to have more than one possible answer.

Here is an early example of the plain, blocked puzzle. In fact it was the first crossword published in the *Daily Telegraph* on 30 July 1925 and you might like to have a go at it.

CROSSWORD No. 8

From the *Daily Telegraph* 1925

ACROSS
1 Author of 'Childe Harold'
5 Author of tales of mystery
8 Will reveal the hidden
13 Incursion
14 Elizabethan sea-rover
16 Lily
17 Succulent plant
18 Useful in haymaking
19 Nap
20 Where cricketers are trained
21 A distinguished order
22 Adverb
23 Chinese coin or weight
25 A seaside pleasure
28 Cut
30 Soothing; product of Gilead
34 A blemish except in a billiard ball
35 Shakespearian character
37 A word from the motto of the Garter
39 A seaside implement
40 Where Sir John Moore died
41 Travellers' haven
42 Selvage
44 Part of a ship
45 First name of famous American author
46 Unadulterated

47 Petition
48 Beverage
53 King of the Amalekites, who came 'delicately'
57 Military abbreviation
59 That is
60 A measure
63 Cromwell's 'Empty bauble'
64 Island home of an ancient civilisation
66 The germ of a building
67 A volcano
68 Guarded by eunuchs
69 Kind
70 Visionaries
71 Applied to anything perfect
72 A people with unalterable laws

DOWN
1 Often 'snatched from the burning'
2 A seat of learning is the key to this
3 Tumult
4 Poems
5 Bears the burden of youth
6 Tree
7 Supplements

CROSSWORD No. 8

1	2	3	4			5	6	7		8	9	10	11	12
13						14			15		16			
17						18					19			
20						21			22		23			
							24							
	25	26	27			28		29		30	31	32	33	
34					35				36		37			38
39				40								41		
42			43		44						45			
	46					47				48				
49					50				51					52
53	54	55	56		57	58		59			60	61	62	
63					64		65				66			
67					68						69			
70						71					72			

9 Transported
10 Air (mus.)
11 An annual festival
12 A fish
14 Fall
15 Greek god of love
24 Mythical founder of a great Empire
25 Country of Europe
26 Not so well
27 Pronoun
28 Indian lemur
29 A district in South London
31 Conjunction
32 River of France
33 Can pick and strike
34 Note of octave
35 First name of famous Highland outlaw

36 Unit
38 An explosive
43 Thank you
45 Exist
49 A king, both first and sixth
50 A German word not used on Armistice night
51 Consider
52 Depressions
54 Bars and is often barred
55 A skin affliction
56 Changed by motorists
58 Rock
59 Also
60 Recess in a church
61 Lump
62 Would apply to the upper atmosphere
65 Before

Was there anything you noticed about the diagram? The symmetry? Yes, of course—the crossword diagram would look the same if it were turned upside down, a feature we will notice in most diagrams. (This particular diagram will also look the same if turned sideways and if reflected in a mirror.) But what else did you notice? What I noticed was that no sooner had I put a few words together than I came to a stop and had to start again. If you look at the diagram carefully, you will see that there are in fact no less than *nine* crosswords all isolated from each other in the one square. This sort of thing wouldn't be too popular with crossword editors today because one of the requirements of a diagram is that all the answers should be *interconnected*. Totally isolated parts won't do! Times change of course and when we look at p.31 of the *Daily Telegraph 50th Anniversary Crossword Book* we see the diagram below (a diagram still used by the *Telegraph* today incidentally).

The clues had become slightly cryptic (as you can see on p.148) and the diagram has a more open look about it, allowing for longer words or even phrases. In each answer we notice that the squares are checked and no words fill themselves in automatically. When you have read Chapter 12 you will realise that even this diagram has its weaknesses, but for the moment let's recognise what an advance it is over the previous one. Now we must look at cryptic clues.

3

Beyond the Simple Definition

The first *Daily Telegraph* puzzle had lots of short words of the type that quickly became hackneyed. The solver of the twenties must soon have realised that poems = ODES, thank you = TA, and before = ERE. Yet even in this puzzle there is a hint of the cryptic in 2 Down: 'A seat of learning is the key to this'. The setter is inviting us to think of Yale University and a Yale lock; and he has offered us something a little more interesting than 'An American University'. Now, as it happens, I don't find this a very sound clue because Yale University can't really be the key to a Yale lock—but the setter's heart was in the right place! The Yale clue has a descendant in the modern puzzle called the *double definition*.

An example of the double definition clue might be this:

[3.1] University name on key (4)

The answer is YALE because it is both a university and the name on certain keys. This may not be a very exciting clue, but it shows a degree of trickery absent from the plain clue. Had we wanted simply to offer two definitions on a plate we might have written 'University, name on key', but the omission of the comma is a legitimate trick and we might just be led astray for an instant to think of some poor Oxbridge undergraduate returning home after midnight unable to enter his college.

Now here are some more examples of double definitions which you might like to try for yourselves:

[3.2] Broken part of body (4)
[3.3] Take notice of Gospel writer (4)
[3.4] Oil film? (6)
[3.5] Tumblers producing spectacles (7)

The answers are BUST, MARK, GREASE (remember Olivia and Travolta?) and GLASSES. In [3.5] the two definitions are joined by a *link word* 'producing'. This link word helps the clue make sense, and it

24

is justified because the word for 'tumblers' produces the word for spectacles. More about link words in due course. Were you misled into thinking of the wrong meaning for tumblers and spectacles? Then you have been the victim of what I call the *misleading context*. The clue has provided you with a phrase about acrobats (the straight-forward reading), but the *cryptic reading* has nothing to do with the circus: you are being given a coded (or cryptic) instruction to find a word with two meanings. Isn't that more interesting than 'Spectacles (7)'?

There is no reason why we should not string together a whole series of definitions as the following clue shows:

[3.6] Left harbour gate bearing drink (4)

The solver may have visions of a sailor sloping off with his rum, but this is simply a series of five definitions for the word PORT.

The double definition can often be entertaining if one of the definitions is fanciful:

[3.7] Sad like the girl who's had a haircut? (10)

Here the answer is DISTRESSED, suggesting that distressed *might* mean having had tresses removed. Because this usage *is* fanciful the clue finishes with a question mark.

Here is an example which yields an idiomatic phrase:

[3.8] Feeling very happy like the mountaineer who's climbed Everest? (2,3,2,3,5)

What phrase suggests that someone is either very happy or at the highest point of Earth? Answer: ON TOP OF THE WORLD.

If it is possible to mislead with two definitions, it may also be possible to baffle the solver with a single cryptic definition. My children are constantly teasing me with jokes like this: What do you take the lid off before putting the bottom on? This joke can be turned into a cryptic definition:

[3.9] You take the lid off it before putting the bottom on! (6)

Because this is an outrageous definition we allow ourselves an exclamation mark to warn the solver. The answer? TOILET!

Here's another one derived from a joke book:

[3.10] Will doing them make a scout or guide dizzy? (4,5)

Answer: GOOD TURNS.

We could perhaps define a SKINHEAD as follows:

[3.11] An extremely distressed youngster (8)

A definition such as

[3.12] A letter demanding money for accommodation (8)

may suggest an unpleasant communication through the post until we remember that it is the LANDLORD (or LANDLADY) who lets out the accommodation. Letter is one of a number of *-er words* often used in a misleading sense; you will meet others.

One or two 'old chestnuts' are deservedly famous and you might like to try them for yourselves:

[3.13] A wicked thing (6)
[3.14] A jammed cylinder (5,4)

If you like this sort of clue, you will find quite a lot in *The Times*, and here is a selection:

[3.15] Keen observer of gulls? (8)
[3.16] Presumably one doesn't run after it? (4,5)
[3.17] He was rushed almost from the start (5)

The danger of the cryptic definition is that it can fall flat or seem too vague. And if the solver understands the sense of the definition straightaway he may feel that he has been denied a truly cryptic clue. (The answers to the last five clues? CANDLE, SWISS ROLL, SWINDLER, LAST TRAIN, and MOSES.) Now you are invited to try a tutorial puzzle based on the ideas in this chapter.

CROSSWORD No. 9

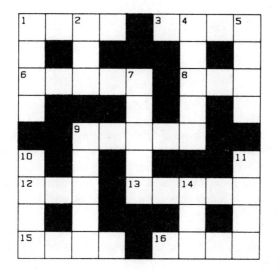

ACROSS

1 This girl is a ruddy gem (4)
3 Roasting device to sputter (4)
6 Marijuana? One notifies the police (5)
8 Six-footer working on a hill? (3)
9 Money for animal (5)
12 Beastly butter! (3)
13 Tree, one of greater age (5)
15 Red wine seen in the marquee perhaps (4)
16 Break? That will do for a card game (4)

DOWN

1 Newspapers showing student pranks (4)
2 Female supporter (3)
4 But it can also play forte! (5)
5 Lyle's partner is displayed in the gallery (4)
7 Parisian flower (5)
9 One like Brutus, upright type (5)
10 Ridge on the guitar may make you worry (4)
11 Holiday accident? (4)
14 Writer of this book, a studious type! (3)

4

The Anagram

In Chapter 3 we saw how fiddling around with definitions could produce an element of 'crypticity' (if I may be allowed to coin a new word). But a word not only has a meaning—or more than one meaning—it has letters too, and these letters offer us many chances for word puzzling. One very popular way of indicating the letters is the anagram, and this is where we begin.

We are forty years on from Don Lemon and his book of puzzles, and we are looking at the *Daily Telegraph* crossword for 21 July 1932. Here is 7 down:

[4.1] 'Meet tired Pa' (anag.)

Although there are millions of ways of arranging these letters, it will only take a minute or two to come up with PREMEDITATE—and of course it may well prove easier if we already know some of the checked letters. Even so, there is something unsatisfactory about this clue because we aren't given any definition of the answer.

However, we must not be unfairly critical when considering clues of over 50 years ago—some progress has been made. The next clue appeared in 1947:

[4.2] Atom plaint farce (anag.) (Yet power can be controlled by it)
      (3,2,10)

This clue offers us an anagram and a definition—and it is a definition that tries to link up with the theme of the letters to be anagrammed (however vaguely!). The answer is ACT OF PARLIAMENT,

An improvement, yes, but this is still a bit on the clumsy side. How much more elegant is this 1973 *Telegraph* clue:

[4.3] Pure ice broken up for the fussy diner (7)

Here again we have an anagram but instead of '(anag.)'we see the phrase 'broken up'. This phrase serves as an *anagram indicator*, telling us that the letters of 'pure ice' must be broken up to yield a word meaning 'fussy diner'. The answer is EPICURE.

In a 1960 puzzle we have this clue:

[4.4] Arrange to send port (6)

Here the anagram indicator is an imperative verb. We are told to arrange 'to send' so that we can get a word meaning 'port'. We've already seen that 'port' has at least five meanings (p.25), and from the way the clue is worded we're probably thinking of an alcoholic Christmas gift. In fact, however, the port is a harbour and the answer is OSTEND.

Anagram indicators are many and varied. Any words or phrases that indicate a jumbling of the letters will do, so long as the clues are grammatical and make sense: 'terribly', 'excited', 'mixed up' are all warnings to the solver that an anagram might be afoot. Now try this:

[4.5] Dicky came top (4)

Doubtless you will think of a clever boy called Richard who beat his classmates in the examination. However, this is another example of the misleading context because the *cryptic reading* of the clue has nothing whatever to do with a successful male. In the cryptic reading 'Dicky' is an adjective (not a proper noun) meaning 'shaky' and 'shaky came' means an anagram of 'came'. The answer therefore is ACME, meaning 'top'. Again we see an example of how a cryptic clue presents you with a series of words which are ostensibly about a particular theme, but you must ignore the theme and concentrate on the words as a series of 'cryptic' instructions to lead you to the answer.

So far we have looked at two types of cryptic clue: the double definition and the anagram. In the following chapters we shall meet other types.

Before that, though, we are going to have a foretaste of 'clueology' to see how the coded instructions are put together. We are going to analyse all the bits and pieces that actually make up a cryptic clue and label them.

We shan't be doing this for *all* our clues, but if we do it now and then, you will see that there is some sense in the cryptic clue, even if it looks like gobbledegook at first sight! Once you appreciate this, you will know what to look for in a clue when you try to solve it—and this is important.

Into clueology we go then, and first of all we take a look again at clue [4.3] and under its different parts you will see that I have placed some letters:

[4.3] Pure ice broken up for the fussy diner (7)

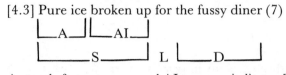

A stands for anagram and AI *anagram indicator*. Together they form S, the *subsidiary indication*. L stands for *linkword* because it links the subsidiary indication to D, which is the *definition* (of EPICURE).

Already in the clues we have seen that A and AI can be the other way round and that L need not always exist, as is the case with:

[4.5] Dicky came top

Now it is also possible for D to come before S, as in this example:

[4.6] Fungus in a crag, I fancy

The linkword 'in' means 'consisting of' so we are being asked to find a fungus which consists of the six letters of 'a crag I' in a fancy way. The answer is AGARIC.

I hope you have enjoyed your introduction to clueology. What you now need to understand is that *the normal modern cryptic clue nearly always consists of a definition and subsidiary indication*. An anagram, however, is only one form of subsidiary indication, and we shall be looking at some others in the following chapters. In the meantime have fun with the puzzles below. Crossword No.10 consists entirely of anagrams, so in each clue look out for the AI, the A and the D (and sometimes the L). Crossword No.11 mixes in anagrams with the sorts of clue covered in Chapter 3. Sooner or later you will have to discern what type of clue the setter has laid before you. At this stage you should be able to recognise a few of the tell-tale signs, but as a help the anagram clues are asterisked.

CROSSWORD No. 10

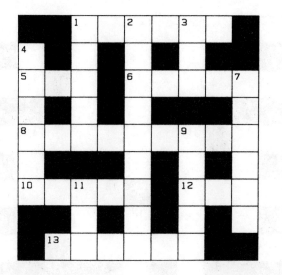

ACROSS

1 Duet is newly adapted (6)
5 Form of art shown by sailor (3)
6 Re tax—it could be more than is necessary (5)
8 Neat prose translated into universal language (9)
10 Aimed to upset TV, press, etc? (5)
12 Weapon destroyed gnu (3)
13 Modern centre, redeveloped (6)

DOWN

1 Use leather to lash unruly prats (5)
2 *Anti*-beer? I may become drunken! (9)
3 Devour tea possibly (3)
4 Master diverted little river (6)
7 Man out, swinging—what's the total? (6)
9 Weird thing in the dark (5)
11 Female creature featured in odd ode (3)

CROSSWORD No. 11

ACROSS

1 How competitors in dead heat cross the line, nevertheless (2,3,4,4)
8 Evangelist? He scores a couple of points (9)
*9 Reg revamped work unit (3)
10 Distinguished airman is a card (3)
*12 A pith gets messy in a food (9)
*14 Hog, sir, is horrible, monstrous (6)
15 Elegance from Warsaw? (6)
17 Gymnast could be thinking the right way (2,3,4)
18 Prosecute a girl (3)
19 I will, badly (3)
*21 Natural manure makes pod spring out (9)
*24 Broken down floor, note, in historic building (5,2,6)

DOWN

*1 A great school! I get excited—I'm very keen on ancient history (13)
2 Money container? (3)
3 The temptress when night approaches? (3)
*4 Rat, say, could deviate off course (6)
*5 More wrath upsets the gardener's friend (9)
*6 Fish die in agony (3)
7 A period when youngsters come to a full stop? (7,6)
*11 Greet funny little bird (5)
12 One who hangs up half a stocking support? (9)
13 Attempts scores in rugby (5)
16 Start to show to advantage (3,3)
20 Vulgar sound of cow (3)
22 In favour of person being paid (3)
*23 Edward makes a bad end (3)

5

More Common Clue Types

Charades, Container and contents, Reversals

In Chapter 4 we saw how the anagram and its indicator could be used as a 'subsidiary indication' to a definition. We now start to look at a few more ways in which a crossword setter can indicate the letters in the answer. For the moment we must leave the history of crosswords behind, and look at some modern examples.

Charades. Have you ever played the game of charades? In Act 1 someone drops the word 'hat' into the conversation; in Act 2 the word 'red' is dropped in; then in Act 3 someone tries to mention the word 'hatred' without your noticing. You have played this parlour game? Well, the charade clue is just like that; you define 'hatred' as 'hat' and 'red' and tell the solver to put the parts together:

[5.1] Headgear on communist evokes intense dislike (6)

CI is a *charade indicator*; the word 'on' is suitable for a down word. The *linkword* L means 'draws out' (i.e. 'provides').

Before we pass on to other examples note how the word 'red' is defined by 'communist'. This is a bit of *crossword jargon* and there are a number of such words that are great favourites with crossword setters. Another favourite is 'ant', which is often defined by 'worker'. You will pick these up as you go along, but some of the more common three-lettered ones appear in Appendix 1.

Now here are some more examples of charades:

[5.2] Man needs essential animal (6)

   (Don)   CI   (key)

   ⌊_____S_____⌋   D

giving don + key = DONKEY. Here is an alternative clue giving the same answer:

[5.3] Stupid person a university lecturer provided with solution (6)

   └──D──┘   (Don)   └──CI──┘ (key)

[5.4] Discharge of lightning on a Lancashire town (6)

Here the 'discharge of lightning' equals 'bolt'; 'on' is simply equal to itself, 'on'; and the Lancashire town town is BOLTON. There is no CI in the clue; the parts just follow on.

[5.5] Dental deposit? Use salt repeatedly (6)

You may use a salt water rinse for that stain on your teeth, but think too much along those lines and you'd be a victim of the 'misleading context'. Think instead of salt as a sailor and use 'tar' repeatedly to get TARTAR.

[5.6] Bridge over loch? That's cunning (8)

This is a down clue and 'arch' (= bridge) is *over* (CI) 'ness' (a loch). Such ARCHNESS from the crossword setter!

[5.7] It's very warm, the Spanish inn (5)

Very warm is 'hot', the Spanish (i.e. *the* in Spanish) is 'el' and an inn is a HOTEL. Again there is no CI. This is a good moment to warn you that you can expect some simple foreign words in subsidiary indications. EL is another bit of crossword jargon. In addition, LE, LA, LES can all be denoted by 'the French'; 'of the French' would be DU; 'the German' is DIE, DER or DAS. We are concentrating on the 'grammar', but we are also picking up some vocabulary.

Container and contents. The charade clue gave us a formula A *plus* B equals C; the container-and-contents clue gives us a new formula A *in* B equals C:

[5.8] Vegetable to stick in the shelter (6)

CCI

Stop thinking about the wilting lettuce and start getting word-conscious! 'To stick' is a definition for 'gum'; the shelter is 'lee'; 'gum' *in* 'lee' gives LEGUME.

[5.9] Finishing with a boxed ear—charming! (9)

CCI

When 'ear' is *boxed* by 'ending' we have ENDEARING. Have you guessed what I mean by CCI? It's the container-and-contents indicator! 'Holds' is a popular CCI and will often tell you what sort of clue you are dealing with:

[5.10] Girl holds information for business programme (6)

'Ada' holds the 'gen' for the word AGENDA.

'Clutching' is another give-away CCI:

[5.11] Members clutching a rota—they insist on proper procedure (9)

'Members' here are 'legs' because we're thinking about members of the body, not MPs in the chamber—a nice piece of crossword jargon in a misleading context. 'A rota' is 'a list' and 'legs' clutching 'a list' becomes LEGALISTS.

Reversals. Turn around the word 'peek' and you get 'keep'. This simple fact can be made the basis for a reversal clue:

[5.12] Have a little look round part of fortification (4)

RI

RI is the reversal indicator, telling us that when 'peek' (= have a little look) is put round (around, backwards) we get KEEP (part of the castle).

For a down clue the reversal word could be said to go *up*, so *up* is another RI as in this example:

[5.13] Bear up: here's a ring (4)

Not 'Cheer up, darling, have a bit of jewellery!', but Pooh (Winnie-the-!) *up* to give HOOP.

Some words are of course palindromes, and so we could have a clue like this:

[5.14] To-and-fro action (4)

Write the word DEED 'to' (forwards) or 'fro' (backwards) and it is the same.

Sometimes the reversed clue can be ambiguous:

[5.15] Expert turned evil (3)

Read this as D, S and the answer is DAB; read it as S, D and it's BAD! (If the setter has offered you __A__ with the first and third letters unchecked, he is no dab and is most certainly very bad!)

You now know about six types of cryptic clue: cryptic definition, multiple meanings, anagrams, charades, container and contents, and reversals. We've still got a long way to go before we've covered all the weaponry at the setter's disposal. Before we go on, however, it's time for you to consolidate what you know; so here's another tutorial puzzle.

CROSSWORD No. 12

(The answer to 14 across is a well-known phrase even though not found in *Chambers 20th Century Dictionary*.)

ACROSS
1 Disease boy has got in fifth month (6)
4 Remarks not heard by fellow players when going around team (6)
8 Plump bird's grumble (6)
9 Cat bothered us more (6)
10 Russian cast? They work on a script (9)
14 Gentry receive guests here making Nanny retreat with rapture (5,8)
16 There's scope in the sultanate for a fervent royalist (9)
20 The curse of an old Egyptian city (6)
21 Repay artist on return (6)
22 American general arranging truces (6)
23 More than one door-keeper rushes around (6)

DOWN
1 Faces shown by simpletons (4)
2 Bring up jemmy, for instance—get the swag (4)
3 Wanted gentleman caught in the act (7)
5 Cost I worked out for philosopher (5)
6 Diana's noble disregard (8)
7 Laid importance on sweets being served up (8)
11 Material dug from pit comes to the surface (5)
12 Coasting aimlessly, uncertain of what to believe (8)
13 'These are corpses' vulgar fellow declares (8)
15 In the belfry they play doubles (7)
17 Death is solemn (5)
18 Revolutionary Dutch cheese produced (4)
19 Does funny poems (4)

CROSSWORD No. 12

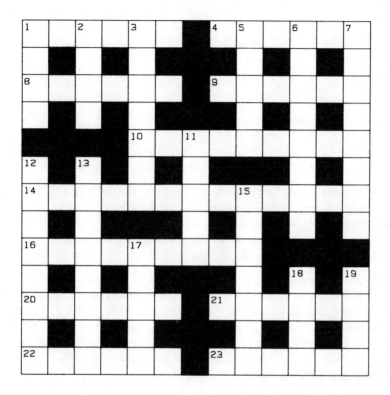

6

Yet More Common Clue Types

Hidden words, Vocal clues, Subtractive clues

By now you can see that there are lots of ways of writing a cryptic clue by using different techniques to indicate the subsidiary indication. In this chapter we inspect some more weapons in the clue-writer's armoury. Note though that the clue-writer is not out to destroy the solver; rather he is out to tease and amuse.

Hidden words. If you take the letters of a sentence in order, a word will often be found lurking. To show what I mean, I invite you to consider the very sentence you have just read. Look at 'order, a word' and you may see ERA spanning the first two words and RAW spanning all three. Look at 'will often' and you can see LOFT. This phenomenon is the basis of the hidden clue and it may best be illustrated by an example:

[6.1] Pub in Pinner (3)

    D   HI   HW

Pub is INN and it may be found *in* Pinner.

The word 'in' is our HI *(hidden indicator!)* and HW is the *hiding word*. The word 'in' is also part of the HI in this clue, where the hidden word spans more than one word (HP = *hiding phrase!*):

[6.2] Rat getting in among children? Egad—exterminate! (8)

    D ⌊____HI____⌋ ⌊_____HP_____⌋

Another common HI is 'some':

[6.3] Some overenthusiastic kissing—one draws blood (4)

This is nothing whatever to do with a romantic love scene. Some (i.e. 'part of') overenthusiastic kissing is TICK, a bloodsucker (defined by 'one draws blood').

Vocal clues depend on how the answer sounds when it is spoken. There are two sub-categories.

The *pun clue* relies on the fact that some words sound like others, e.g. PAIR and PEAR, HEIR and AIR. They are *homophones*, to use the technical jargon. Here is a pun clue:

[6.4] Feature of Scotland where there was a vicar we hear (4)

The two words 'we hear' form a very common pun indicator (PI!). Where was there a vicar? Bray of course, and it's 'Bray' that we hear when we get the answer which is a feature of Scotland—BRAE.

Can you find the PI in the following clue?

[6.5] Post for a man it's said (4)

It is the phrase 'it's said'. A man (= male) is *said* but the definition refers to 'post', which we also call MAIL. One more:

[6.6] Shakespeare in speech? It should be precluded (6)

Shakespeare is the 'Bard'. What sounds like 'Bard'? BARRED, meaning 'precluded'. (Would you have spotted the PI?)

The *accent* clue relies on oddities of speech. Such a clue could also be regarded as a special type of two-definition clue. Here are some examples:

[6.7]   Animal is warmer according to 'Arry (5)
[6.8]   Correct, but in a refaned way? Scold angrily (4)
[6.9]   A f-fellow somewhere in Jordan (5)
[6.10] Bird gettin' dressed for ceremony (5)
[6.11] Not thin and thuffering from a complaint? (5)

In [6.7] 'Arry is an 'aitch-dropping cockney' who talks about things being 'otter (hence OTTER). In [6.8] our awfully 'nace' person is never 'right' but 'rate', which prompts us to RATE him. [6.9] is a combination of an accent clue with a simple charade. Our unfortunate stutterer is unable to talk about 'a man'; instead he refers to 'a m-man' (AMMAN is Jordan's capital). In [6.10] 'robing' without the final 'g' leads to a bird (ROBIN) and in [6.11] our lisping (or 'lithping') friend is 'sick' (THICK!).

Subtractive clues. In several of our clue types we have been involved in adding words to other words or putting words into other words. In a charade, for example, the formula has been

$$A + B = C$$

Well, equally we can use the idea that

$$B = C - A$$

In the 'average daily cryptic' the most common way of subtracting is by removing a head or a tail and the indicator is usually fairly obvious. Thus:

[6.12] Mama, topless, is something else! (5)

Concentrate on the words please, reader, not the misleading pornography! Mama is mother. Remove the 'top' letter and we get OTHER. 'Topless' is a give-away 'beheading indicator': 'headless' is another. (The suggestion of 'top' means that this clue would probably be suitable for a *down* word, rather than an across one, by the way.)

Here's a clue involving truncation at the other end:

[6.13] Endlessly talk about the field event (6)

Nothing to do with David Vine boring the pants off us ('Remember, he needs 173 metres for the bronze and that is a *big* throw!'). Concentrate on the words, please. When 'discuss' is presented 'endlessly' it becomes DISCUS. 'Endlessly' and 'endless' are give-aways for this type of clue.

If words can lose their first and last letters, they can also lose their hearts:

[6.14] Get the better of the heartless monster (4)

The monster is a 'beast'—remove the heart ('a') to give BEST, a verb meaning 'to get the better of'.

In a *very* sophisticated puzzle you might come across:

[6.15] University lecturer is   an ass   ignoring the solution (3)

    └───D───┘ L (Donkey) └─SI─┘   (key)

'Donkey' minus 'key' = DON (SI = subtraction indicator) or even:

[6.16] Arousing affection, having had ear removed, dying (6)

    (Endearing)   └─SI(i)─┘ (ear) └─SI(ii)─┘ └─D─┘

Answer: ENDING

On that gruesome note we are ending this chapter, but not before you attempt another tutorial exercise.

CROSSWORD No. 13

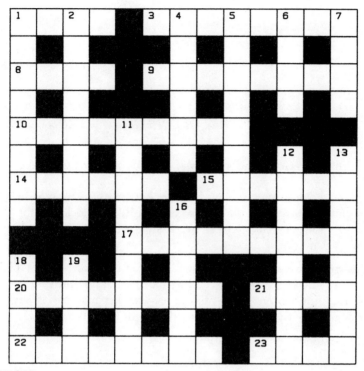

ACROSS

1 Animal sounding like an organ (4)
3 Philosophers? They can't thwim! (8)
8 Title held by certain American (4)
9 Vine-crop is exceptional in particular district (8)
10 Nun's dirge played for parting (9)
14 Looked only briefly—decapitated —killed with a spear? (6)
15 Terrible 'arvest—get desperately hungry (6)
17 A cake before the social function is more than enough (9)
20 Repertory company gets up musical repeats (8)
21 Side of blade useful for cutting 'awthorn barrier? (4)
22 Drunk one coming to entrance? Seek help from the law (8)
23 Requests jobs not using the head (4)

DOWN

1 Sincerely pious outside the home (8)
2 Booze inside worker—one to bring something up! (8)
4 Drug cut short a courageous girl (6)
5 Worked out a route and gave it out (9)
6 Wilderness shelters this eagle (4)
7 Left-wing Tories upset, in a sweat (4)
11 Exhilarating tale given twists (9)
12 See grand exploding bombs (8)
13 Young hares? Permits needed for catching at all times (8)
16 Treasure stored? Not completely, that's most certain (6)
18 Said of country life—it must put aside the past (4)
19 Heartless Jack, who couldn't eat everything, expectorated (4)

7

Non-word Elements in Subsidiary Indications

Abbreviations and symbols, Numbers, Bits and pieces

Over the past four chapters we have looked at all the main clue types, but so far we have used whole words as building-blocks for the clues. We can, however, use letters or clusters of letters as we shall see below.

Abbreviations and symbols. Consider the word PRATTLED. This may suggest 'p + rattled', but can the setter indicate 'p' in a subsidiary indication? The answer is yes, because 'p' is short for 'piano' or 'quietly', so a charade clue might read as follows:

[7.1] Gossiped quietly   in a fluster   (8)

In the world of crosswords there are a vast number of common abbreviations, and you will find a fair number in Appendix 1. This list is by no means exhaustive though, and one of the joys of learning how to solve is in coming to recognise the language of abbreviations and symbols.

In the clues that follow we can introduce only a small number in various types of clue.

[7.2] Miss West embraces novice man

Answer: MALE—'Mae' embraces 'L' (= learner, novice).

[7.3] Good man, a sailor lying on bed, wounded (7)

A good man is a saint (St.); a sailor on this occasion is an AB (on other occasions he's a tar or something else!). Put it all together (in a down clue) to give STABBED.

[7.4] Bob has to study for the exam—buzz off! (5)

A bob is a shilling (= s); 's' + 'cram' = SCRAM!

[7.5] Slant in Conservative policy (7)

A simple charade: 'in' + 'C' + 'line' = INCLINE.

[7.6] Poet edited religious education book (6)

This is a bit trickier. Religious education = RE and an (edited) anagram of RE book is BROOKE.

Asking the solver to form an abbreviation which is then incorporated into an anagram is regarded as fair only where the abbreviation is obvious. Even so it is a technique better left to the more advanced cryptics. On fairness and advanced puzzles, more anon!

Numbers. In 'crossword land' we still use Roman numbers when convenient. Thus I = 1, V = 5, X = 10, L = 50, C = 100, D = 500 and M = 1000, with of course the possibility of combinations. Thus:

[7.7] 100, very old and shut in (5)

And glad to get the Queen's telegram ? Forget it! 'C' is a hundred; very old becomes 'aged'. Answer: CAGED.

[7.8] Amiss gets 50 less than ex-Aussie opener (4)

With apologies to those who detest cricket: the answer is AWRY ('L' less than 'Lawry').

Numbers may be combined with the abbreviations:

[7.9] About 50 inhabiting beautiful Devon village (8)

gives 'C' (= about, an abbreviation which will become familiar) + 'L' in (inhabiting) 'lovely'. Hence CLOVELLY.

'Love' and 'duck' are useful speaking terms for zero which is regarded as the shape of O. Thus:

[7.10] The lady's love is a very brave man (4)

Answer: 'her' + 'O' gives HERO.

[7.11] Cricket ground where there's a duck, 5 and a 50 (4)

Answer 'O' + 'V' + 'aL' = OVAL.

Bits and pieces. In this chapter we've seen two ways in which the crossword setter can get rid of odd letters. There remains a third, very important way. A letter can be defined by the position it occupies in another word. A few examples will suffice to illustrate this:

More on Crossword Terminology

The 'cross word puzzle' has become the 'crossword' puzzle or plain 'crossword'. But what about the 'realm' of crosswords and the people who participate in it? Could we agree on 'crosswording' and 'crossworders'? Maybe, but neither of these words has found a regular place in the dictionaries.

A word that came into vogue in the 1970s was 'cruciverbalism' (from the Latin *crux, crucis,* a cross, and *verbum,* a word). This would mean 'the realm of crosswords', and a 'cruciverbalist' would be someone interested in crosswords. From there we could also presumably deduce the adjective 'cruciverbalistic'. None of these words has yet gained entry into the dictionaries, though they do seem useful however much critics may describe them as 'pretentious'.

'Cruciverbalists' are of course in two categories: those who make up the crosswords and those who solve them. The latter are clearly 'solvers', but what about the former? The word 'compiler' has been much used, but it suggests that puzzle construction only involves *collecting* the material together and underplays the aspect of creativity. What about 'composer'? This is quite good, but would be viewed by some as too grandiose. *The Listener* calls its crossword contributors 'setters', since anyone making up a crossword is 'setting' a puzzle for the solver. 'Setter' therefore is the ideal word.

[7.12] Look at bee for example round end of cowslip (7)

The words 'end of' will tell us that we want the last letter in the word that follows, i.e. 'p'. Put insect around 'p' to get INSPECT.

[7.13] Craftsman is good initially—then not working so hard (7)

'Initially' is a tell-tale word and 'good initially' gives 'g'. When the craftsman is not working so hard he is 'lazier'. Answer: GLAZIER.

'Finally' is also a tell-tale word:

[7.14] Climbing plant with flower finally providing fruit (4)

'Climbing plant' is 'pea'; 'flower finally' is 'r' ('r' being the last letter of 'flower'). Answer: PEAR.

[7.15] Head of school, many years a wise man (4)

'Head of school' is 's'; add 'age' to get the answer: SAGE.
     Initial letters can often be put together in a charade, as follows:

[7.16] Leaders of firm are terribly obese (3)

Take the three leaders (leading letters) to get FAT. (Alternatively final letters may be joined together, but this is much less common.)
     Now try this one:

[7.17] A bit of trouble with relation's reproach (5)

A bit should always mean the first letter—this is a convention which has become a useful rule. So add 't' to 'aunt' and get TAUNT. There's one other thing to notice about this clue. The apostrophe-plus-s combination denotes a possessive to give the clue sense, but means 'is' when we're thinking about the construction of the clue ('t' with 'aunt' *is* TAUNT).
     Though a bit, a head and an end always have single letters a 'heart' may have one letter or more:

[7.18] Chap with heart of steel, bit of a lion? (4)

The heart of steel is 'e'; add it on to 'man' and you have MANE.

[7.19] Stupid fool in middle of road, beginning to fluster (3)

The beginning to the word 'fluster' is 'f' and the middle of the word 'road' is 'oa', giving OAF.
     Half-words can be useful to the crossword setter:

[7.20] Famous performer is semi-naked (8)
'Semi-starkers' is STAR.

     Now it's time for another tutorial puzzle where you will meet some new 'bits and pieces'.

CROSSWORD No. 14

ACROSS

1 Loud oriental celebration (5)
4 Start to tamper with gun—it's only a toy (6)
9 Girl about ten may receive radio waves (7)
10 Agents bringing food aboard (5)
11 Unusual combination of gunners and engineers (4)
13 One drawing southern vessel, *The Queen* (8)
14 Doctor, endless pain is something monstrous (6)
17 Be a chap like George and start to slay monsters (6)
19 To make one's way takes a very long time in these corridors (8)
21 Five—the age for a girl (4)
25 Make a song about the West—jazz? (5)
26 Grass pots are falling to bits (7)
27 Don't have all the lemonade sister! Leave off! (6)
28 Happening that's not odd at the end of August (5)

DOWN

1 Learner in the amusement park shows instinctive skill (5)
2 Performer is a hundred—over the hill (5)
3 Look after what would now be about 4p! (4)
5 Badge labelled 'First Prize'. It's specially presented to steer (7)
6 Fifty trapped in conflicts—ways of escape needed (7)
7 Makes certain unfavourable judgements, the head having left (8)
8 Note 500 pairs perhaps on Noah's boat (4)
12 Tune is first class? Right! (3)
13 Star in revolutionary students union (3)
14 Deprived of top position (given drugs to capture record) (7)
15 Attacks a ship about to travel (7)
16 Fruit, very large, seen around the open country (7)
17 Public transport almost broken down (3)
18 Salt submerged in Antarctica (3)
20 Former prime minister in the garden (4)
22 Mountain-top home—Jane's taken around one (5)
23 Sailor not at home, abroad (5)
24 Some chap serving in part of church (4)

CROSSWORD No. 14

8

The Orchestration of Subsidiary Parts

Complex clues, Linking clues together

You now should be able to solve the following clues, recognising a different type of subsidiary indication in each one:

(a) [8.1] Put up with a rude person (4)
(b) [8.2] Goose's mate ruined garden (6)
(c) [8.3] The French shelter is hidden (6)
(d) [8.4] Fast and quiet in sudden attack (5)
(e) [8.5] Show contempt perhaps—gratuities sent back (4)
(f) [8.6] Sea-eagle in her nest (4)
(g) [8.7] Despatched perfume we hear (4)
(h) [8.8] Senior is more daring, losing head (4)

The clue types are:

(a) TWO DEFINITIONS   (answer: *bear*)
(b) ANAGRAM   (answer: *gander*)
(c) CHARADE   (answer: *latent*)
(d) CONTAINER AND CONTENTS   (answer: *rapid*)
(e) REVERSAL   (answer: *spit*)
(f) HIDDEN   (answer: *erne*)
(g) VOCAL   (answer: *sent*)
(h) SUBTRACTIVE   (answer: *older*)

Complex clues. Each of the eight clues above could be described as a *simple* cryptic clue (however hard it is to solve!). A *complex* cryptic clue, on the other hand, includes some combination of more than one technique. Here is a random selection (keyed by the letters above):

(b,c) [8.9] Trails along with legs collapsing after wearisome task (8)

An anagram of 'legs' is 'gles'. Add it to 'drag' and we get DRAGGLES. If you like you can add the S/D notation to see how the clue works, but it's about time you understood the shorthand way that setters use to explain a solution. In this case the solution note would read (drag + anag.). Other notes will be explained as we go along.

(c,h) [8.10] The man has almost finished paved area around a plant (7)

Here the charade incorporates a subsidiary component which has been clued 'subtractively'. The man is 'he'; an 'almost finished paved area' is 'pati' (not quite a patio!) and around is 'c'. The answer is therefore HEPATIC (a liverwort). The note would read (he + pati(o) + c).

(c,d) [8.11] You get dry around bottom of tongue with an American disease (7)

You get 'TT' around 'e' ('bottom' because it is a down clue) with 'an' plus 'us': (e in TT + an + US) gives TETANUS.

(b,d) [8.12] Secular lot are somehow besieging politician (8)

Here we have an abbreviation inside an anagram (MP in anag.) gives TEMPORAL. Alternatively we could have an anagram inside something else:

(b,d) [8.13] Palatable fruit nasty lice will get into (8)

Here 'nasty lice' = 'elic', and so (anag. in date) gives us DELICATE.

(b,c,d) [8.14] Sweetmeat—kitchenware contains small amount, cool possibly (5,9)

'Plate' contains 'inch' plus an anagram of cool, 'ocol': (inch + anag. in plate) gives PLAIN CHOCOLATE. In this clue we have the formula A contains BC, with both B and C placed inside A. However it is quite possible for A contains BC to mean 'A contains B, then add C' as in this example:

(b,c,d) [8.15] Mathematician worries terribly about Northern fisherman (6,8)

A strange bringing together of concerns? No matter—put an anagram of 'worries' around N, then add 'angler': (N in anag. + angler) gives SENIOR WRANGLER, Cambridge's best maths graduate. You, the solver, would have to sort out whether to put the fisherman inside the anagram or outside. This sort of ambiguity adds a distinct spice to a crossword clue.

(b,c,e) [8.16] Signified dire need after doctor returned (6)

Signified means OMENED and the clue works like this: (MO, rev. + anag.).

(e,f) [8.17] Fairy coming back in dire pantomime (4)

Here we have to look for a word hidden in reverse, and it isn't too hard to spot PERI (hidden, rev.).

(b,h) [8.13] Bread in short supply—unusually scanty (4)

Take (anag. of brea(d)), i.e. an unusual presentation of a short rendering of 'bread', and you get BARE.

(d,e) [8.19] Chaps turned up in the American agency—it should be entertaining (6)

Our note would read (men, rev. in CIA) and the answer is CINEMA.

(c,d,e) [8.20] Women's Libber swallows man up, one man who'd fight (9)

Poor chap! The man is Dan (he could be Les or anybody else, but he isn't). When one (1) is added on and (Miss) Greer does her swallowing, the answer is GRENADIER. Our note would read (Dan, rev. + 1 in (Germaine) Greer). We add the bracketed Germaine, because Ms Greer won't be found in the dictionary.

Clearly we could find yet other combinations of our eight clue techniques, and you can expect to meet others not given here. Deciphering a complex clue is one of the joys of crossword solving.

Linking clues together. In most daily puzzles each clue is separate and independent. The solver has to manage (say) 28 or 32 clues and any linking occurs in the checking of the letters. Sometimes though a setter will attempt to find connections between *clues*. For example, successive clues may be linked together by three dots to suggest a common theme:

[8.21] Now for the give away . . . (7)
[8.22] . . . from me, perhaps, a Spaniard with gold (5)

The answer to the first clue is PRESENT, a simple two-meanings clue—which we would explain in the notes as (2 mngs). Who does a present come from? Answer: a DONOR (don + or). You may not *yet* have learnt that gold = or (the heraldic colour) or possibly Au (the chemical symbol), but I can't tell you everything at once!

Answers may spread across several words at different sites in the puzzle. This was a clue I used in the *Birmingham Evening Mail* (starting at 9 across):

[8.23] 9, 5 down, 1 across, 25 down, 27 across, 22 across. Claim of our paper—exceptional deal, this fine blend reveals many great things (2,3,3,7,7,4,2,3,8).

Three Amazing Stories

The Times did not decide until 1930 to include a daily crossword, and when the go-ahead was given there was no one readily to hand to produce the puzzle. Robert Bell of *The Observer* was approached (he was producing the Everyman puzzle) and he delegated the task to his 28-year-old son Adrian. Adrian had never *solved* a puzzle before, let alone set one! He had ten days to learn and continued setting for over 40 years. Bell's identity was kept secret until a BBC interview in 1970.

One of the early *Daily Telegraph* setters was L. S. Dawe. In 1944 he was visited by members of MI5 who pointed to six suspicious words in his recent puzzles: MULBERRY, NEPTUNE, OMAHA, OVERLORD, PLUTO and UTAH. These words just happened to be code-words for the impending D-Day. Dawe was fortunately able to show MI5 how his crosswords were constructed, thereby convincing them of his innocence.

The Guinness Book of Records tells the story of a lady in Fiji who completed a *Times* crossword in May 1966. What's amazing about that? The puzzle was published on 4th April 1932 and she had been working on it for 34 years!

An anagram of the last eight words gives the catchline on the front page: BY FAR THE LARGEST EVENING SALE IN THE MIDLANDS.

Sometimes there will be cross-referencing between clues all linked by a common theme. Thus, 30 across and 9 down could be linked as follows and the solver may be (mildly) misled into treating 9 as a number in its own right rather than a clue reference:

[8.24] 30. Looked after 9 somehow (6)
[8.25] 9. Separate revolutionary students in rising (6)

9 gives the answer SUNDER (red NUS, rev.) which can somehow give NURSED (anag.), the answer to 30.

This is a simple example. In some puzzles the cross-references can cover half the clues.

It's time for another tutorial. This time you have a complete 15 × 15 with a few complex clues thrown in.

CROSSWORD No. 15

ACROSS

1 Band possibly took horses we hear—route going around city? (4,4)
5 Soul manifest in tipsy cheering (6)
9 Terrible collapse with love deserting—I'm in the operating theatre (7)
10 Fellows in the wrong causing anguish (7)
11 Bit of excitement with a glass of beer he had in frolic? A risky venture (4,2,3,4)
13 Mad artist's characteristics (6)
14 Lessons from the school chaplain? A source of help (8)
16 'Ostel allowed unlimited tea and food (8)
18 Smooth ambassador endlessly getting round (6)
21 Novel with Indian going to America? (5,3,5)
23 Conflict and bombast—what's the justification? (7)
24 Cunning one is turning singer (7)
25 Garden tool has some little worth when brought back (6)
26 Quietly abode—was in the chair (8)

DOWN

1 Concerning the answer you need determination (10)
2 Falls once more upset artist (7)
3 Hate made rip go wild in fit of passion—one should have to make amends (6,3,6)
4 Silver allows metal ornaments to be produced (6)
6 After meal a person gets lively making attempt to do something novel (6,4,5)
7 The scrutineer was a twister in the sixties (7)
8 'Enrietta, a painter (4)
10 Propositions from the session just over half way through (6)
12 Part of watch that isn't new (not seen in digital variety!) (6,4)
15 Start of storm—and oak perhaps will come down on top of the thoroughfare (6)
17 Order to forbid some who grab men turning up (7)
19 A long time before Edward got 'airy'? (7)
20 Examiner of films possibly upset crones (6)
22 Marbles must be given up—prepare for exam (4)

Additional Challenge

Take the word PALE and see if you can use each of the clue types listed on p.48 to write a clue for it. The reverse clue can be a reverse charade *(e, c)*. For good measure, try two charades and a reverse hidden. Then compare your list with mine on p.66.

CROSSWORD No.15

9

The '& Lit.' Clue

Take a good look at this clue:

[9.1] I'm one involved with cost (9)

Can you solve it? Where is the definition? Well, it reads like one, doesn't it? In that case where's the subsidiary indication? Perhaps it's an anagram of 'I'm one' all mixed up ('involved') with 'cost'—which *would* give nine letters. But if that's the case, where's the definition? Let's pursue the anagram line. Keep juggling and you'll see ECONOMIST. Now read the clue again and you'll see that the whole clue is *also* a definition. If we use our S/D notation we can analyse the clue thus:

I'm one involved with cost (9)

A clue like this is known to crossworders as an '& lit.', and this particular clue would be given the solution note (anag. '& lit.'). What this means is that the clue offers us an anagram *and* a literal definition all in one. The '& lit.' clue has a special sort of appeal all its own. Before we consider some other examples let's look at a clue which is *not* an '& lit.':

[9.2] Mint perhaps in gel? It can be refreshing (7)

The answer is SHERBET: (herb in set, v.).

The letter v. denotes 'verb', by the way. Now the statement inherent in the clue *may be literally true* when you eat a glacier mint, but that does *not* make the clue an '& lit.' because the part up to the question-mark is S and the remainder D. *Only* clues when the S and the D are together are true '& lits.'. What about the following clue, then?

[9.3] Denomination spreading abroad 'Christ doeth much'? (9,6)

The last three words may be spread abroad and we see that they are an anagram of METHODIST CHURCH. The first two words are clearly a definition and yet the whole clue also gives a definition—an 'enhanced' definition, in fact. We could analyse the clue as follows:

Denomination spreading abroad 'Christ doeth much' (9,6)

where D^e stands for 'enhanced definition'. Since in this clue D^e and S overlap for much of the clue I will term this a 'semi & lit.' rather than a true '& lit.'. It can be turned into a true '& lit.' though:

[9.3] It spreads abroad 'Christ doeth much' (9,6)

In this case I prefer the '& lit.' version to the 'semi & lit.', but the 'semi & lit.' is a legitimate type of clue which may be preferred, especially if the '& lit.' definition is deemed too vague (more on this later). Now we have seen what an '& lit.' is and what it is not. We have also seen that there is a sort of halfway-house between a normal clue and the '& lit.' which we have called a 'semi & lit.'.

Now let's continue the chapter looking at some more 'pure' '& lits.':

[9.4] Leaders of various individual congregations (alternatively rectors sometimes) (6)

Take the first letter (leaders) to give VICARS. This is not (anag. '& lit.') but (first letters '& lit.'). A very easy clue, this—not just because it is easy to pick out all the initial letters, but because the definition sense is completely obvious. This is a danger with the '& lit.' clue—it can sometimes look like a childishly simple definition rather than a cryptic clue.

Another danger with the '& lit.' clue is that the intended definition sense can be too vague. Here is an extreme example:

[9.5] Andrew could become this (6)

This is a very bad attempt at an anag. '& lit.' to give WARDEN. Little Andy could become a bus conductor or a brain surgeon (or even a crossword setter!). The definition is somewhat remote, to say the least! But the clue becomes perfectly respectable (even if uninspired) when we stop trying to be too clever and put in a definition:

[9.6] Andrew could become a guard (6)

In the last page or two we have started to criticise clues, and there will be more of this to come in the next chapter. Before we get to that, however, let's have a look at some better '& lits.' using different clue types. Then it will be time for you to do a little more work:

[9.7] Part of it 'it an iceberg (7)

Answer, TITANIC (hidden '& lit.').

[9.8] This language would be strange for Senor (5)

This semi anag. '& lit.' gives NORSE.

[9.9] One may be found in church (8)

(I in MINSTER '& lit.') gives MINISTER.

[9.10] The reverse of a divine fellow? (3)

DOG is the reverse of a god in more ways than one, so this is (rev. '& lit.').

You'll find a few '& lits.' in the puzzle that follows.

CROSSWORD No. 16

Games and Puzzles Competition winner by D. F. Manley, June 1977

ACROSS

1 Rooms on view in publishing house favoured by crossword fans (8)
5 Difficulty can be severe, going around centre of maze (6)
9 There's mud—it's a messy sports ground (7)
10 Spiteful woman's dad was primarily a stooge (7)
11 Reptile upsetting a girl a lot (9)
12 Low in generosity to some extent, being in debt (5)
13 Two-faced crook who would spoil his ballot paper? (6-7)
16 True leader of rectors always to be found at the close? (5,8)
20 Something for ploughing an allotment? (5)
21 Disturbances due to unruly brute in horse race (9)
23 Resentment from someone ineffective having gone mad (7)
24 Girl, East European, is dance's centre of attraction (7)
25 Wine can make you reticent about sin (6)
26 Vague notions from learner in fashionable Cambridge college (8)

DOWN

1 Wise man taking vehicle around Bath perhaps (6)
2 I went ahead after girl helped (7)
3 Uses the telephone at that place in the pub—gets through finally? (6,2,3,4)

CROSSWORD No.16

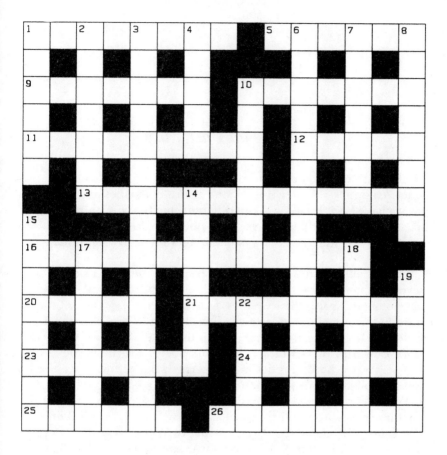

4 Set up a watch maybe—or relax (5)

6 Moon or a star? Ryle would get excited, being this (10,5)

7 Adult w-works vigorously—tries for new job? (7)

8 Imposing old ladies arrange bets (8)

10 Boat specified by Conservative pundit (7)

14 Offer no resistance, confess, having told fibs at first (3,4)

15 Editor, one turning up surrounded by journalists, takes the chair (8)

17 Dreadfully enraged nobleman (7)

18 Fierce character embracing love is a soldier (7)

19 Estimate the worth of a female twit? (6)

22 Tiny chap broadcasting, an Athenian (5)

10

More on Fair Play

In the last chapter we found ourselves criticising particular '& lit.' clues. And now we are going to look critically at clues in general. So far we have been learning about different clue types. This is all rather like learning about parts of speech—nouns, verbs, adjectives and so on. Now we must consider something rather like grammar and syntax.

First of all, another historical diversion. We left the history six or seven chapters ago with the advent of the cryptic clue and its gradual development from the twenties and thirties. Is is now time to introduce three famous names. The first is Torquemada of the *Observer*. He is the setter credited with the advent of the cryptic clue. Born Edward Powys Mather, he dominated the scene in the thirties so far as extra hard cryptics are concerned, but at times his puzzles were unsolvable. We shall return to Torquemada later.

While Torquemada was teasing the *Observer*'s readers in the thirties another crossword setter was exploring new crossword possibilities in *The Listener*. Prebendary A. F. Ritchie of Wells Cathedral took the pseudonym Afrit (an Arabian demon), and he too on occasion was able to produce puzzles that attracted *no* correct entries! But Afrit was a pioneer, and when after the Second World War he turned his attention to the theory of crosswords he laid the foundation on which Ximenes was to build so successfully.

Torquemada died in 1939 and his eventual successor was Derrick Somerset Macnutt, a classics master 'of the old school' who took the name Ximenes (another inquisitor). We shall meet Ximenes and his successor Azed in Chapter 16. Afrit and Ximenes can be regarded as the 'lawmakers', the codifiers who brought order and discipline to a pastime that might otherwise have got out of hand. Inasmuch as many papers and magazines still 'break the rules' Afrit and Ximenes have not entirely succeeded. Indeed there are some crossword setters who positively delight in being non-Ximenean (unorthodox) against those who are Ximenean (orthodox). Your writer is firmly in the Ximenean camp.

Afrit's book of *Armchair Crosswords* was published in 1949. In a preface Ximenes commended Afrit thus: 'The crossword world may be trivial, but like greater worlds it needs standards, and Afrit is the man to set them.' The next few pages contain an Introduction by Afrit which mentions *The Book of the Crossword*, an 'exhaustive treatise' which 'has not been written'. In his section on clues we discover Afrit's Injunction, appropriately culled from Alice (how appropriate indeed when Lewis Carroll was such a marvellous forerunner of the modern crossword setter!). This is what Afrit says:

> We must expect the composer to play tricks, but we shall insist that he play fair. *The Book of the Crossword* lays this injunction upon him: 'You need not mean what you say, but you must say what you mean.' This is a superior way of saying that he can't have it both ways. He may attempt to mislead by employing a form of words which can be taken in more than one way, and it is your fault if you take it the wrong way, *but it is his fault if you can't logically take it the right way.* The solver, for his part, is enjoined to read the clues in an anti-Pickwickian sense. This also requires explanation. To take a remark in a Pickwickian sense is not to take it literally; therefore, to read a clue in an anti- Pickwickian sense is to close the mind to the acquired metaphorical meaning of the words and to concentrate upon their bald literal significance. If you do so, you may find you are being presented with an anagram of the solution, or that the solution is 'hidden' in the clue, or a bit of jugglery with its component parts is being done.

In other words: the solver who follows the structure of a clue literally should expect to discover a grammatical set of coded instructions leading to the answer.

A crossword clue is rather like a mathematical sum. The symbolism must be fair to lead the solver to the correct answer. The concept of fairness was further developed by Ximenes through his clue-writing competitions in the *Observer* and his book *Ximenes on the Art of the Crossword*. In fact the post-1949 developments now make many of Afrit's own clues in *Armchair Crosswords* look suspect! We shall follow in Ximenes' footsteps by looking at unfair clues and comparing them with fairer equivalents. Here we go.

[10.1] Small pebbles—English (7)

This is supposed to give an anagram of English, namely SHINGLE, but the clue is a breach of Afrit's Injunction because the clue-writer has omitted an anagram indicator. This is a case of the *unindicated anagram*. The clue may be rendered 'sound' by the addition of a suitable indicator:

[10.2] Small pebbles—possibly English (7)

might do, though 'possibly' is weak—and, incidentally, most Ximeneans would find 'perhaps' too weak. The clue might be better as:

[10.3] Broken English pebbles on the beach (7)

By no means a great clue, but a sound one, and this is important. Indeed it is particularly important for the novice setter who, like an overkeen young fast bowler, may be included to lose 'line and length'.

Here is a clue which may look all right at first sight, but which a Ximenean would regard as a no-ball:

[10.4] English mixture on the beach (7)

Two things are wrong here. First we have an *unsatisfactory noun as anagram indicator*. There is no grammatical or syntactical justification to suggest that 'English mixture' can mean 'mixture of English'. In contrast, 'gin cocktail' which *means* 'a mixed gin' could be used to indicate 'ing'. Similarly 'train crash' would be acceptable as a subsidiary indicator for RIANT (an example given by Ximenes himself). Secondly 'on the beach' is an *unsatisfactory definition*. An adverbial phrase (which this is) cannot be used to define a noun. Here is [10.4] rewritten:

[10.5] Mixture of English pebbles on the beach (7)

A clue such as the one following should cause the umpire to have a word with the bowler's captain!

[10.6] Small pebbles possibly coming from the country (7)

This sort of structure has often been referred to as a *clue to a clue* and this particular example is an *indirect anagram*. The solver is expected to equate 'coming from the country' with 'English' and *then* work out an anagram. He may get *the* right answer from the definition and the checked letters but to deduce 'English' and then work out an anagram is too much, because there are simply so many alternatives to English: Turkish and bucolic are just two! And of course any letters already in the diagram cannot easily be fed into the working out of the subsidiary indication. However, some would find the following clue quite defensible:

[10.7] Concerning what diet might become, it's seasonal (5)

Written by your author for the *Radio Times* this clue was meant to suggest TIDAL (i.e. of tide, which is an anagram of diet). Since 'diet' can only become two different words ('tide' and 'edit'), *perhaps* the clue may be deemed fair. [10.7] may perhaps be termed an *indirect definition*.

Here is another one sanctioned by *The Times:*

[10.8] Country with its capital in Czechoslovakia (6)

The capital concealed in Czechoslovakia is 'Oslo', so the answer is NORWAY. Hmm! Better though an indirect definition than none at all:

[10.9] What English could produce (7)

The answer is again supposed to be SHINGLE, but we have no indication of the definition—an *undefined answer*! Even worse would be the *indirect, undefined answer* in a case like this:

[10.10] What English could produce (6)

where the setter intends the answer to be GRAVEL! The inexperienced clue-writer might argue thus: ' "English" could produce "shingle", and "gravel" means "shingle". What's wrong with that?' Let me tell my hypothetical friend! (1) There is no definition in the clue and (2) the subsidiary indication leads not to the answer but to a clue to the answer. All *very* unsatisfactory!

Sometimes a clue-writer will provide an *inaccurate definition*. One way of doing this is by *false generalisation*. A couple of examples will suffice to illustrate this:

[10.11] Month in East for the saint (9)

clearly gives Augustine (August + in + E), but now look at this clue:

[10.12] Dreadful stain produced by Augustine (5)

The intended answer is clearly SAINT, but this won't do because while 'saint' can define a particular saint (i.e. Augustine), 'Augustine' cannot define 'saint'. Because the saint (who produced this mysterious stain!) might have been Matthew, Mark, Luke or John we must qualify 'Augustine'. Three common ways of doing this are:

[10.13] Dreadful stain produced by Augustine? (5)
[10.14] Dreadful stain produced by Augustine maybe (5)
[10.15] Dreadful stain produced by Augustine perhaps (5)

Another way of providing an inaccurate definition is by indicating an *incorrect part of speech:*

[10.16] What's hidden by Fred afterwards? He must be stupid! (4)

The S part of this clue is straightforward. The answer is DAFT. But what about the last few words? They suggest a definition that is a noun rather than an adjective—say TWIT or FOOL. A clue-writer will often want to 'dress up' his clue to make sense but won't know how to tie in the D with the S. In difficulty he adds extra words ('He must be'), then tries to convince himself that the clue is really quite good by sticking an *unnecessary exclamation mark* at the end (an additional fault in itself). When you think about it, clue [10.16] is indeed daft. If we must stick with this idea, though, and we want to produce a sound clue we could try this version:

[10.17] What Fred afterwards conceals is stupid (4)

Clue [10.16] is evidence of another affliction suffered by the inexperienced, the *redundant word syndrome*. The following clue is supposed to give the answer DORSET:

[10.18] Strode out to where Hardy lived (6)

The trouble is that 'to' fulfils no syntactical function in the clue. It is not a legitimate link word between the S and D parts denoting equivalence (such as 'for' or 'in'); it is merely there to make the whole clue read better. A better version is:

[10.19] Strode out where Hardy lived (6)

Before we leave the subject of redundant words, let's take a fresh look at two clues from an earlier chapter:

[7.3] Good man, a sailor lying on bed, wounded (7)

The answer, remember, is STABBED (St. + AB + bed). Isn't the 'a' redundant? In a sense it is, but by a long-standing convention we may allow ourselves to introduce the indefinite or definite article when defining a noun.

[7.4] Bob has to study for the exam—buzz off! (5)

SCRAM consists of S + cram, and here we have defined cram by '*to* study' in the way that a dictionary might. In fact the 'to' in the infinitive could be deemed redundant, but convention allows us to use it.

Here is another wide delivery from our overkeen and wayward fast bowler:

[10.20] Sykes is found in the United States of America (4)

This hidden clue to ERIC can't justify all those extra words where our comedian *isn't* lurking, so let's make it snappier:

[10.21] Sykes is found in America (4)

If a crossword setter can put too many words in his clue he can also put in too few:

[10.22] Fred in a bad way? A mate is required (6)

An anagram of 'Fred in' suggests itself fairly quickly: FRIEND which means mate. But look carefully. The word 'in' is doing *double duty* as part of the phrase to be anagrammed *and* the anagram indicator. The clue should really read 'Fred in in a bad way'—it is 'Fred in' that is 'in a bad way', not just Fred. What about the right-hand side of the clue. After all I have said about redundant words, wouldn't 'mate' suffice. Yes—but the extra words can be justified syntactically. The solver is telling you 'You require a word meaning mate,' so the extra words do fulfil a function as a legitimate instruction to the solver. If we want to rewrite the clue soundly let's try this version:

[10.23] Fred in muddle. A mate is required (6)

At first sight this may look like another example of double duty: 'Fred in' in (a) muddle. Or it may look as though we have an unsatisfactory noun as the anagram indicator (see [10.4] above on p.60). But this clue *can* be justified: 'muddle' is an *acceptable intransitive verb:* the words 'Fred in' muddle, i.e. 'potter about', to produce the answer.

Contrast [10.23] with this:

[10.24] Fred in difficulty—a mate is required (6)

A clue-writer might try to argue that 'in' is *not* doing double duty. The clue is meant to suggest that there is difficulty with the words 'Fred in'. This is not Mr Macmillan's 'little local' difficulty but a 'Fred in' difficulty. A true Ximenean will regard this as stretching the language too far: the clue suffers from the same fault as [10.4].

Here is another way in which an anagram could be improperly indicated:

[10.25] The East has lad striking a bargain (4)

The word 'striking' is the anagram indicator and we are supposedly asked to form an anagram from E and lad to give DEAL. The word 'has' is quite unfairly misleading however. It is true that East is somehow 'involved' with lad in the anagram, but 'has' is grammatically misleading.

It's easy to make the clue sound:

[10.26] Eastern lad striking a bargain (4)

and

[10.27] Lad involved with Eastern bargain (4)

are both possible.

In [10.26] we have treated 'has' as a redundant word; in [10.27] we have integrated the anagram letters with the anagram indicator in a syntactically accurate way.

The unsatisfactory anagram indicator is a particular example of what we might call *word abuse* (for want of a better phrase). Types of word abuse are best illustrated by individual examples:

[10.28] An accomplishment indeed to be beaten (8)

This is supposed to give FEAT in DEED = DEFEATED. Ximeneans say that 'indeed' in a clue does not equal 'in deed' (two separate words). Not all setters agree (alas).

Here are two clues with similar difficulties:

[10.29] Peruse in Gateshead—or somewhere in Berkshire (7)

The intended answer is READING (read in g) but Gateshead = G is taking too great a liberty with the language say Ximeneans (even if G is head of the word 'gate').

[10.30] The cold season now in Bury (5)

This is supposed to suggest INTER (winter with no W). The Ximeneans rightly assert that 'now' cannot equal 'no W' in a clue. Notice too that Bury has a capital B which it shouldn't really have. The *false capital* is a very minor offence (if it is an offence at all), but see how we can overcome the difficulty and the 'now' problem by putting Bury at the beginning of the clue:

[10.31] Bury in the cold season, no hint of warmth (5)

The cold season (winter) with no hint of warmth (w) gives INTER.

The same convention applies to 'hint' and words of that type as applies to 'bit' (see p.44). It should indicate *only* the first letter. Similarly with the tail. Ximenes has an amusing example of an unsound clue where this is not so:

[10.32] There's a horse in the stable with a lion's tail (8)

The answer is STALLION (stall + (l)ion), but as Ximenes says, 'why should a lion have a tail three times as long as the rest of him?'

Middles must be precisely middles, too, says Ximenes, so this would not pass muster:

[10.33] Active learner at heart of Universe (4)

The supposed answer is LIVE (L + (Un)ive(rse)) but the *heart* of UNIVERSE is 've' or even 'iver', *not* 'ive'.

The next example is perhaps the most oft-quoted of all clues adjudged unsound by Ximenes:

[10.34] I am in the plot, that's clear (5)

The intended answer is PLAIN ('i' in 'plan'), but 'I' is the letter, not the pronoun! To overcome the deliberate ambiguity we can change the form of the verb and of course we can change 'I' to 'One'. Here are just some of the ways by which [10.34] can be rendered sound:

[10.35]

$$
\left\{ \begin{array}{c} \text{I} \\ \text{One} \end{array} \right\}
\left\{ \begin{array}{l} \text{will be} \\ \text{must be} \\ \text{can be seen} \\ \text{should be} \end{array} \right\}
\quad \text{in the plot, that's clear (5)}
$$

Curiously enough, though Ximeneans do *not* allow the word 'I' to assume a personal status, a word or cluster of words can develop human characteristics:

[10.36] Rescue reviled drunk (7)

The word 'reviled' is 'drunk', i.e. in a disorderly condition, giving the answer DELIVER. Notice how 'reviled' is an adjective in the meaning reading of the clue and 'drunk' is a noun—but in the actual cryptic reading these parts of speech are reversed. This is a nice example of Afrit's Injunction.

One very common error is that of the *wrong direction*. Consider this clue for example:

[10.37] Dull poet coming back (4)

This is all right for an *across* clue but *not* for a *down* clue. The letters of 'bard' are 'reversed' to form the answer DRAB, but they should go back in an across word and up in a down word. So a better version for a down clue would be:

[10.38] Dull poet turned up (4)

If for some reason a crossword setter had a brilliant clue involving 'up' (and 'back' would not do), he could change the diagram by making all the across words 'down' and down words across. A drastic measure, but one which your author has resorted to a few times.

NINE CLUES FOR PALE
(see Challenge on p.52)

(a) Whitish stake of wood.

(b) Leap frantically looking ill?

(c) Soft drink wanting in colour (p + ale).
Friend needs a bit of expertise to make part of fence (pal + e).

(d) Albert in Physical Education is not looking well, maybe (Al in PE).

(e, c) Eastern circuit goes around wooden post ((E + lap), rev).

(f) Sup ales—partly making you lose colour? (pale, verb).

(g) Bill coming out of palace looking ashen (palace minus a/c, a/c = account, bill).

(h, c) Wooden post in hotel apparently rejected (rejected = sent back).

In some crosswords you will find almost any Roman numeral defined by 'many' (L possibly, C, D and M certainly). Thus:

[10.39] Many aged suffering from hypothermia? (4)

Here 'many' is supposed to suggest C (= 100); C + old = COLD. But by what criterion is a hundred equal to 'many'? Ximenes certainly didn't like this practice, and I don't think he would have liked this clue either:

[10.40] Note ancient brave (4)

Here you are presumably invited to take cognisance of a revered figure by his tepee, and B + old = BOLD. But a note could be A, B, C, D, E, F or G (not to mention DO, RE, MI, FA, SO, LA, TI with all their variant spellings!). If notes are plentiful, so too are directions:

[10.41] Direction to have a meal—get a chair (4)

It's quite easy (S + eat = SEAT), but there are lots of directions if you box the compass from N, NE round to NW! I haven't got a name for what is wrong with these last three clues. Shall we call it the *many/ note/direction syndrome*?

Finally we must say a few words on punctuation. You will already have noticed how the D and S parts of a clue can be juxtaposed without any punctuation (as in [10.36] above). The Ximenean convention is to allow the omission of punctuation but not to allow inaccurate punctuation. This would amount to word abuse. The presentation of 'Gateshead' for 'gate's head' could be deemed an example of this, but there are other dreadful possibilities usually reserved for the more difficult cryptics with the words 'Punctuation may be misleading' in the preamble.

Watch out for this sort of thing:

[10.42] Stage love-in—Shakespeare setting initially? (6)

'Stage' is the definition for BOARDS (O in bard + s). The addition of the hyphen and the dash undoubtedly helps to make sense of a sequence of the six words, but this constitutes a case of *unfair punctuation* in breach of Afrit's Injunction. The clue must be recast to make it sound.

I have dwelt on the matter of fair play at some length, because the crossword solver who aspires to become a crossword setter often gets into great difficulty in creating a sound clue. If you should ever attempt clue-writing for yourself, I hope this chapter will point you in the right direction. Now try the tutorial puzzle, where I *hope* all the clues are sound!

CROSSWORD No. 17

By Duck from *The Hamlyn Books of Crosswords*

ACROSS

1 V.I.P.s (big ones usually) with lots of money (4)
3 Pointed remarks about commotion in the West Indies (8)
9 Idle talk about someone at tea-party (7)
11 Remove muck from vessel—bend over into it (5,2)
12 Item of clothing left on far side of wood (5)
13 Creature's taken in by deception —they offer a chance for easy money (9)
14 Simply erase deal—it's all wrong —I'll keep quiet about it (2,4,3,6)
16 Notice in certain gardens offering a caution to would-be drug-takers? (4,3,3,5)
19 Rumour that could make a V.I.P. green (9)
21 Tidy hospital somewhere in Wales (5)
23 Dismissed actors one's ejected from society (7)
24 Arrange quantity of medicine—horrible sip must be swallowed (7)
25 Character in middle of Colditz escaping, causing deception (8)
26 One of 13 perhaps attending a Greek character (4)

DOWN

1 'Gregorian' kisses? (5)
2 Hard work—try for the most part to get help (7)
4 A quiet unending stream—and a suitable time to appreciate it? (5)
5 Projecting features making it hard for one to say 14 across? (4,5)
6 See in seedling strange things that could move you (6,7)
7 Boy we hear gets laid up—one with shadowy face? (7)
8 Record is accompanied by poems giving separate interesting incidents (8)
10 Tell lone chap 'e must mix, find a way to communicate (9,4)
14 Compensate state of gloominess bringing in a barrel (4,4)
15 A loud film never finishing—Edward is terribly distressed (9)
17 Dean, etc. will have become ordained (7)
18 Writer offering anecdotes to the French? (7)
20 The Spanish gentleman—Griffiths?! (5)
22 A hysterical laugher whose laugh conceals deep longing (5)

CROSSWORD No.17

11

Crossword Lingo and Tips for Solvers

Definitions, Anagram indicators, Other indicators, Some 'give-away' words

We have now covered all the main clue types that you can expect to meet in a 'daily cryptic' crossword. Much of our attention has been focused on the 'grammar' of crossword clues. In this chapter we are going to focus briefly on vocabulary. When faced with the series of words in a clue you need to know what to look for. You will ask yourself lots of questions: Are these words the definition? Is the setter telling us to put one word inside another? What does 'about' mean here? The comma comes here, but is this where the definition and subsidiary indication are divided? Why has the setter used a question mark here? And so on.

Definitions. For the most part we have concentrated on subsidiary indications and taken the definition for granted. Take the word CAPTAIN. A dictionary definition begins thus: 'a head or chief officer: the commander of a troop of horse, a company of infantry, a ship, or a portion of a ship's company.' In providing a definition for a cryptic clue we can either (i) provide a *straight definition:*

[11.1] Commander with army in awful panic (7)

(TA in anag.)

or (ii) provide a *cryptic description* (based here on a cricket captain's function):

[11.2] 'Pa, I cant! That's wrong!' he may declare (7)

(ptai in can with the misleading context of George Washington?)

or (iii) provide a *definition by example:*

[11.3] Cook? Starts to prepare the added ingredients to be put into container (7)

(ptai in can with another misleading context—think of Captain Cook).

[11.3] shows us how the crossword setter's lingo often relies on *double meanings*. Vocabulary may be specially selected to mislead—but only within the framework of Afrit's Injunction!

Anagram indicators. It is not long before a crossword solver learns to recognise anagram indicators. There are hundreds of words at a crossword setter's disposal: 'strange', 'unusual', 'terrible' are common adjectives; also used are the corresponding adverbs ('strangely' etc.). A setter may refer to 'a mixture of' something or talk about something being 'cooked' or 'ruined'. And so on. But beware of 'upset' which can indicate reversal in a down word.

'Upset' is indeed an ambiguous word as the following examples show:

[11.4] Light at night has upset these rodents (4)

Answer: RATS (star, rev.).

[11.5] Rats upset Russian emperor (4)

Answer: TSAR (anag.).

'Around' and *'about'* are likewise ambiguous—even more so in fact. Consider these clues with 'about':

[11.6] Banter about a fibber (4)

Answer: LIAR (rev. of rail).

[11.7] The manner shown by chaps about one (4)

Answer: MIEN (1 in men).

[11.8] Fastening device about source of light (5)

Answer: CLAMP (c + lamp).

[11.9] About to get single girl, being lax (6)

Answer: REMISS (re + miss).

In these four examples we see how the word 'about' can indicate two types of clue or be part of a subsidiary indication.

'In'. This too can be a troublesome little word, which the solver must learn to interpret:

[11.10] Girl found in cloisters (4)

Answer: LOIS (hidden).

[11.11] Mean not to go in the river (6)

Answer: DENOTE (not in Dee).

[11.12] Setter let loose in thoroughfare (6)

Answer: STREET (anag.) with 'in' simply acting as a link word between the subsidiary indication and the definition.

Other indicators. You now know that 'we hear' means a pun and you will spot reversal indicators such as 'returning' and 'coming back' quite easily. Something 'getting' something might suggest a charade and something 'outside' something could suggest a container-and-contents clue. Recognising the indicators, like everything else, comes with practice.

Some 'give-away' words for short subsidiary components. Attempt a daily cryptic and you will enter a world preoccupied with directions (north = N, etc.), numbers (hundred C, etc.), and a more-than-usual interest in the French (LA, LE, LES). American soldiers may have gone home after the War, but the good old GI still appears in the back pages of our papers. Indeed there is something of a military preoccupation with gunners (RA), engineers (RE), volunteers (TA) and so on. Crosswords may be square, but they often have sex-appeal (IT or SA) which may please a sailor (AB or TAR usually). A worker is regarded as less than human (ANT), but great consideration is shown to the doctor (DR, GP, MB, MD, MO—a health centre practice where you don't know which one you will get). 'Political' neutrality is achieved with a fair balance between left (L) and right (R), though the Conservative (C) party has more seats in the grid than Labour (LAB) which still lags behind the Liberal (L) party.

If you want a longer vocabulary, look at Appendix 1. The bibliography (Appendix 2) also includes crossword dictionaries. It is impossible, however, to tell you *everything*—and I only hope that I haven't told you too much, for one of the joys of crossword puzzles is to learn the language for yourself. Before your next tutorial, though, here are some tips for solvers.

TIPS FOR SOLVERS

1 Don't spend all day on 1 across! If I am solving a 15 × 15 standard cryptic, I read through the clues in order, spending no more than 15 seconds (roughly) on each and solving where I can. As I start on the down clues I can expect help from checking letters. After this first run-through I concentrate on clues relevant to a particular part of the diagram and follow wherever that leads.

2 Remember that the definition will always be at the beginning of the clue or at the end. If you can separate it out easily, the remaining words in the clue may suggest the clue type.

3 Hidden words and anagrams offer beginners the easiest start. Some crossword jargon shouts 'Anagram!' (as we have already discussed on p.71).

4 Look out for other crossword jargon. Something 'going around' something may alert you to a container-and-contents clue. The worker may well be an 'ant'.

5 Look out for opportunities to fill in individual letters on the diagram in pencil. The definition of a plural may allow you to fill in an 's'. Similarly you may see opportunities for 'ing', 'ed' and other common endings.

6 Don't be afraid to use a dictionary, especially when you are learning. It is *not* 'cheating'!

7 In addition to a dictionary you may find other reference books helpful, especially a one-volume encyclopedia and an atlas. (More about this on p.274.)

8 If you get desperately stuck, have a break. Let your brain tick over on 'automatic pilot' and after a night's sleep the answer may be obvious.

9 If you fail to finish a puzzle, try to learn something by reading the answers.

10 Keep a sense of proportion, and don't let solving crosswords dominate your entire existence!

CROSSWORD No. 18

By Duck from *The Hamlyn Books of Crosswords*

ACROSS

1 The French doctor and essayist (4)
4 A cricket club's umpire saying 'Exit sir'! initially points the finger (7)
10 Possibly a group of extremist pop fans is coming around the party afterwards (9)
11 See nurse rummaging to some extent for fluid to inject (5)
12 See thin fragments in food being obtained beside a street—this sort of food? (7,8)
13 There's a shortage of salt passing through a plant (6)
14 A boy stuck in marsh plant used logic (8)
16 Whole large tin exploded (8)
18 Nothing in swimming pools? That's an anticlimax (6)
21 A long struggle. Representing us: Edward R. and a Henry (7,5,3)
23 Ignorant learner must have external restraint (5)
24 Firm newspaperman, anything but apathetic (9)
25 Relax almost completely in lodgings and introduce red herrings (7)
26 Artist left cathedral city (4)

DOWN

2 Rousing a fellow in a side-section of the building (9)
3 He produces booze in a little brown jug (6)
4 Satisfy an appetite perhaps with grilled sausage (7)
5 Actors we hear in the class (5)
6 Sign of future developments in London street appearing round top half of window, ghastly white (5,2,3,4)
7 The dog will reform someday (7)
8 Endlessly talk about a field event (6)
9 Party putting up for election makes 'class' the issue (6, 8)
15 Tries messing about with wall—a difficult region for the home decorator (9)
16 A bloke at first opulent, losing head—the glory has departed (7)
17 Forcibly removes tar on pipes (7)
19 Violins producing sort of jazz on board (6)
20 Plant's a sensation with double dose of nitrogen in (6)
22 Mountain range, head of Glencoe—make journey round (5)

CROSSWORD No.18

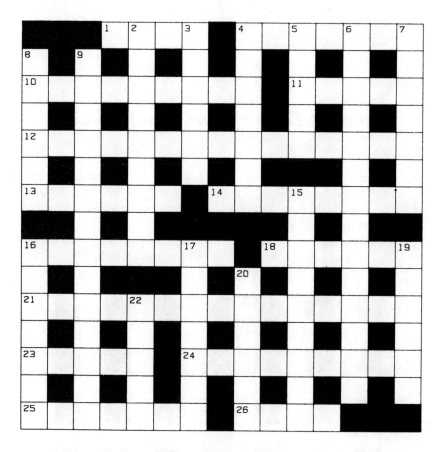

12

More on Diagrams and Tips for Setters

In Chapter 2 we defined what we meant by 'checked' and 'unchecked' squares and we said how the cryptic puzzle moved quickly from a closed diagram to an open diagram. It is time to look at diagrams in a little more detail and in doing so give you the chance to have a few more tutorials.

The most common size for an everyday cryptic is 15 × 15 and the diagram will usually be based on the lattice shown below:

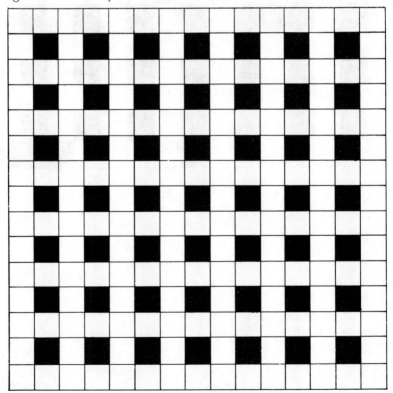

Extra squares will then be blocked out to divide words off and the result will usually be a puzzle of 28 or 32 clues. The 28 formula is regarded as ideal because it offers four long words or phrases and a range of answer lengths down to 4 or 5 letters. It is also possible to blank out the squares in either of these ways:

(a)

(b)

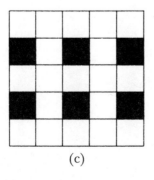

(c)

(Diagram (c) amounts to the same thing as Diagram (b) turned through 90 degrees.) The two puzzles which follow show grids based on these lattices.

CROSSWORD No. 19

By Duck from *The Hamlyn Books of Crosswords*

ACROSS

5 Wave a bowl at the breakfast table? (8)
8 To steal? To steal we hear is something easily done (6)
10 After start of July I prune ragged shrub (7)
11 Withered bit of corn rejected? It might have concerned her (5)
12 Dean once involved in expounding Exodus (4)
13 Craftsman and dedicated man—a certain TV detective (5-5)
15 Air Arne built rousingly around nation's leadership (4,9)
17 Mother joins crew going round garden—does some good but not much (10)
18 Animal in which tip of nose shows up? (4)
20 South African metal, lustrous material (5)
22 Fashionable period restricts one—it's temporary (7)
23 It may be swung in church obscuring screen (6)
24 Backed last 'ack putting on five hundred (8)

DOWN

1 Roman emperor and Indian prince beset by extremes of tradition (6)
2 Diana's poor half-missing fur is fit to be thrown out (10)
3 Eastern picture that's short? It's a *long* film surely (4)
4 People scattered with one snake in road writhing (8)
6 The occasion—presumably R.C. or free church? (5)
7 Gruelling period for the farmer? (9,4)
9 Draught-excluder, short one at home (7)
14 Correctness—show it insincerely and outwardly ooze (10)
15 A great noise surrounds Ted's awful bike (8)
16 Shakespearean character set Lear in a frenzy (7)
18 A printer's measure presented to this engraver would be one to last (5)
19 Etherised digit? (6)
21 What is your name, catechumen? This reply is standard (4)

CROSSWORD No.19

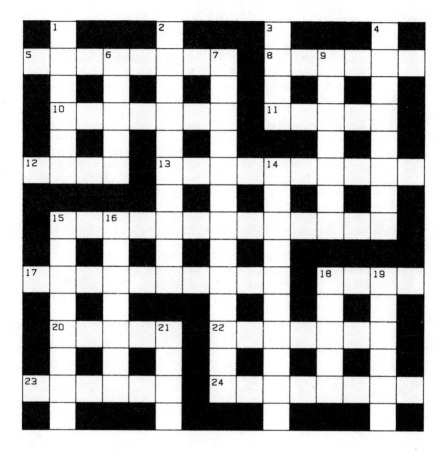

CROSSWORD No. 20

By Duck from *The Hamlyn Books of Crosswords*

ACROSS

7 Builders, etc. hang around a monument in Scotland (9,6)

10 Symbol displayed by 'Arry's picnic basket at the seaside? (9)

11 Kind but terribly green (5)

12 Master to make a study of wine (5)

13 Rows with beet sown by middle of patch—and here's a place for the runners (3,6)

14 Airmen stayed up endlessly—a chancy business (6)

16 Powerful joke about Henry (6)

17 Form of art—while there's this there's hope (5,4)

19 Rascal in Society party (5)

21 Pervert asked for more (5)

22 Author—one to sample but only a minor literary figure (9)

23 Get very angry wanting insect removed from part of machine (3,3,3,6)

DOWN

1 Bring stillness to city area, bring stillness around (6)

2 Fairy appearing in October only (6)

3 Introductory comment—blame rep if it's wrong (8)

4 Advertisement in exhibition for spirit (6)

5 Father going to inn got drunk somewhere in Devon (8)

6 Riding up on the green, turn back (6)

8 Climb tricky with ice? A pity—faultlessness will be required (13)

9 Showing feeling for what a nice lettuce should be? (6-7)

15 Almost entirely deceitful Welshman, character created by Shakespeare (8)

16 Comes before President goes back (8)

17 South-eastern gent to begin journey (3,3)

18 Charge mischief-maker with upsetting trade union, leader of extremists (6)

19 Beetle making mark on seaman (6)

20 Hospital worker providing beer (6)

CROSSWORD No. 20

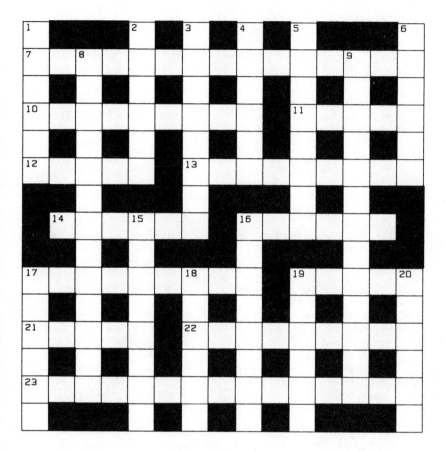

Yet another possibility is the partially closed/partially open grid and the next puzzle shows a common example:

CROSSWORD No. 21

Radio Times by Duck from *The Hamlyn Books of Crosswords*

ACROSS

1 TV programme in which b.f. (fully calm) may go wrong (4,2,5)
9 See 33 Across
10 DJ presenting cat maybe and bird to R-Robin (4,6)
11 Miss Bakewell? England's leader, big noise making a come-back (4)
13 Germaine may appear something of an ogre (erroneously?) (5)
16 Help a confused Hebrew character (5)
19 One with anger at onset of rain? Put clothes on this indoors! (5)
20 A mother's broadcasting—Joy? (7)
21 Material for basket-making from tradesman in Bow? (5)
22 Former African president overthrown initially, to be tortured afterwards? (5)
23 Broadcaster appears to be a revolutionary leader (7)
24 Unusually p-play? Give close attention (5)
25 Additional features in next race (5)
26 32's half confused, making insinuations (5)
29 Politician to right? Yes primarily! (4)
32 TV presenter and Stewart returning to nasty noisy hut (5,5)
33 & 9 Respond to chimes in TV programme? (4,4)
34 Seers wander around—they tell us what's happening (11)

DOWN

2 Correct error? Not entirely. Let it be so! (4)
3 Sly look from the French Queen (4)
4 DJ inexperienced? Yes and no! (5)
5 Comedian like Emney? (5)
6 It could be for letting you in (5)
7 Former cricket commentator not loth to get rollicking with jar? (4,6)
8 Ex-bowler, originally fiery and hot? Genuine bloke (4,7)
12 Chap who likes to do things having a dreadful moan, contentious party (3,2,6)
14 Bring up academic—he'll get involved in Pot Black (7)
15 Ted loses head and clutches a gun somewhere in London (4,3)
17 Actor appearing in *Little by Little*, one with a burden (4,6)
18 Pester Mr Worth? (5)
19 A hard lump, essential part of battery (5)
26 Plant border to the south (5)
27 Novelist wants a touch of elegance staying in hotels (5)
28 First items of evening news— Miss Lawley perhaps is to follow (5)
30 Lest one should leave Trevor, Roy is here (4)
31 Overcook the fish? (4)

CROSSWORD No. 21

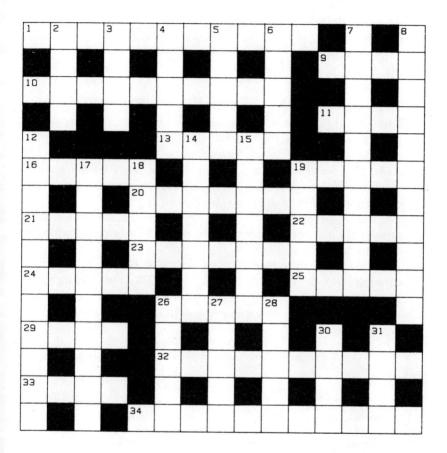

Whatever basic grid is used the setter should try to keep to certain standards of fairness:

1 *No part of the grid should be completely cut off* from another part of the grid (remember the nine mini-crosswords on p.21).

2 *The number of unchecked letters (unches) in an answer should be a half of the total or less.* It won't matter too much if 7 letters out of 13 are left unchecked, as here:

$$\_\_R\_\_S\_\_O\_\_R\_\_V\_\_R\_\_$$

Knowing that the answer should give you a football team (7,6) you will soon get BRISTOL ROVERS. In the diagram on p.22, though, one may be left trying to solve e.g. 13 across with __A__E__ and this can simply pose too many possibilities for comfort. (It should be added that lattice (a) makes the observance of this convention easier than (b), (c) or (d).)

3 *The triple unch (and worse!) should be avoided.* This means that no answer should contain three consecutive letters not checked by crossing letters.

4 *Normally the diagram should be symmetrical if given a half-turn* (i.e. through 180 degrees). Some diagrams also give symmetry if turned through 90 degrees. Sometimes a mirror symmetry will be preferred to a half-turn symmetry, as in the puzzle below.

CROSSWORD No. 22
Yuletide Special by Duck from *The Hamlyn Books of Crosswords*

ACROSS

1 Sort of plant seen over the stable? (4,2,9)

9 Places like Eden with awful dangers (7)

10 Girl featured in a joke—religious type (7)

11 Mitty, in getting excited, wished everyone God's blessing (4,3)

14,33 Seasonal animal—helped noted hurrier with a special distribution (7,3,8)

17 Seasonal decorations around 'olders (7)

19 Christmas food makes awful n-noise being swallowed by dog (7)

21 Spreads out decorations everywhere, putting lights on yuletide spruce initially (7)

24 Two ducks mater cooked in a place of refreshment (7)

28 Magistrate and engineers on Dec 24? (5)

29 A tree has been arranged—one may have a feast (5)

30 Seasonal music made possibly by 101 smart scholars (9,6)

33 See 14

DOWN

1 Expression of relief with first bit of turkey—something worth seeing (5)

2 A quiet little chap. (Is he tied to mum's _____ strings?) (5)

3 Voter might be out of place—if he made his vote this (5)

4 Vehicle or vessel turning up (3)

5 What a parcel! You can get a knocking sound from it (3)

6 Centrepieces of blue and red attracted attention (5)

7 It's very warm, the Spanish Inn (5)

CROSSWORD No. 22

8 Chew a lot, swallowing end of the chicken (5)
12 I scold, being very cross (5)
13 Sing melody, except for the beginning, very oddly (5)
15 Senior is more adventurous with leader gone (5)
16 *Yearn With Love*—a seasonal entertainment (5)
18 Some tinsel you see (3)
20 Employment in houses (3)
21 Sort of Greek party with endless rice (3)

22 Seaside place of entertainment with rubbish provided by clown (7)
23 Look over some poetry in Old English (7)
25 Declare what women like to hide? That's mean! (7)
26 Dismiss giver heartlessly—not in the house
27 Whose Gospel is the shortest? (You get points here) (5)
31 Miss West? It's not *oll* dreamy, coming up (3)
32 Boy is a shiner we hear (3)

That's as much as you need to know about diagrams for the moment, but before we go 'mountaineering with Chambers' here are some tips for setters.

TIPS FOR SETTERS

1 Begin with the diagram. You have a choice:

   (a) Use an existing diagram.
   (b) Make up one of your own before starting on the answers to be entered.
   (c) Make up one of your own concurrently with fitting in the answers.

   If you are setting for one of the dailies, (a) is the normal option but you will have a choice between several different diagrams. Option (a) is recommended for the beginner, but some existing diagrams do not conform to the standards laid down in this chapter and option (b) offers some scope for originality. Option (c), though, is the preferred method for experienced setters. It is also a very flexible method, allowing changes to be made to the diagram when a word will not quite fit.

2 Use an interesting variety of words and phrases. The long answers need to go in first. They should not be boring to define and/or difficult to break up (e.g. STRENGTHLESS). You will be forced to have dull words when there is no other choice, so do not make life difficult for yourself. Make sure that any *phrase* used is standard and well-known: YELLOW SHIRT is not acceptable, but YELLOW FEVER is!

3 If you are setting a number of puzzles choose diagrams that cover all lengths of words from 4 to 15 letters (or more, by joining answers together). Words with 3 letters are best avoided in a 15 × 15 puzzle but this can mean that 11 letter answers are unduly neglected unless you make a policy of including them.

4 Use a pencil and a rubber for the diagram. Don't be too obstinate—be prepared to start again, especially if you end up wanting a long word ending in J!

5 In writing clues concentrate on sound Ximenean principles rather than try to be too clever (read Chapter 10). Include in your puzzle a good variety of different clue types. For tutorial purposes in this book I have constructed some puzzles which use a disproportionate number of anagrams. In a 15 × 15 puzzle try to ration yourself to five full anagrams plus a few clues that are partially anagrams.

6 Know your solver. In a 15 × 15 puzzle try to use everyday words

and phrases. (When we go 'mountaineering' in the next chapter you will begin to learn what is acceptable for harder cryptics.)

7   Check your clues and diagram carefully. Check one thing at a time (e.g. the number of letters in brackets). Don't try to do it all at once.

8   Use a 'guinea pig' wherever possible to try out your puzzle for you. Better still, use two such—an ordinary solver to test the level of difficulty and an 'expert' to check for soundness.

9   If your crossword is to be published, be willing to listen to a crossword editor's criticisms, but do not allow him or her to enforce a non-Ximenean alternative! Instead suggest a new clue yourself. Always ask to see proofs.

10 You will make mistakes, and you may face criticism. Learn from your experience, and keep a sense of humour.

13

Mountaineering with Chambers

It is time now to progress from the blocked diagram to the barred diagram. We are about to scale the heights of Crossword Mountain. Farewell to Definition Plains and farewell to *The Times* Foothills. Ever on, ever upward to the rarefied atmosphere of Azed, *The Listener* and the Crossword Club. For our journey we need a guide book, and if you have not already done so you will need to purchase a copy of *Chambers 20th Century Dictionary*.

Hitherto we have used common knowledge, common words, common abbreviations. From now on we will meet unusual words and ancient language that rarely survives in a single-volume dictionary—except *Chambers*.

This is not just a commercial for my 'sponsor'—*Chambers* is indispensable. Where else can you so easily find the probable misprint in Shakespeare (EALE)? Where else, in such a concise volume, can you find a supposed 'cross between a male yak and a common horned cow' with ten different spellings (though some are male only, some female only)? If you don't believe me, look under ZHO in the big red book where you will also find: ZO, DSO, DZO, ZHOMO, DSOMO, JOBO, ZOBO, ZOBU, DSOBO. Also in its 1500-odd pages you will find everything from ancient words for 'grievous' (DEAR, DEARE, DEERE) and a Scotticism for a hanging clock (WAG-AT-THE-WA') to WORD PROCESSOR (a cryptic definition of a clue-writer?). If you pause to *read Chambers Dictionary* while solving a puzzle, you may also find some quirky definitions in the best Johnsonian tradition: try ECLAIR and MIDDLE AGE for example.

As you progress to the barred puzzle you will need to learn the abbreviations in Chambers. You will still be meeting MA indicated by 'master', but that abbreviation may also be clued by Morocco, the International Vehicle Registration. Copper may still be Cu, but you had also better know that beryllium has the symbol Be. And so on.

gaff¹ *gaf, n.* a hook used esp. for landing large fish: the spar to which the head of a fore-and-aft sail is bent (*naut.*).—*v.t.* to hook or bind by means of a gaff.—*adj.* **gaff'-rigged** (of a vessel) having a gaff.—**gaff'-sail** a sail attached to the gaff; **gaff'-topsail** a small sail, the head of which is extended on a small gaff which hoists on the top mast, and the foot on the lower gaff. [Fr. *gaffe.*]

gaff² *gaf,* (*slang*) *n.* a low theatre: a fair. [Origin obscure.]

gaff³, gaffe *gaf, n.* a blunder. [Fr. *gaffe.*]

gaff⁴ *gaf,* (*slang*) *v.i.* to gamble.—*ns.* **gaff'er; gaff'ing.** [Origin obscure.]

gaff⁵ *gaf,* (*slang*) *n.* humbug, nonsense.—**blow the gaff** to disclose a secret, to blab. [Prob. connected with **gab²** or **gaff³;** cf. O.E. *gegaf-spræc,* scurrility.]

gaffer *gaf'ǝr, n.* originally a word of respect applied to an old man, now familiar (*fem.* **gammer**): the foreman of a squad of workmen. [**grandfather,** or **godfather.**]

gag¹ *gag, v.t.* to stop the mouth of forcibly: to silence: to prevent free expression by (the press, etc.): to choke up.—*v.i.* to choke: to retch:—*pr.p.* **gagg'ing;** *pa.t.* and *pa.p.* **gagged.**—*n.* something put into the mouth or over it to enforce silence (also *fig.*), or to distend jaws during an operation: the closure applied in a debate: a nauseous mouthful, boiled fat beef (*Lamb*).—*n.* **gagg'er** one who gags.—**gag'-bit** a powerful bit used in breaking horses. [Prob. imitative of sound made in choking.]

gag² *gag,* (*slang*) *v.t.* to deceive.—*v.i.* to practise imposture.—*n.* a made-up story lie. [Possibly **gag¹.**]

gag³ *gag,* (*coll.*) *n.* an actor's interpolation into his part: a joke: a hoax.—*v.i.* to introduce a gag: to joke.—*v.t.* to introduce a gag into.—*n.* **gag'ster** (*coll.*) one who tells jokes, a comedian. [Possibly **gag¹.**]

An extract from *Chambers 20th Century Dictionary,* showing lots of definition possibilities for the crossword setter.

Buy your *Chambers* then—and buy a few more books if you can, as indicated in Appendix 2. But if you only have money for one reference book it must be *the* Dictionary. Use it and enjoy it. End of commercial!

The tradition of using bars was established in the early days of British crosswords and became the hallmark of Torquemada, mentioned briefly in Chapter 10. One of his puzzles from his 1934 miscellany *The Torquemada Puzzle Book* is shown overleaf.

I provide the grid with the answer because in my humble opinion no one in his right mind should be expected to attempt a solution! By today's standards this is a work of misdirected genius with its unsound clues and difficult references. Note too the lack of symmetry and reversed words which strike us as very odd.

TORQUEMADA PUZZLE

ACROSS

1 Buddy gets a head on him and becomes peevish
7 American law-giver sets a Scottish standard
12 Waited for by Brutus but not by Pilate
14 I wrote Terminations when I started and The Trimmed Lamp when I ended
15 *rev.* 36
16 I take those who do not take themselves
17 37's
19, 21 Confirm officially
20 City found in a town
23 I'm already fashionable and if you add the difference between six and sixteen I'm an erroneous overcoat
24 Genus of worms in a heretic
25 *rev.* French fleet in English waters
27 Shepherd's bad companion
29 11
30 You may discover us in a trick but you had better shake to make sure
31 34 dn
32 *rev.* Shortened
34 Relying on a large scale
38 Trim is my county town
39 Epitaph in bad verse
40 I can hold a candle—to 26

DOWN

1 Behead this old clothesman for a murderer
2 Bisected drawback
3 e.g. squire
4,11 One boot that helped another to dish a cake
5 Clouded with brown from unfaces it
6 Walked on by people in coloured shirts
7 Solomon's eight-bottle man
8 *rev.* I said: "The purple flowers droop: the golden bee Is lily-cradled: I alone awake"
9 A German might associate this piece of lead with 22
10 Novelist not encouraged to write at Cambridge
13 *rev.* Scottish stout that becomes musty when it crosses the border
18 Next will help in
22 Should come after 27
26 *rev.* 29
28 *rev.* Noah's care has become anyone's old care
32,33 All but the play by Maugham
34 31
35 My first is unchecked in 13 and my second in 11
36 *rev.* 15
37 One 17

TORQUEMADA PUZZLE

¹F	²R	³A	⁴B	B	⁵I	⁶T	⁷J	⁸E	⁹D	¹⁰G	¹¹E
¹²R	E	P	L	¹³Y	N	¹⁴H	E	N	R	Y	R
¹⁵I	T	¹⁶H	U	F	F	E	R	O	¹⁷A	P	¹⁸S
¹⁹P	R	E	C	²⁰F	U	N	²¹O	N	I	²²S	E
²³P	O	S	H	²⁴U	S	A	B	E	L	L	A
²⁵E	D	I	²⁶R	T	²⁷C	R	O	O	²⁸K	²⁹E	R
³⁰R	U	S	E	³¹S	A	³²L	A	³³T	R	U	C
³⁴S	³⁵C	³⁶U	³⁷T	A	T	E	³⁸M	E	A	T	H
A	³⁹T	R	I	P	E	⁴⁰T	O	R	C	H	E

Notes

Across: 7. Two meanings; 12. Julius C., III, 2, 37; Bacon, Essays, Of Truth; 14. Henry (James), (O.) Henry; 23. Post.-teen, posteen; 24. Sabell(i) a(n); 25 *rev.* French borrowing; 30. R-us-e, anag.; 39. T-R.I.P.-e; 40. Candelabrum when put to 26.

Down: 1. Jack the (f)Ripper; 2. Draw back; 3. Esquire; 4 and 11. Wellington, Napoleon; 5. Anag.; 6. And others; 7. I Kings, xii, 28; 8 *rev.* Tennyson, O., 28; 9. Trail; 13. *rev.* Two meanings; 28. *rev.* C-ark; 32 and 33. (The) Letter.

It would be very easy for us to write off this puzzle completely, but two aspects of it have survived: the difficult vocabulary and the barred diagram. Clue- writing has become more disciplined and this has allowed the difficult solution to be more solvable (thanks to the pioneering work of Ximenes); the barred diagram has become more orderly. A typical 12 × 12 Azed diagram is shown below.

The basic permitted parameters for the 12 × 12 'plain' puzzle were laid down by Ximenes in his book *On the Art of the Crossword:*

1   Number of unches in a word:
  4 and 5 letters, 1 unch
  6 and 7 letters, 1 or 2 unches
  8 and 9 letters, 2 or 3 unches
  10, 11 and 12 letters, 3 or 4 unches
2   Number of words in a barred puzzle: 36, usually with six rows and six columns containing one word and the other twelve two words. 'Four of the twelve one-word rows and columns will contain your four long words: the other eight will be reduced in length by bars to fit shorter words.'

Note how the Ximenean formula leads to a tidy balanced-looking diagram with no 'multiple unches'. You can see that there is more checking in a Ximenean diagram than in a blocked diagram, and this is a distinct asset for the solver. Suppose you are faced with a clue such as this:

[13.1] Vegetable, very black inside—it grows in the tropics (6)

and you have all the crossing words to give you

LEB__E__

By the time you get that far you should be able to work out BB in leek = LEBBEK, but if you cannot you can always look up *Chambers*, find the only word that will fit and work backwards to see how the clue works. With L__B__E__ or __E__B__K it would be a shade harder.

For the most part, clues in plain barred puzzles are similar in concept to those in blocked puzzles, but to give you a flavour of the different language due to *Chambers* here are some examples and answers all from Azed and his competitors (we shall look at the Azed competition again in Chapter 16):

[13.2] Pour out Jock's shin-bone soup (5)

Answer: SKINK which has two meanings—hence the note reads (2 mngs). Skink is a Scottish word for that form of soup—hence the label 'Jock's'. Jock is a familiar person in Azed!

[13.3] Zinc sulphide to mix with einsteinium (6)

Answer: BLENDE (blend + E). You've been warned about abbreviations.

The next clue won S. L. Paton first prize in Azed No. 1:

[13.4] Before the heart ensnares one, one likes to go on a binge (7)

Answer: ORGIAST (a in or + gist). Note two things: (1) before = or, a rare usage which would be too obscure for the average cryptic: (2) one = a (quite justifiable but in less advanced cryptics 'one' = 'I' usually).

[13.5] Campaigner in old company holding steadfast to right (8)

Answer: CRUSADER (sad in crue + r, 'semi & lit.'). This too was an Azed first-prizewinner from M.L.Perkins. Note the use of 'old' for the obsolete word 'crue'. Many words in *Chambers* can be labelled 'obsolete', 'stale', 'traditional' or 'as before'. In this clue also note 'to' meaning 'besides', a useful 'throwaway' in a charade.

[13.6] Gee surrounded by at least four more dashes (6)

Answer: SPANGS (g in spans). 'Gee' is a spelling of the letter 'g' (as well as a suggestion of a horse). Look out for el, em, es and others!

[13.7] Oily swimmer has success on lake–goodness me, born genius (9)

Answer: GOLOMYNKA for a down clue (go + L + O my! + n + ka). An interesting assemblage of obscure bits and pieces combining to make an obscure word—but genius = ka is soon learnt with experience!

In 'advanced cryptics' the answer often describes itself in the first person. This prize-winning clue from C.O.Butcher uses this convention to achieve an '& lit':

[13.8] I form bulges erected on a defence's sides (9)

The answer is GABIONADE (I bag (rev.) + d e '& lit.').

This *personification* goes back to the Victorian riddle (see p.2). This sort of thing is definitely allowed, even if the personal I cannot be allowed in the plan (see p.65)!

Solvers of an Azed puzzle will need to know that familiar words can take on unfamiliar meanings when used as indicators. If you are familiar with the hymn 'There is a green hill far away', you will know that 'without' can mean 'outside' as well as 'lacking'. Here's an example from Ximenes:

[13.9] Rural spot without excitement (8)

giving MOFUSSIL (fuss in moil).

Did you know that 'on' can mean 'getting drunk' and that 'over' can suggest a word being *rolled* over (i.e. reversed)? No examples here, but you will meet them soon enough!

From unusual words and unusual usages of usual words to unusual word order. Most of us think and write like this:

I hate people who flatter me with lies.

But a poet does not always write his sentences in the order 'subject/object/verb'. Thus William Cowper:

The lie that flatters I abhor the most.

And thus William (W.J.M.) Scotland, an Azed prizewinner demonstrating another verbal art form, that of clue-writing:

[13.10] The jungly mass one cleaves (7)

The answer is MACHETE (anag. in mace, because in fact 'mass one' is cleaving 'the jungly'!).

*wide-spectrum	*wooden-headed	*yellow-billed
*wife-swapping	*wooden-tongue	*yellow-footed
*wiggle-waggle	*wood-hyacinth	*yellow-hammer
*wild-williams	woodlessness	*yellow-headed
williewaught -s	*wood-offering	*yellow-horned
*will-o'-the-wisp	*woolly-haired	*yellow-legged
*willow-grouse	*woolly-headed	*yellow-necked
*wind-changing	*word-building	*yellow-rattle
*winding-sheet	*word-painting	*yellow-ringed
*winding-stair	workableness	*yellow-rumped
*window-screen	*working-class	*yellow-yowley
*Windsor-chair	*working-house	yieldingness
*wine-coloured	*working-model	youthfulness
*wine-glassful	workmistress -es	
*wine-merchant	*world-beating	Z
*wing-shooting	*world-wearied	zalambdodont -s
*winnowing-fan	worshipfully	*Zantedeschia
*winter-beaten	*Woulfe-bottle	*Zarathustric
*winter-bourne	wranglership -s	*Zeitvertreib
*winter-cherry	wrathfulness	*zenith-sector
*winter-clover	wretchedness	*Zeuglodontia
*winter-garden	*writer's-cramp	zincographer -s
*winter-ground	*writing-paper	zincographic
*winter-weight	*writing-table	zoochemistry
*wire-stitched	wrongfulness	zoogeography
*wire-stringed		zoographical
wisecracking	X	zoologically
*wishing-stone	xanthochroia	zoomagnetism
*witches'-broom	xanthochroic	zoopathology
withdrawment -s	xanthochroid -s	zoophytology
witheredness	xanthomatous	zoospermatic
withholdment -s	xanthopterin	zootomically
wollastonite	xerodermatic	*Zwinglianism
womanishness	xeromorphous	*Zwinglianist
*woman-queller	xiphisternum -s	zygapophyses
*wonder-monger	xiphophyllus	zygapophysis
*wonder-struck	xylobalsamum	zygodactylic
*wonder-worker		zygomorphism
wondrousness	Y	zygomorphous
woodburytype	*yankee-doodle	zygomycetous
*wood-engraver	*yellow-backed	zymotechnics

An extract from *Chambers Words*, compiled 'for the benefit of all who play in fun or in earnest with words'. (Asterisks denote words not permitted in Scrabble®).

Finally a subtle pair of clues from Azed linked by leader dots:

[13.10] Cunning but timorous if losing head . . . (5)
[13.11] . . . To these fools, given which they *would* have heads (5)

[13.10] gives LEERY and [13.11] OAVES. Transfer the L from the first clue to the second and you would have 'eery' (timorous) and 'loaves' (heads). Clever stuff!

The time has come for two small tutorial puzzles. Then we must look at some of the more sophisticated clue types common to barred puzzles. Are you using your oxygen yet?

CROSSWORD No. 23

ACROSS

1 Poppy and a stone in Jock's gutter (8)
7 Greek character will shortly become invalid (4)
8 Arsenic arrives from geological formations (4)
10 Source of hope in troubled times? (6)
12 One in old age not yielding milk for Mac (4)
13 Fruit giving dog energy (4)
16 Man at table shows orange stain (6)
17 Unit attached to bit of sound (4)
18 Scottish boy shows spirit (not square) (4)
19 Watching over five couples on the floor? (8)

DOWN

1 Pa eats nut rudely rejecting superior old appetiser (8)
2 Flower that's tender, hurt when upset? Not entirely (4)
3 Bard puts touch of magic in E.lang. and E.lit. (7)
4 Master sermon amplifies a message from the heavens maybe (5)
5 One in love is secure (4)
6 Die with a tear destroyed in shoot out... (8)
9 ...killed with gun outside American institute (7)
11 Workers appearing before newspaper boss complained as before (5)
14 Instrument with nothing in order (4)
15 Touches of obvious talent in crossword in 'The Listener' (4)

CROSSWORD No. 24

ACROSS

1 Plant tissue shows tree is 2000 roughly (8)
7 Dedicated man retired, no longer with us (6)
8 Bird's old garment (4)
9 Townsmen linger endlessly around (4)
11 Do is producing an old-fashioned racket (4)
12 What Jumblies went to *sea* in—or river we hear (4)
15 'urried along and declared (4)
16 Poet heard to be in prison? (4)
17 Girl gets hold of hard Azed—36 lines of skilled writing? (6)
18 The old weaken and come in about to die (8)

DOWN

1 I am great, fantastic—superior's right! (8)
2 Beetle story upset Her Majesty (6)
3 Heartless bird's mutter (4)
4 Fallen angel, one with happiness curtailed (5)
5 Bird eating a wee portion (4)
6 A month in old Paris requires my French, second language, right? (8)
10 Cordyline has two birds in it (6)
11 Old city governor is in the city (5)
13 A bit of mutton to devour? (4)
14 Expert turned up admitting learner's lacking in literary style (4)

14

Advanced Clues

Moving, Substituted and Alternate letter(s), Subtractive container-and-contents

Ximenes once recommended that hard words should have easy clues and easy words hard clues. Much of the 'hardness' in clues is due to the subtlety of wording, but there are clue types used in advanced puzzles that you probably will not meet in the everyday cryptic. The examples that follow are culled from Azed puzzles and Azed clue-writing competitions in the *Observer*.

The moving letter(s). In this clue type the solver is invited to find a word and then move a particular letter (or letters) to discover a new word:

[14.1] See me in N. European water, tail moving? (6)

N. European water is WASSER: move the tail (r) to get WRASSE. Note that an '& lit.' effect is also achieved since a wrasse is a fish.

[14.2] I disapproved of the unseemly skunk, tail foremost (4)

Move the c of atoc (a skunk) to the front to obtain the censor CATO.

The substituted letter(s). Here you are invited to find a word and substitute one letter (or set of letters) for another. Thus in this clue:

[14.3] Vigorous? Love yielding to East in source of drowsiness (5)

We find a source of drowsiness (poppy) and substitute e for o (love) to arrive at PEPPY (meaning 'vigorous').

Here is another example, a first prize in one of Azed's competitions, from J. P. H. Hirst:

[14.4] Given unconventionally for Jack's head (7)

Jack is tar. Replace his head ('t') with 'vineg' (anag. given) to give

VINEGAR, which you will remember was accompanied by brown paper (hence the '& lit.').

Alternate letters. The solver is asked to discard every other letter in a clue such as the following:

[14.5] Outings in which you find chain keeps losing odd bits (5)

A ride on a shaky bicycle? Maybe—but forget the 'misleading context' and remove the odd letters ('bits') from 'chain keeps'. The result is HIKES.

The words 'odd bits' and 'even bits' usually give the game away but here is the technique given a new subtlety by Azed:

[14.6] Ancient Syrian one regularly placed among king and troops (8)

Place A alternately among R and MEN and you'll get ARAMAEAN.

In the following clue (which won a first prize for N. C. Dexter in a 1984 Azed competition) the alternate letters are anagrammed:

[14.7] By it 'truth' and 'lie' looked alternately interchangeable (11)

An anagram of BITUHNLEOKD is DOUBLE THINK (another '& lit.' of course).

The missing-words charade is best illustrated by some examples:

[14.8] Opening gambit at parties is hard if shyness _____ inhibits one (7)

The first word here provides the definition. The remainder is a sentence into which you must insert some words which make sense. The words required are 'or if ice' ('ice' meaning 'reserve'). Put them together in a charade and the answer is ORIFICE.

[14.9] 'Adam's _____', said archaic Eve, *very* old crone? (6)

The answer is RIBIBE. Can you see why?

Sometimes the charade provides a 'letter formula' telling you how to get from one group of letters to another:

[14.10] Highland cattle put with this will become quiet (4)

The answer is NOUT (highland cattle) because 'put with no ut' equals 'p' (an abbreviation for 'quiet'). A relatively unusual type of clue this, and the example given threw more than one solver when perpetrated by Azed.

The subtractive container-and-contents clue is a combination of techniques (d) and (h) in Chapter 8. Here's an example of my own, hitherto unpublished:

[14.11] This minor when put in bed is happy (4)

It's nothing to do with a compliant child when you read the clue cryptically. You want a word which when put in bed gives you 'blessed': hence LESS.
     Here's one from Azed:

[14.12] What'll those enthralled like us in Market get? Mare's-nest (5)

The word you want, hidden in the 'mart' (or market) of mare's nest is ESNES, who are enthralled as slaves. Quite simple really!

The composite anagram was revived by Don Putnam in a *Games and Puzzles* magazine article in 1975 (how sad the demise of that monthly which for ten years provided some splendid advanced puzzles!). He described a clue from Afrit's book which read as follows:

[14.13] You could make this whale seem quarrelsome, but hold it up by its tail and it begins to laugh (7)

Forget the words after 'quarrelsome' and concentrate on the first seven words. Afrit is saying take 'this word for whale' plus 'seem' and you could make 'quarrelsome'. The answer is RORQUAL (hence the 'lau' in the reversal, the beginning(!) of 'laugh'). Quite soon after Putman's article Azed and *Listener* puzzlers were faced with the rediscovery of the composite anagram. The clue-writer was saying in effect 'If A won't form a decent anagram, I'll add B and define it as an anagram of C.' A way had been rediscovered of combining the anagram with the subtractive clue.
     This type of clue normally appears as an '& lit.', as the following examples illustrate:

[14.14] Ecuadorans, broke, might produce a _____ and nothing else (5)

ECUADORANS is an anagram of 'a, _____, and, o'. The missing word is SUCRE.

[14.15] Some sprinkling with this could give a tame meal gusto (9)

This won B. Franco a first prize from Azed in 1977. The word 'some' has to be sprinkled with a word to give 'a tame meal gusto'. Answer: MALAGUETTA (look up its meaning in *Chambers* if you don't know it).

4 -UZZ

stay	bley	Esky ®	ismy	espy	oosy	gazy
quay	fley	yuky	fumy	I-spy	posy	hazy
away	gley	paly	cany	nary	rosy	jazy
M-way	sley	waly	many	oary	upsy	lazy
sway	joey	ably	wany	vary	busy	mazy
tway	drey	idly	zany	wary	maty	vizy
baby	grey	rely	deny	scry	city	cozy
gaby	prey	ugly	reny	adry	mity	dozy
inby	trey	lily	miny	aery	pity	fozy
goby	stey	oily	piny	eery	doty	oozy
go-by	quey	wily	tiny	hery	arty	Z
toby	defy	ally	viny	very	duty	Geëz
upby	affy	illy	winy	airy	cavy	chez
orby	cagy	inly	bony	miry	Davy	trez
ruby	edgy	only	cony	wiry	navy	oyez
lacy	eggy	holy	mony	skry	wavy	phiz
pacy	bogy	moly	pony	dory	bevy	whiz
racy	dogy	poly	tony	gory	levy	friz
ricy	fogy	duly	puny	lory	envy	quiz
fady	orgy	guly	tuny	pory	movy	swiz
lady	hugy	July	awny	rory	yawy	Günz
wady	achy	puly	gyny	Tory	dewy	lutz
eddy	ashy	ruly	ahoy	spry	nowy	Druz
tedy	caky	owly	pioy	'Arry	towy	jazz
tidy	laky	gamy	cloy	bury	waxy	razz

An extract from *Chambers Back-Words for Crosswords,* a reverse-sorted word list, ideal for the crossword fan who is stuck with (say) ____TZ : LUTZ is the only answer!

My own prize-winning Azed clue for PICKLE (which can mean 'steal') read as follows:

[14.16] Kleptomaniac: a man to _____ indiscriminately?

(Incidentally 'A man to pickle indiscriminately' is a rather good clue for KLEPTOMANIAC, don't you think?)
    The composite anagram does not *have* to be part of an '& lit.' clue; as in this case of mine 'very highly commended' by Azed near St Valentine's Day:

[14.17] A little romance? Such fun with cryptic letters may show it is fourteenth.

In other words take a word possibly meaning 'a little romance', combine it with 'fun' 'cryptically' to give 'it is fourteenth'. The answer comes out as HISTORIETTE (a short story). In the first of your next tutorial puzzles all clues are based on the clue types described in this chapter. Quite often though you won't find a single example of any of them, even in an Azed—but there are just a few in the full-size puzzle. Remember, too, that the setter will always be looking for a new and subtle way of telling you how to deal with the letters in front of you.

CROSSWORD No. 25

ACROSS

1 Might _____ malfunction to make light smear? (5)

5 This snake with ring around is making grating sound (3)

8 Fragments to classify, first to last (4)

10 Work of art's loud, not soft and languishing (8)

11 Plans—utter odd bits showing what man's made of? (5)

12 Plundered—one gets a hanging (dead towards the end) (5)

17 Offering amnesty—a little time given for four (8)

18 Jock's cattle oddly shifting round —it's a habit (4)

19 An unseemly place like this could be nasty (5)

20 Bell sounds pierce, start to finish (5)

DOWN

1 Look fit selecting odd bits in the attic (4)

2 It's Bahrain: see _____ in his setting? (4)

3 Dot boozes with a touch of sadness coming to the fore (7)

4 See girl ruin tea—odd bits served (4)

6 Numbers switching ends in ecstasy (4)

7 Horror writer has a bit of ghastliness for his middle bit of book (4)

9 Special errand: _____ might be attracted to Mr Electron! (7)

12 Ogres half twisting into fabulous birds (4)

13 Lean sceptic may interject with _____ (4)

14 Write in _____ or ... alternatively presented as 'orient'? (4)

15 _____? It is possibly to sing (4)

16 Big _____'d produce bad sting possibly (4)

CROSSWORD DINNERS

Crossword dinners have been held in honour of *The Listener* and *The Observer*. At *Listener* dinners the solvers meet the setters, but at *Observer* dinners solvers meet *the* setter. *Observer* dinners have celebrated Ximenes Nos. 100, 200, 500, 750 and 1000, Azed Nos. 250, 500, 750. The 'D-AZED' menu is shown below for the Azed 500 held in Oxford in 1981. The conventional menu is on p.110.

D-AZED MENU

Ten common beers? No! (8,8)

★ ★ ★ ★

Eel's fins? Tell no fool! (6,2,4,6)

★ ★ ★ ★

A crab trifle left? Come often! (11,2,4,7)

Heat a cat-toe soup . . . (7,8)

. . . Ill at our tea? (11)

Boil croc (8)

★ ★ ★ ★

Mum's choice lemon cheese (we'd hot treat) (9,6,4,5,2,6)

★ ★ ★ ★

The finer men ate stiff cow-rind (6,4,5-6,5)

CROSSWORD No. 26

ACROSS

1 Look around mountain pass—it will have hard mass of igneous rock (9)
10 Chemical coming from a chimney in Glasgow? (4)
11 Black crew in underground layer (8)
12 Tropical dish maid can cook—not all right, fantastic! (9)
13 Strong liking for eating a bit of garlic and salad (6)
14 Black mineral has resistance? This will pierce a hole (5)
17 Feminine English woman's felt hat (6)
19 Small cask in pub attracting glance, not half! (7)
20 Hobo languishes holding a coin not worth much (4)
22 Advance payment for penniless pre-1971 poet (4)
24 Artist put back silk in cupboard (7)
26 You can't play cricket without _____ ball! This intruder's taken possession (6)
29 Praying not to get gee-gee as present (5)
30 Garbled matins—one only *appears* to pray (6)
31 A learner needs library service—never on a permanent basis? (9)
32 Cold sea bit tricky, around zero? Such may be the answer (8)
33 Account by army for the official minutes (4)
34 Softly touching woman—not entirely kind to be a grasper (9)

DOWN

1 Bean produced in the biologist's workplace repeatedly? (6)
2 A loser primarily, an 'orse not finishing sadly (7)
3 Water-carrier wasn't fit, with wooden joints somehow? (12)
4 In room a ghost lurks somewhere in Ireland (5)
5 Antiseptic appearing as yellow crystals—ten sufficient for the chemistry class? (8)
6 Wife featured in educational paper organised communities (6)
7 Mother 100—having modern technology around one is key to prolonging life (12)
8 I don't go to matins *and* evensong —what'll do for collection? (5)
9 A time in Israel with actors turning up (4)
15 Torment losing every other part —allowance for waste required (4)
16 Fish become frightened—I had *one* caught (8)
18 Be a success? Ali was with his (4)
21 Wine that's yellow I vote 'nasty' (7)
23 Where you'd see British go on jaunt—and the king? (6)
25 Some of the fens, earthed, dry up as before (6)
27 Fine French child for rude eruption after meal? (5)
28 Would a non-conformist Scot primarily inhabit me? (5)
29 Handle of kettle perhaps or bucket (4)

CROSSWORD No. 26

15

Special Crosswords

All the crosswords so far have had 'normal' clues (however complex) and the words have been entered in a 'normal' diagram. In a special crossword something is abnormal—either the form of clue *or* the grid you are presented with *or* the way you must enter letters in the grid. In extreme cases you may be faced with several forms of abnormality. There are a number of standard special crossword types and beyond that there are the 'special specials'! In this chapter we shall look at some of the well-known specials. In each case we shall look at the standard 'rubric' which accompanies that type of puzzle and then illustrate with a tutorial.

Printer's Devilry. This form of puzzle was invented by Afrit (see pp.58–9). Here is the rubric in its classical Ximenean form:

> Each clue is a passage from which the printer has removed a hidden answer, closing the gap, taking liberties sometimes with punctuation and spacing, but not disturbing the order of the remaining letters. Thus in the sentence *Now that it's so much warmer, can't I let the boiler go out?* MERCANTILE is hidden. The printer might offer as a clue: *Now that—it's so much wart, the boil : ergo, out!* Each passage when complete makes some sort of sense.

The clue Ximenes chose has an extreme case of shifting word breaks along the line. A PD clue with a simple break and no shifting letters is also possible, as in this beautiful example which won Mrs E. M. Pardo a first prize from Ximenes:

[15.1] Children taking piano lessons soon learn the sign ff (6)

The break occurs in ff giving the undevilled version '. . . for a clef', and the answer is therefore ORACLE. In Azed competitions this additional advice is given to PD clue-writers:

N.B. Preference is given to PD clues in which breaks before and after the word omitted (before *and* after omission) do not occur at the ends or beginnings of words in the clue.

Hints to solvers. Sort out any obvious space shifts. Then try to find the point at which the clue looks strained and insert a pencil stroke. See if you can add new letters to the 'stranded' letters either side of the stroke to produce a word which fits in with the theme of the clue. In the Ximenean example above you should be able to see 'the boiler go out'. In that context a 'wart' doesn't make much sense. By trial and error you might decide to break thus: war/t. In the context of the clue and perhaps with some help from checking letters you should arrive at 'warm' and 'warmer'. Then if all else fails, you can look up the 10-lettered MER words in *Chambers Words* and work backwards. Solving PD clues can be very hard, but this tutorial puzzle offers generous checking and should present few problems.

CROSSWORD No.27

Printer's Devilry

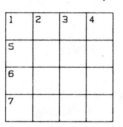

ACROSS
1 Royal Academy will only display the bet (4)
5 If you're going in for driving, Tess, son might help (4)
6 Got a big success? Banks should be pleased! (4)
7 In a gale you might see town (4)

DOWN
1 Towards end of game do play 'ere (4)
2 Sleep's needed by one living in busy street-bus? 'Tis impossible with traffic noise (4)
3 Cats are crossbred by American ranchers (4)
4 Ties—dress in the latest fashion (4)

Misprints is a form of puzzle invented by Ximenes and the rubric explains all:

Half the clues, both across and down, contain a misprint of one letter only in each, occurring always in the definition part of the clue: their answers are to appear in the diagram correctly spelt. The other half, both across and down, are correctly printed: all their answers are to appear in the diagram with a misprint of one letter only in each. No unchecked letter in the diagram is to be misprinted: each twice used letter is to appear as required by the correct form of at least one of the words to which it belongs. All indications such as anagrams, etc., in clues lead to the correct forms of words required, not to the misprinted forms.

The Ximenean rubric does not give an example of a misprinted clue, but we can illustrate from Ximenes himself:

[15.2] Rummy sort of girl—see the old-fashioned bun (6)

The answer is GINGAL (gin + gal), and the misprinted word is 'bun' which should be 'gun'. It is a curious feature of the misprinted clue that it always makes much better sense than the so-called 'correct' version!

Correctly printed clues are like any other clue but you need to work out by process of elimination where the misprint occurs.

Hint to solvers. Fill in unchecked letters in ink, but divide the squares diagonally, putting the across letter in pencil in the top corner and the down letter in pencil in the bottom, thus:

When you have settled the priority work out the implication for the crossing words, inking in where possible. And if two letters agree, use ink straightaway. Put a pencil line through each misprint in the clues, and beside the number of each misprint clue mark C (for *clue* misprint). If the misprint is in the *diagram*, mark D. Thus a sequence may read as follows (supposing that 'work' is a misprint for 'word'):

Down
C 1........work.......
D 2.....................
D 3.....................

In each section of clues you will probably be looking for 9C's and 9D's. This may help you categorise some of the clues as you tussle with the last one or two.

In the tutorial puzzle that follows, checking is generous, which should be helpful.

CROSSWORD No. 28

Misprints

ACROSS

1 Here's a little to eat and a little to drink, dear (6)
7 Dagon has limb in the drink (6)
8 Jock's mysterious disease—the unemployed won't get it (6)
9 With five rings perform a touch of oriental magic (6)
10 Ale not bad? I get tight coming in (6)
11 Leaves again being terribly restless—ship sails off (6)

DOWN

1 Corn Street, somewhere in Bucks (6)
2 Dean produces sort of tract about the Old Testament (6)
3 Sheep perhaps beginning to play before long on mountain range (6)
4 Community work interrupts footballer (6)
5 Musical composition rendered by for example French artist, not English (6)
6 Claps a lot, one with half-century having been caught (6)

Playfair. The Playfair code was invented by the famous Victorian scientist Charles Wheatstone (you may remember his famous electrical bridge for measuring resistance if you took physics at school). But it was his friend Lyon Playfair who publicised it: hence the name. Used by the British Army in the First World War, this code is rather more difficult than the simple substitution code where one letter is replaced by another. Afrit it was who introduced Playfair codes to crosswords, and this is the now-familiar rubric using the sample codeword favoured by Azed:

MENU

CONSOMMÉ BRETONNE

★ ★ ★ ★

FILLET OF SOLE NELSON

★ ★ ★ ★

CONTRE FILET OF BEEF CLAMART
CHATEAU POTATOES
RATATOUILLE
BROCCOLI

★ ★ ★ ★

CHOCOLATE MOUSSE WITH CRÊME DE MENTHE

★ ★ ★ ★

COFFEE WITH AFTER-DINNER MINTS

Wine kindly provided by *The Observer*

(see page 103)

In a Playfair word square the code word (in which no letter recurs) is followed by the remaining letters of the alphabet, I doing duty for I and J (see below).

```
O  R  A  N  G
E  S  T  I  C
K  B  D  F  H
L  M  P  Q  U
V  W  X  Y  Z
```

To encode a word split it into pairs of letters, e.g. CR IT IC AL. Each pair is then seen as forming the opposite corners of a rectangle within the word square, the other two letters [at the corners of the rectangle] being the coded form. Thus CR gives SG (not GS which RC would give). When a pair of letters appears in the same row or column, the coded form is produced from the letters immediately to the right of or below each respectively. For last letters in a row or column, use the first letter of the same row or column. When all pairs are encoded the word is joined up again, thus: SGCICEOP. Answers to clues are to be encoded thus in the diagram. Solvers must deduce the code-word from pairings determinable by cross-checking letters, thus enabling them to complete the diagram.

This rubric nowhere states that the remaining letters are in alphabetical order, but this is always evident from the example. In a typical Playfair puzzle there are four words to be encoded. Often they are of six letters each with two pairs of letters coded and one pair unchecked.

Hints to solvers. The first stage is to solve the Playfair clues—without help from any checked letters! Because of the lack of checking the setter should give you easy clues (e.g. a hidden word, a simple anagram, a two-part charade all help). For solving these codes Scrabble® tiles can be a great help, enabling you to shift around the letters more quickly than with pencil and paper. The setter should give you some straight line coding and once you can decide whether the straight line is a row or column you are well on the way. Remember always to point your diagonals consistently upwards or downwards rather than sideways (see the note about CR above).

If you come across a sequence such as PQR, you may reasonably assume that it comes horizontally among the 'remaining letters'. This can be a great help. *Expect* to find XYZ on the last line—but beware the tutorial puzzle that follows!

CROSSWORD No. 29

Playfair by Duck from *Games and Puzzles* (see rubric on p.111)

Coded words are asterisked

ACROSS

1 The Devil's old catalogue (6)
6 Hamlet, for example, is mostly tragic in retrospect (5)
10 That is associated with rugby(masculine, rough game?) (9)
11 Showing ribs weakened, lacking energy (7)
12 Front half of gym shoe can make you swell (4)
13 Somehow became lower once (6)
*15 Leave a club perhaps and join up again? (6)
17 Epic dual is thrilling (6)
18 Introduced quietly, showing embarrassment and hiding effrontery (8)
22 Organ's something awful—it may be full of sand (8)
24 Yarn found in old magazine? (6)
*25 Gate—it often falls on sports field in summer (6)
27 Local girl collecting seaweed in abundance (6)
29 One with little height, circling, came down (4)
30 Delay coming through old Czech province (7)
31 A number could be revolutionary in combat (9)
32 Remain b-bad, old, backward (5)
33 Inflicted injuries—horrific—with weapons (6)

DOWN

1 Not in sorrow as previously—start afresh (5)
2 Salt drink, sort of soup, taken about noon—Sal usually has it (9)
3 There's semblance of disorder as before with shortage of oil (4)
4 Plant with two currents? One must have *a*! (6)
5 French lady in ermine, etc.—they can provide material for heat (8)
*6 Mace-bearer has to live with raw deal (6)
7 Schoolboys' punishments—bottoms must turn over. It's a handicap (6)
8 Bitterness is slightly excessive? You can do this to wine (7)
9 New horses in mire are slithering around (6)
14 Restaurant's dreadfully lurid inside and lifeless according to Mac (9)
16 A pet lamb? Mickey isn't half taken in school (8)
19 Riding over Somerset ditch is likely to make you sneeze (7)
20 Man who supposedly demonstrates 'god-power' upsetting conventions in party (6)
21 Drawing no. 50 at least? (6)
*22 Inwardly hard, outwardly spiteful, inclined to gossip (6)
23 Region in South Africa where men were tough (6)
26 Mass of flowers round top of loom once used for weaving (5)
28 Dice game without name initially—did Caesar go to work on it? (4)

CROSSWORD No. 29

Letters latent. Here is the appropriate rubric:

> From the answer to each clue one letter must be omitted whenever it occurs in the word, before entry in the diagram. Definitions in the clues refer to the full unmutilated answers; subsidiary indicators refer to the mutilated forms to be entered in the diagram. Numbers in brackets show the full lengths of unmutilated words.

Then usually is added something like this:

> The letters omitted, read in the order in which the clues are printed, form an appropriate message/quotation from the *Oxford Dictionary of Quotations*.

Curiously a sample clue is rarely provided, but that is no reason for you to be deprived:

[15.3] Politicians monkey with society repeatedly (8)

The diagram (from Azed) shows that the mutilated form has five letters, so we are looking for a word with three letters the same, all missed out. The SI consisting of the last four words gives us 'sai' + S + S = SAISS and since 'ists' looks like a possible ending for a word meaning politicians, we try to find some way of constructing a word with three t's. There is one, STATISTS, so we put a T in the margin to contribute to the message or quotation.

The generous checking in the puzzle that follows should make your task reasonably easy. The missing letters spell out a name to which we must all be grateful, but there is one proper name missing from *that* book!

CROSSWORD No. 30

ACROSS
1 Burglars finally grab a bit (5)
5 Orchestra completely English (5)
6 Navy'd name rowing boat (6)
7 Measured part of carpet edge (5)

DOWN
1 Times for bringing up a sword (5)
2 Right and left, with hints of national tragedy, soften (6)
3 Tree, possible supplier of deal (5)
4 Jock's vaulted passage to shed (5)

9 EEE

eeeenprrst	eeffoprrr	eefhoorrs	eefinorst	eefoprrrv
presenter	profferer	fore-horse	firestone	perfervor
represent	eefforstt	foreshore	forestine	eefoprrty
eeeenprrtv	off-street	eefhoortt	eefinprsu	ferrotype
preventer	setter-off	three-foot	superfine	eefprssuu
eeeenprsuv	eefghiorw	eefhorrtu	eefinrrst	superfuse
supervene	foreweigh	three-four	renfierst	eegghorsw
eeeenpssst	eefghirrt	eefhrrrtu	eefinrstu	whore's-egg
steepness	freighter	furtherer	interfuse	eeggiilnt
eeeenqrssu	eefgillnr	eefiillnp	eefioprrt	gelignite
queerness	refelling	fillipeen	profiteer	eeggiklnr
eeeenrrstw	eefgillny	eefiilmtx	eefioprrw	Greekling
westerner	feelingly	flexitime	fire-power	eeggilmnr
eeeenrrsuv	eefgilnnu	eefiilnrt	eefiossuw	gemel-ring
unreserve	unfeeling	infertile	sousewife	eeggilnnt
eeeensssst	eefgilrss	eefiilqru	eefipprrr	negligent
terseness	griefless	liquefier	fripperer	eeggilnss
eeeensssstw	eefgimruv	eefiilrst	eefiprstu	legginess
sweetness	vermifuge	fertilise	stupefier	eeggiloos
eeeeoprrtv	eefginorr	eefiimnty	eefiprsuv	geologise
portreeve	foreigner	femineity	perfusive	eegginnpu
eeeeoprsst	eefginrrr	eefiimrrt	eefirrrtt	pug-engine
poetresse	referring	metrifier	fritterer	eegginnrv
eeeeorrstv	eefginrrt	eefiinrss	eefirrrtu	revenging
oversteer	ferreting	fieriness	fruiterer	eegginrrs
eeeeorrtvx	eefgiortv	eefiiprtw	eefirrstu	sniggerer
overexert	forgetive	tripewife	surfeiter	eegginrst
eeeeppprtu	eefgiprru	eefiirrsv	eefirrttu	gee-string
puppeteer	prefigure	versifier	fruit-tree	eegginrtt
eeeeprrrsv	eefglnrtu	eefiirstt	eefkllttu	gettering
preserver	refulgent	testifier	kettleful	eeggiorsu
eeeeprrrtv	eefglrrtu	eefiklmrv	eefknoort	egregious
perverter	regretful	milk-fever	foretoken	eeggoorrv
				overgorge

An extract from *Chambers Anagrams,* for those who are solving in a hurry perhaps!

The Common Theme. Perhaps this is the most common of all special puzzles. The rubric simply reads as follows:

The unclued answers have something in common.

(Sometimes the word 'lights' is used instead of 'answers', but since this word has also been used on occasion for actual letters, I have avoided using it in this book.) If you finish solving all the clues you might be left with a set of unfilled answers as follows:

CAL__IO__E, CLI__, ER__TO, EUT__RP__, __ELP__MENE, PO__YH__NIA, TE__P IS__HOR__, THA__IA, __RANI__

It should not be difficult to spot that these are the nine muses (Calliope, Clio, Erato, Euterpe, Melpomene, Polyhymnia, Terpsichore, Thalia, Urania). The following puzzle is a fairly typical example from *The Spectator* (though the diagram isn't quite 'Ximenean'!).

CROSSWORD No. 31

Looking Up by Duck from *The Spectator*

The unclued answers have something in common. A clued answer could be said to have given them a start.

ACROSS

9 Going in for comp again and making deeper impression? (10 hyphened)
14 Boxer landed one short (3)
16 Part of empire—gold carriage (6)
18 Some benzole ICI supplied—oily (5)
20 Burning is constant hazard known to Lloyd's (7, hyphened)
22 Interferometers and other things assigned to Head of Science (7)
24 One (late) taken aback by certain heavenly bodies? (7)
25 Tangle—what fools must finally suffer (5)
26 Valley with coal-dust, black (5)
28 Terrible ordeal around noon in controversial play (7, two words)
31 He may travel in it over it (7)
33 Cowper's work has Greek character endlessly blue (7, two words)
37 Dead serious crime? Answer's hanging (5)
39 Stale vinegar is penetrating fish—end of meal (6)
40 Narrow projecting part 'urt (3)
41 Ixtle's been woven and elastic (10)
42 Secluded lanes with hollow tree among other trees (6)
43 Wyatt rejected eminences—magistrates (8)

DOWN

1 Blades in country cycle, dress and hat carefully arranged (13, hyphened)
2 Go off having relaxation without hint of anxiety (5)
3 Punch is nothing after sharp pain (6)
4 What's in poisonous air showing up somewhere in Paraguay (5)
6 Alluring commander is incompetent (7)
7 Boy to remain cuddling Dad, upset (6)
8 What's this—is seen possibly? (6, two words)
11 Bird in wavy bit of déshabillé with few people around (9)
12 Mean women fool these society suckers (13)
13 Canine sight—peer hard (8, hyphened)
15 Beautifully thin having eaten nothing (7)
21 Element of thrillers produced by South American writers with energy (8)
28 Obliquely, like philosopher (6)
30 Rivers in depressed old pasture (6)
32 Bring down medic—to free from pain going round (6)
34 Soft, pure, terribly superior (5)
35 Prison dance (5)

CROSSWORD No. 31

Looking up

Theme and Variations. A development of the 'thematic' puzzle is the theme and variations puzzle, for which the rubric is as follows (the numbers may vary):

> Four theme words have something in common. Each of them has two variations connected to it, though the nature of the connection differs with each set of variations.

In the puzzle some of the clues read 'Theme-word A',' Variation of A', and so on. To give you some idea of how this works, here is a listing of some answers from an early Azed puzzle:

Theme: 4 Stomachs of ruminants
Theme-word A Rumen. Variations: Lions, Wasps (R.U.men)
Theme-word B Reticulum. Variations: Bonnet, King's hood (alternative names, see *Chambers*)
Theme-word C Bible. Variations: Vinegar, Breeches (names of famous bibles)
Theme-word D Read. Variations: Solve, Study (definitions)

A theme and variations puzzle appears as No.53 on p.176.

Carte Blanche. With this sort of puzzle you are presented with a blank diagram, usually 12 × 12, and asked to fill in the bars as well as the letters. Instructions are in the form:

> The symmetry of the diagram is such that it would be the same if turned upside down, but not if given a quarter turn. The proportion of checked to unchecked letters is about normal. The clues are in their current order.

In other words you have a normal Ximenes/Azed diagram of 36 clues with the usual conventions on the number of checked letters (see p.92).

Hints to solvers. You would be well advised to avoid using the printed diagram initially. Start solving the puzzle on a large sheet of squared paper, until you have defined the tops of the diagram's two sides. Concentrate very carefully on the first three or four across clues, and a few down answers will suggest themselves. When you are able to fill in a bar, fill in the one symmetrically opposite. Remember that the nth across clue will be in a symmetrical position with the nth counting from the end, but the same is not true of the downs. By the end of the sixth row of the diagram there should be space for nine across clues since there are usually 18 in total.

119

Ximenes (Derrick Macnutt)
wearing his Ximenes tie, 1971

Jane Bown, *The Observer*

Afrit (Preb. A. F. Ritchie)
Headmaster of Wells Cathedral School, 1948

The Headmaster, Wells Cathedral School

Azed
(Jonathan Crowther)
wearing his Azed tie, 1981

Oxford and County Newspapers

CROSSWORD No. 32

Carte Blanche by Duck from *Crossword*. The clues appear in the correct order. Solvers are asked to fill in the bars (but need not bother with the numbers). Symmetry is such that the diagram would appear the same if turned upside down but not if given a 90 degree turn.

Clamorous priest stirred up the Northern worker

A talent to contain what's original, not going to an extreme?

Some speeches drag out in Shakespeare

Violent poetry translator's immersed in

Field of activity—what the book records in this place

River needs raised bank, removing rapid current in duct

Scottish observer—creeps nervously about, very Scottish

Poisonous plant from Uruguay, thin short one

Genus of monkeys—see returning missionary with one

The most evil character in Indian police station detained by security force

Part of opera: what's central in it?

Note aphis spurting ... what comes from a _____?

Look in farm vehicle, see old peasant

Bashed lout in revenge

Communist always rejected Thatcher

The prize in old game

Onset of crisis and I go a greeny yellow

The pan is shaken in the specified place—is this a precious ore here?

Group of armadillos look heavy coming up round end of plateau

Animal in tangle with short tree, right between the branches

'To the garcon' (He got a _____ split up?)

Old woman wanting common time in the gutter

Aquatic organisms lunge uncertainly in canal

What the intrusive newsman says: Here's a monetary advance

CROSSWORD No. 32
Carte Blanche by Duck

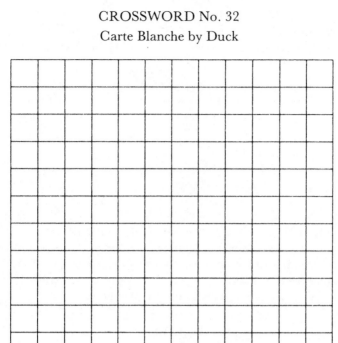

As before you should stifle onset of
  excessive laugh
Eye cut with lancet and chemical
  often used in cutting
What laugh may produce, we hear,
  spreads
Murmuring softly instead of loudly in
  excessive nicety
Marine creature from old civilisation
  kept in an American city
Certainly old Duck is not absurdly
  hard...
...Eagerly aimin' to provide what
  overstressed solvers need?
What you get in *Private Eye*? It bores
Porgies—what one receives aboard?
Low character in airship
Public shelter keeping out the cold....
...Nevertheless one ... one probably
  won't feel it!

Right and Left was invented by Ximenes, who also set several examples under his other name Tesremos for *The Listener* (for the uninitiated Tesremos is the reverse of Somerset, Macnutt's middle name). The rubric says all:

Apart from 1 across, which is normal, each clue is really two clues, side by side but not overlapping, leading to two answers, one for the numbered space on the left of the central line and one for that on the right: the clue for either side may come first. The division between clues is not necessarily marked by punctuation.

Hints to solvers. It is worth spending several minutes on 1 across. Quite often it is a straightforward anagram clue and it may be related to the peculiarity of the right and left puzzle. Solve as many clues as you can in the upper half of the puzzle and expect the break to be cunningly concealed in many cases. If the worst comes to the worst, arrange clusters of answers together on one side of the central divide and be prepared to transpose the letters across the divide when everything becomes clearer. Alternatively you might consider using a copied diagram before working on the printed one.

The puzzle below is one from Ximenes:

CROSSWORD No. 33

CROSSWORD No. 33

Right and Left by Ximenes from the *Observer*

ACROSS

1 Fruit bolter being terribly sick in rowing-boat (12)

6 Every one of these fish is to pass the Rear Admiral safe and sound—a close shave (6,6)

7 There's starchy stuff in half the arm-bone and in half the guts—in half of each more than a pound (6,6)

8 With pride old Nelly embraces an Apollo with a head of gold caught like Apollo himself on the rebound (6,6)

10 Slow down: there's a danger signal about road-surfacing with lumpy projections not firm edging second-class road (6,6)

12 This predatory bird hasn't quite got the dash to catch carp, or scarlet-backed carp-like fish (6,6)

16 Mum, a mercenary Venus, needs to be got up in the old, old way, i.e. long curls innumerable (6,6)

17 A thing which stands for Britain, with what's British in it, to provoke a shy creature around America (6,6)

18 Preserve one bed for each: this fertiliser is not quite at full strength (6,6)

19 A dark blue cloth—something unique I got in jumble-sale—a short yard, with a margin to spare (6,6)

DOWN

1 Jet flyer crashes bridge—G.W.R. link with east disorganised: single line remains—verb. sap. (7,7)

2 It's the Cup—grand—half the second half's gone—all the tricks —blaze away—the ball's in—it's a goal (5,5)

3 Spanker's near me! I've terrible Latin, little Greek—I'll be kept in—not well up in courses about oxygen: we're downtrodden, but na tanned the noo (8,8)

4 I stagger along: I might remind you of the cricket tests—those paragons of patient effort (6,6)

5 Great violinist, having to give a recital among you, renders no less than fifty odd pieces (5,5)

9 A night-flier with strength to diminution can hardly fly at all—pulls up, being about to fit sails (8,8)

11 Saintly man in France has his prime interrupted by the Nine wild and eery busting the clerical domicile (7,7)

13 She'll advise you, for example, up the river to go slowly and take it easy with little work (6,6)

14 An Admiral, born to be on the water, that's to say a fatherly man where there are ships (5,5)

15 The organ stops: part of the woodwind has perished and rings sharper: some of the cellos elope (5,5)

Definition and Letter-Mixture.

In a DLM puzzle each clue consists of a sentence which contains a definition of the answer and a mixture of the letters (beginning with the beginning or ending with the end of a word in the clue) of the required word.

That, more or less, is the normal rubric. A typical clue might read as follows (without the underlining provided of course!).

[15.4] I can't sleep 'cos I'm an insecure sort of person (9)

The first three words here give the definition and COSIMANIN is a mixture of INSOMNIAC.

Here is a DLM clue where the mixture ends at the end of a word:

[15.5] Tango theme is rendered by octet (9)

Can you see a mixture of EIGHTSOME working back from the 's'?

Unlike with strictly hidden clues, a certain amount of verbal 'cottonwool' is encouraged to produce an interesting context. Often three DLM clues are run together and an example of this from Azed is given below. A puzzle consisting entirely of DLM clues becomes quite easy once a few words have been put in, because you soon learn exactly where to look for the answer.

CROSSWORD No. 34

CROSSWORD No. 34

Radio Times by Azed from the *Observer*

Each 'programme synopsis' contains both a definition (one word or more) and a mixture of the letters (beginning with the beginning or ending with the end of a word in the clue) of the three words indicated by the clue numbers (in the correct order). Both indications of the first word precede both indications of the second, and so on. In each case either the definition or the letter-mixture may come first.

ACROSS

1 }
7 } *The beat glides up.* George Melly shows how rhythm has been put
10 } on disc and film since the Beatles were seen prancing through Yellow Submarine land (8, 4, 10 (2 words))

11 }
12 } *What were we wearing?* A panel of fashion experts examines how to
14 } get back those old styles, i.e. rare clothes from the clothes-horse, or make copies of old garments ('U', of course) (6, 5, 8)

17 }
18 } *The Stage is Set* (play). Country shepherd cannot refuse scheming
19 } city bird, abandons sheep, ewe lambs and all, in exchange for the inevitable lost innocence (6, 6, 6)

20 }
23 } *Lifting the veil.* In a downright uncompromising look at what is
25 } going on in a modern convent, Rory Pinstripe seeks to explain unceasing devotion to the 'habit of centuries' (6, 6, 6)

27 }
29 } *Pins and Needles.* See Charmian Purl knit a shawl from yak hair
30 } (matted) and sew a flimsy dress in bombazine (her class assisting in this) (8, 5, 6)

31 }
32 } *Punk—Inspiration or Babel?* Lower end of music scene scrutinised
33 } by Ted Grope, a chap with no liking for glib appraisals or easy slants (10, 4, 8)

DOWN

1 }
2 } *Comic Book Art—Pop or Op?* Examining the role of
3 } Superman, Penny Numbers checks on what may be salvaged from the original concept (4, 10, 5)

4 }
5 } *Lines in Maroon Ink.* Dundee poet Hamish Thible seeks to bare his
6 } soul and thus give a Gaelic ring to the phrase 'go metric' (6, 6, 6)

7 }
8 } *A 'Pink' or a 'Purple'?* Giles Painter's talk is not so rash as to
9 } try to get at what liberalism really means but it should help to clear the system (8, 6, 8)

13 }
15 } *Everything About it is Unfeeling.* Representing show business in
16 } declamatory lingo, puts off the comic mask, warning of that elusive 'slot in the bill' (10, 8, 8)

21 }
22 } *New Arrangements.* A conducted tour through the maze of
23 } modern dance orchestrations by that skilled Scot king of the ballroom pas, Hew McOrnes (6, 6, 6)

24 }
26 } *Here let me lie.* Panel-game in which contestants repair to the
28 } Truth Booth to see flagrantly fictitious experiences dispensed with as objects of fun (6, 5, 4)

Wrong Number. This, perhaps, is the least common of the standard specials, and it is very hard to start off. Here is the rubric:

> Each clue includes a one-word definition of the word required at the number where it stands but belongs as a whole to a word of the same length elsewhere. Method recommended is to find, after solving a clue, a definition of the solution in one of the other words of its length: this will show where the word is to go.

Here are two clues from such a puzzle by Azed:

[15.6] 28 across. The old woman's blue over end of relative (5)

[15.7] 9 down. Glum youth soft-headed, one kept in trim no longer (5)

It turns out that the answer belonging to 28 across is UNCLE (the clue for which is at 25 down and the definition for which at 28 across is 'relative'). 28 across gives ANILE (anil + e) which means soft-headed, so the answer fits in at 9 down. The answer to 9 down is PROIN (p + i in Ron—remember Ron Glum in the radio programme 'Take It from Here'?). This fits in at 2 down which contains the definition word 'prune'. Thus each WN puzzle consists of a number of circular chains, one for each word length.

See how you get on with this one from Ximenes:

CROSSWORD No. 35

CROSSWORD No. 35

Wrong Number by Ximenes from the *Observer*

Each clue includes a one-word definition of the word required at the number where it stands but belongs as a whole to a word of the same length elsewhere. Method recommended is to find, after solving a clue, a definition of the solution in one of the 5 other clues to words of its length: this will show where the word is to go.

ACROSS

1 Grape contains centre of pulp, a conical body (5)
5 I'm from the isle—I'm too small to pull a coach (7)
11 I'm fleecing a bird that's swallowed champagne, perhaps: you can have a slice (7)
12 To take prolonged looks at a TV is to flounder (5)
13 The Navy in America are used in state elections (4)
14 Rail being far from broken is together in one piece (8)
15 East China must slough off N.America and welcome in minor officer, Turkish official (6)
18 What's divine about novelist revered a good bit (7)
21 Crown, and less valuable coins, contain a mineral coated with copper carbonate (9)
22 To intrigue disloyally with her is horrific, just a bit (9)
24 Held head in an awful state, covered with blood (7)
28 Have a crack at the French in the hollow (6)
29 Putter-in of good work in bar, being in debt, behaves like bird-fancier off to Gretna (8)
30 Aromatic condiment kept in pukka vases (4)
31 Fastener—here's part of the clasp right in view (5)
32 Meal dear in Paris: he'll pinch your pony and sock you (7)
33 Socialist votes stuck together—shows herd instinct (7)
34 The flower of creation, its appetites and its food (5)

DOWN

1 Unusual ernes in flight, to reach which one must cross part of the Channel (8)
2 The activity of a fly-by-night round that location could be learnt as the result of a pick-up (8)
3 If it luxuriates on a lawn, spray is in vogue (5)
4 Take sly measures, lacing one tea with another (9)
6 Hiding-place on shore where seceding party receives envoy representing Navy (6)
7 This cherry split's nice, not 'arf—swell (6)
8 Affected by storm tortile tellurium is laminated (9)
9 Rising prima donna, wanting meals supplemented (4)
10 Make declarations and talk rubbish in the 'ighlands (4)
16 With endless rush I beat: my force fairly staggers (9)
17 She's in arch, short shows never filmed by BBC—they gave lots of people the sack (9)
19 ITV arias out of tune must have got the bird (8)
20 Once passionate wench in only part of garment (8)
22 Ham recipe is wrong—result's slimy, often salt (6)
23 Product of juice of red fruit spoils a metal (6)
25 Lobe of whale's tail's eaten mashed—that's lucky (5)
26 To separate brawlers, flushed with start of drink (4)
27 Economised—only half keen—in a limited edition (4)

Other specials. In addition to the specials just described there are a number of other specials which have become standard (e.g. Justyn Print by Zander in *The Listener*, see pp.190–1). Some, though, are very much 'special specials'. A 'special special' may exploit a different clue type, a different way of entering words on the diagram, a different shape of diagram—or even all three. Some advanced solvers feed on such a diet of puzzles almost exclusively, and their needs are well catered for by *The Listener* and Crossword Club—not to mention the occasional new special from Azed in The *Observer*. (Roughly one puzzle in six from Azed is a special, but new specials are usually reserved for particular occasions.)

In difficulty such puzzles vary enormously, and the setter can overload the dice against the solver by leaving too many possibilities for the answer's mode of entry on to the diagram. 'Special specials' lie at the top of Crossword Mountain. Only you will ultimately decide how far up that mountain it is worth going and whether the setter is launching an unfair blizzard directly at you. But keep trying and you will soon conquer some exciting new peaks!

16

Crossword Competitions

Although solving crosswords is often a solitary occupation, it is possible to introduce a competitive element. Many periodicals limit their competitions to the level of chance, by inviting solvers to send in their solutions and then awarding prizes for the first three 'out of the hat'. This at least reassures the editor that there is someone 'out there' solving the puzzles—though it is surprising how many of Afrit's *Listener* puzzles in the 1930s attracted no correct entries. The best competitions, though, must be those that have an increased element of skill. The best-known of these is undoubtedly *Collins Dictionaries/Times* Crossword Championship (formerly sponsored by Cutty Sark). Here one has to solve a standard puzzle plus a very hard elimination puzzle in *The Times* before progressing to a regional final and the national final. Speed of solving and accuracy are the keynotes.

If *The Times* championship is the best-known competition, then the *Observer* clue-writing competition is probably the most significant in terms of 'good done for crosswords'. Started in 1945 by Ximenes it continued until his death in 1971, then resumed under Azed (Jonathan Crowther) in 1972. Solvers are required to solve the puzzle, then write a cryptic clue for a specified word (usually replacing a definition-only clue in the puzzle itself). Through the competition Ximenes developed the theory of cluemanship from Afrit's basic ideas to a fine art (culminating with the publication of *Ximenes on the Art of the Crossword*). Azed has carried on where Ximenes left off, and although he takes his name from the reverse of a Spanish inquisitor (the reverse of Deza) he is no less tolerant of latter-day 'heretics'!

Associated with the *Observer*'s competition have been annual honours lists and periodic dinners to salute the setter. As the competition now stands the submitters of the three clues judged best by Azed are rewarded with book tokens and 2 honours points; the next 20 or so best are labelled VHC (very highly commended) and gain one honours point; and a further 70 or so are deemed HC (highly commended). A cup passes between first-prizewinners and a silver salver between annual champions. Prizewinners and VHCs are listed in the *Observer*, and in a competing year there are 13 competitions (12 monthly, plus one at Christmas when VHCs are awarded 'extra prizes'). Solvers sending a stamped addressed envelope receive slips detailing successful clues plus a commentary from Azed on the competition, often with details of clues that didn't make it and why they didn't.

For the rest of this chapter we will look at some extracts from the slips, with Azed's comments. Some of the names on them have become legendary with regular solvers, with competitors such as C. Allen Baker, C. J. (now Sir Jeremy) Morse, Mrs L. Jarman, D. P. M. Michael and N. C. Dexter providing gems for over 30 years. Your author has had a measure of success himself, but is still quite a 'new boy', having begun as recently as 1970!*

Ximenes No. 79
SALOME—1. Maj. G. W. Shephard (Scarborough): Perplexed damsel wanting a head and requiring nothing more (*amsel-o* and *literal mng.*)...
... An interesting point of 'cluemanship' was raised by a regular and expert solver. Was 'insist' for 'in sist' without a hint of division, sound in the clue to SISKIWIT? . . . the practice had better stop. . . .

Ximenes No. 148
FILIBUSTER—1. A. N. Clark (Portsmouth): I rifle tubs at sea . . .
Mr Clark's *multum in parvo* is, I think, superb; he has brilliantly seized a rare chance.

Ximenes No. 162
TITANESS . . . 'A hardy girl to go against a goddess.' Unsound in *many* ways! It is meant for 'Tess anti' anag., but no anag. is indicated, the wording being vague and unhelpful: this is particularly unfair in an *indirect* anag., the actual anag. words not being given: on top of that Hardy uses its capital—this is deliberately unfair, as it *cannot* be a true clue; the converse process is allowable—a writer may *give* a word a capital for its own purposes without incorrectness. . . .

Ximenes No. 229
MASCOT—1. C. Allen Baker (Milnathort): Up in the morning and

---

* This and other diffident statements here do no justice to DFM's importance in the crossword field. Over the past decade it is he himself who has been the undoubted star in the Azed competitions, for which he has produced a stream of clues to 'fill the eye' (as the judges say of champion dogs at Crufts!). NCD

'with the sun and early bed is said to bring good fortune. . . . May I repeat what I have said before several times, that when I quote unsuccessful clues, I do so not to hand wooden spoons to the authors but to help not only the authors but the competitors, especially newcomers.

Ximenes No. 275 (Printer's Devilry)
ESTOVER—1. J. B. Filburn: True! Man's fasts are inconsistent even with Len there to inspire. . . . COMMENTS—375 entries, 354 correct . . . I must repeat two principles about devilled clues. (1) The formal sense must *not* be sacrificed to the devilled sense . . . (2) The hiding can be *too* well done. An example is 'A good coke heats water in no time' . . . *Very* difficult . . . no fun at all. . . .

Ximenes No. 460
ASTONISHMENT (Misprints)—1. H. S. Tribe: Open winder? Then no mats is shaken (*wonder*). . . . By the way, my wife assures me that Mr Tribe's delightfully neat clue presents a strong household hint... Indication of anagrams. There were a good many which I couldn't accept as sound, e.g. 'fraught', 'separation of', 'critical', 'it appears'.

Ximenes No. 634
BEDSTEAD—1. C. J. Morse: To be still is not enough here: both sides of the sheet must be tucked in (be-d-st-ead '& lit.'). . . . It seems clear that posting on Friday is no longer safe, even in London itself. One solver has written, he tells me, to the P.M.G. to complain, and has so far received no satisfaction but a brief acknowledgement.

Ximenes No. 647
MADCAP—1. E. Gomersall (York): Cake with nuts on top (*cake = madcap, Chamb.*)

Ximenes No. 690 [A 'trick' puzzle for 1 April]
ASCERTAIN—1. Miss D. W. Taylor (Worthing): Find the right answer? Sure—the first of April's over! (A-'s-certain) . . . 263 entries, 229 mahoganies . . . the leg-pull was far, far more successful than I meant.

Ximenes No. 945
OBLITERATE 1. N. C. Dexter (Biol.) Treat defective end of a tube (*anag. plus e '& lit.'*) . . . R.Postill: Wipe out Beatle and disorganised trio remains . . . [Mr Postill] says in his note 'out, vb'; that leaves 'blot' [sic] alone as the definition, and I don't think it will quite do without 'out'.

Ximenes No. 967
CREMOSIN—1. N. C. Dexter: Colour of the Skie, perhaps, with Morne [sic] breaking (*anag. '& lit.', F.Q.* 11, 3 *'Early before the Morne with Cremosin ray'*) [F.Q. = Faerie Queene.]

Ximenes No. 1115
FLESHPOTTERY—1. Mrs B. Lewis: Product of the Tory's pelf, snarls the prosy left (*anags. '& lit.': snarl = tangle*)... COMMENTS— Just under 300 entries, nearly all correct. Was it too hot? Am I, quite unconsciously, becoming more difficult? Or were people upset by not finding Jethart staff (s.v. Jeddart)? This arbitrary omission of cross-references in C is annoying (and, I think, inefficient). . . .

Azed No. 70
. . . If the misprinted clue is as much a definition as its original it cannot be considered to be misprinted. Ximenes made the point in the slip to No.1131 for those who keep scrap-books.
. . . I would always regard 'a bit of', 'a piece of' as coming from the front of the word. . . .

Azed No. 92
BRAINWASH—1. L. May: Bust down reason? (bra in wash).

Azed No. 100
CENTENARIAN:—1. D. F. Manley: An ancient the Queen may get excited (*anag. '& lit.', royal telegram*)... 'Azed achieves his for when he drives around Muswell Hill chased by two? (EN TEN (N.10) in CAR + I + AN (1 + 1 = 2). Dreadfully unsound, I'm afraid, and virtually unsolvable. There is no indication of the part of speech required; 'When he drives' will never do for 'car'; Muswell Hill is only one part of N.10; and 'two' for 1 + AN is surely unacceptable.

Azed No. 430
TEGULA: 1.—C. G. Millin: What the fiddler might have played on, in the film (*gu in tela '& lit.' 'Fiddler on the Roof'*) . . . Is a tela a film? I examined this question very carefully . . . *Chambers* definition somewhat inadequate . . . turned to the new *Collins English Dictionary* for the reassurance I needed . . . Finally a reminder that I still have small stocks of Azed ties, all three colours. The price is now £3 each inclusive of V.A.T. . . .

Azed No. 482
BODY-SNATCHER: 1. C. J. Morse: Stiff collaring, that's my trade—shows what can be done by starch (*2 mngs and anag*).

Azed No. 500
BEFOOL (with 2 extra D's) = I. D. Ashcroft: Admass imperative: get fund at others' expense (*be-fool* imp. form of am-ass). . . . Very few of you noticed that the style of the down clues was such that they made reasonable sense with and without the superfluous D's. . . . The Azed 500 Dinner was a spectacularly successful affair . . . I look forward to meeting many of these friends at No. 750.

Azed No. 662
BARGE-COUPLE: 1. R. J. Hooper: Sawyer's contribution to topping story shows the lighter Twain (barge-couple; ref. Mark T.) . . . [This following clue] is probably the most unsolvable clue I've ever received. ' ''O Attic shape!'' Sounds like naughty Keats may have been involved in this.' Explanation (I quote): 'Quotation from ''Grecian Urn'' by Keats. Naughty = no ''T''. Keats without T sounds like KEYS. Keys open locks, as do couples on a barge.' Need I say more?

Azed No. 679 (see also Ximenes No.275, p.131)
ESTOVER ('P.D.')—1. T. J. Moorey: 'Dry' minister organising party left-winger. . . . COMMENTS:—A mammoth entry—702 in all. . . . I also failed to notice that Ximenes used ESTOVER as a P.D. competition word over 30 years ago (his No.275), and there are still regular solvers who remember that earlier occasion . . . the Ximenes competition attracted a much smaller entry.

Over the past thirty years N. C. Dexter has probably been the most brilliant clue-writer, but C. J. Morse has been the most *consistent*. If you want to know what makes a good cryptic clue, simply look at his two clues above (Ximenes No. 634 and Azed No. 482). One is a great '& lit.'; the other shows how a clever definition can be combined with a subsidiary indication in a totally misleading context. Aspiring crossword setters would do well to enrol in Azed's correspondence school!

17

The Complete Crossworder

Tell anyone that you are a crossword setter and you will be met with one of three stock responses:

1. 'I suppose you do *The Times* in twenty minutes.'
2. 'Which do you do first—the diagram or the words?'
3. 'How long does it take you to make up a puzzle?'

I usually continue the discussion as follows:

1. 'Yes, by now I can break the back of *The Times* puzzle quite quickly (*seven* minutes is my fastest time), but even after years of experience I can get stuck and have to leave the last word or two. *Sometimes* I think it is the setter's fault because either his clue is unsound by the proper standards of fairness or because I can't be expected to know Keats off by heart.' Then there follows a discussion about the standards of Ximenes and so on. However, I try to make the point that even if I take only twenty minutes, it might be worth their while to keep trying. 'Look for anagrams or hidden words,' I suggest, 'and don't give in too easily. We all have to start somewhere.'

2. The answer to this one is glaringly obvious—or is it? Often the inspiration for a crossword comes from an idea—or perhaps a couple of long phrases you want to put in a puzzle. In that sense the words might come first. Overall though you must get the diagram right and you will finish up filling in whatever words will fit. Then you must write the clues.

3. 'Never less than a few hours and sometimes quite a few evenings.' In terms of 'pounds per hour' from editors crossword setting is not a well-paid hobby—but it provides its own satisfactions. Solving puzzles is much the same in terms of time spent. Some people only want to devote 10 minutes on the bus every day. Others will gladly spend a few evenings with a tough puzzle if they know it will work out.

The complete crossworder will, I suppose, be a setter *and* a solver, but not all will want to be setters and the opportunities for getting puzzles published are often few and far between. There is one respect, though, in which everyone can become a more complete crossworder. Share your hobby with a friend; find a colleague or two to look at the back page of the *Guardian* during the lunch break. If you are an Azed solver or a *Listener* solver, you may meet new friends from further afield at special crossword dinners. I have made many new friends this way.

Solving a crossword is normally a duel between the lone solver and his favourite setter. But it need never be a totally selfish occupation, as my father taught me thirty years ago. Happy crosswording!

18

A Crossword Romp

This final chapter contains 45 puzzles ancient and modern. Some are easy; some are hard; a few might seem impossible. They have been chosen within three different categories: (i) 'historical' puzzles, (ii) representative puzzles of the modern era, and (iii) some of my own puzzles reprinted for a larger audience. Since I am writing the book, I had better contribute at least half the puzzles overall, but this proportion by no means reflects my significance as a setter! Not all the clues printed here will necessarily match Ximenean standards (though I hope my own will not be found wanting); but all the puzzles should have something interesting about them, so I hope you will enjoy the romp.

Nos. 36–38 take us back to the early days. No. 36 was a discovery in a second-hand Oxford bookshop while I was writing the earlier chapters of this book. In 1924 C. Arthur Pearson of WC2 published a book of 'word squares', but these were in fact primitive crosswords. Our No. 36 was Word Square No.12. The individually numbered puzzles, overlapping words and unclued pairs (e.g. 49–50) are evidence of a new word puzzle form coming alive. The idea of a pretty picture was taken up by Torquemada and his first puzzle in the *Observer* (No. 37) illustrates the 'feelers' which the Sunday paper was putting out to its readers. Subsequent puzzles featured a marionette, 'all the world's a stage', 'Mrs Porter and her daughter' and other intriguing themes. Notice how many of the clues offer something a little more challenging than a straight definition (with a misleading context in the very first clue). No. 38 shows an early example of a Bible crossword from the *Sunday Companion* of 1 May 1926.

No. 39 is a 'quick crossword' from the *Daily Telegraph*, slipped in for sentimental reasons (see p.xi) and No. 40 takes us back again to the early days of the *Telegraph* with a full version of the puzzle promised on p.23.

No. 41 was my first published cryptic crossword from the *Radio Times* of 1964, and I offer apologies to solvers who weren't watching

TV in those days. Clue scrutineers should be warned that I hadn't yet discovered Ximenes.

We turn now to *The Times*. Nos. 42 and 43 are both from finals of the Crossword Championship. (By the way it took me four times as long as John Sykes to finish No. 43 on the train from Oxford to London.)

Unlike *The Times,* the *Guardian* discloses the names (or at any rate pseudonyms) of its setters. The most Ximenean of these is Alec Robins, who masquerades as Custos. Alec Robins's output has been high in quantity and quality—and not just for the *Guardian.* On alternate months he is 'Everyman' of the *Observer* (No. 45), and in that capacity he helped Ximenes write his book about crosswords before writing one of his own (see p.273). We shall also meet him later as Zander (No. 60).

According to *The Guinness Book of Records* the world's most prolific setter is Roger F. Squires. To *Guardian* solvers he is known as Rufus, but he sets puzzles for many papers and periodicals, including the *Financial Times* (No. 46). Perhaps the most popular *Guardian* setter is Araucaria (John Graham) who shows flair in his puzzles but who is by no means a strict Ximenean in his cluemanship (No. 47).

Prospective setters may find it difficult to place their puzzles in the London dailies, but until a few years ago the *Birmingham Evening Mail* welcomed all comers. Two of my own puzzles appear here as Nos. 48 and 49. My pseudonym 'Duck' comes from Donald Duck, in line with my philosophy that ultimately crosswords should be fun rather than inquisitorial.

One of my favourite puzzles as a teenager was The Skeleton in the *Sunday Express* (No. 50). It is a particularly interesting puzzle for anyone wanting some early lessons in how a grid can be constructed.

Nos. 51, 52, 53 and 54 are all puzzles of mine published by Quality Magazines, first with *Quiz Digest*, then with *Tough Puzzles* (see p.275). Nos. 55 and 56 are two of my puzzles from *Games and Puzzles,* a magazine that broke new ground in 'crossword journalism' in the 1970s. No. 55 was the first Duck puzzle.

The Listener crossword began unpromisingly on 2 April 1930 with a 'musical crossword'. One clue was 'Last three letters of Christian name of a great composer'. The answer (without notes) was IAN—I wonder who the setter had in mind? Mr I. Cresswell of 40 Hamilton Road, Colchester, provided the only all-correct solution but he didn't get a prize. The first pseudonymous setter appears to have been Doggerel, but the running was soon taken up by Proton (A. McIntyre) and Afrit. Before the Second World War prizes were often given to all winners, but the setters of a pre-Ximenean era confessed in print that they could not always gauge the appropriate level of difficulty.

Afrit's first 'Printer's Devilry' was published on 2 June 1937 (No. 57). Some breaks came at the ends of words; unrelated pairs of words are to be inserted; the checking is not as good as it looks because of unclued letter pairs; and there are numerous references to literature. Despite these difficulties there were 30 correct entries. Can you solve the puzzle? I couldn't, but reading the solution was interesting! During the War, *The Listener* introduced an easier (and rather poor) puzzle every other week; Afrit (none too pleased) dropped out. After the War, Afrit re-emerged, and No. 58 is his last *Listener* puzzle. Afrit's *Armchair Crosswords* has already been noted for its contribution to 'clueology' (see pp.58-9). The book's puzzles, though, look very old-fashioned, and (as we have already noted) some of the clues do not match the standards subsequently set by Ximenes.

Thanks largely to the work of Ximenes, *Listener* puzzles have become more even in standard and difficulty. Only three prizes are given each week, and the number of correct entries is now usually between two and three hundred. Nos. 60–63 are examples of *Listener* puzzles. Zander is Alec Robins (whom we have already met); Hen is Vince Henderson; Virgilius is Brian Greer, who also sets for *Puzzler* and *The Times*.

Much has been made in this book of the Ximenean tradition, so for Nos. 64–67 we return to the master himself. No. 66 was the first Letters Latent puzzle and No. 67 marked the end of the Ximenes era. Ximenes' successor Azed is represented in Nos. 68–71. Azed is perhaps wittier than Ximenes and he has developed his own range of specials, some of which are seen here. In the plain puzzle (No. 69) Azed concealed the name of his fiancée (details at the back!). The Mephisto puzzle in *The Sunday Times* is only rarely a special. The first Mephisto (Richard Kilner) died in 1973 and was succeeded by Richard Whitelegg, coincidentally an exact contemporary of Jonathan Crowther (Azed) at Cambridge. Mephisto II is far better than his predecessor and much closer to the Ximenean tradition (No. 72).

In 1977 Azed's solvers contributed to *The Azed Book of Crosswords*. Nos. 73 and 74 formed a tribute to Azed by myself and Bristol office colleague Merlin (Richard Palmer). One or two of my clues now look dated—including the value of the top prize (£20, as I write).

No. 75 is a puzzle by Apex, Eric Chalkley from Croydon, who became a 'disciple' through reading Ximenes' book. Eric learnt not only how to 'ape X(imenes)' but to develop a style of his own. He contributes regularly to the *Guardian* and *The Listener*. At Christmas

Apex circulates a private puzzle to about forty 'top crossworders' including Stephen Sondheim and Leonard Bernstein. Few in Britain probably realise that Sondheim is a crossword setter who has done much to further the cryptic crossword in America. No. 76 is a narrative puzzle, of a type probably invented by Torquemada.

Barred cryptics also appear in the *Spectator* (No. 31 on pp.116-7) and in the *New Statesman* once a month (No. 77). Salamanca (Michael Freeman) is a particularly inventive setter, who also appears in *The Listener*. Like Araucaria, he worries the orthodox Ximeneans! No. 78 by Mass (H. W. Massingham) reminds us that crosswords need not be 'square' in any sense of the word. Look out in *The Listener* for all sorts of shapes, including hexagons.

No. 79 is undoubtedly the hardest puzzle I have managed to complete. Published in *The Listener* to celebrate the Queen's Silver Jubilee, it provided me with over 20 hours of alternate frustration and enjoyment. It is three-dimensional, and I suggest you make a box. Leiruza (A. E. Hughes) has produced a number of puzzles involving knight's moves. Finally we come to No. 80, a fitting tribute to Ximenes.

CROSSWORD No. 36

From *The Word Square Puzzle Book* (1924)

HORIZONTAL

1–14 Pertaining to the Church
12–17 The young of cows
18–23 Wild sheep of Nepaul
22–24 Refuse (noun)
25–27 Low marshy land
26–31 Unfriendly disposition
32–37 An intimate acquaintance
38–41 A kind of vermin
47–48 One of the bovine genus
54–56 An expression of affirmation
57–59 A girl's name
60–62 Part of the verb 'to be'
66–68 Nothing
69–72 A common beverage
73–76 To cause to fall
77–79 A snare
83–85 A kind of tree
87–91 Pertaining to the law
92–95 A heavenly body
95–97 A strong-smelling plant
100–103 A valley
105–109 An appointed meeting
110–115 To select
116–120 The top room of a house
122–127 To impress
128–133 A kind of poetic foot
140–142 To go astray
143–151 A section of the Government
152–154 Diminutive of Henry
155–157 Part of a clergyman's address
158–160 A loud sound
159–166 Guiltless
167–168 Latin for 'and'
171–172 An obsolete pronoun
173–179 A one-horned animal
182–184 Opposed to no
186–191 An ambassador
190–192 A beverage
196–200 A sailing vessel used for pleasure
200–212 Having four seeds
205–209 Frog spawn

VERTICAL

1–122 To set free
2–55 To convey
3–100 Cut or hewn
5–36 An age
7–24 A pronoun
11–25 The title of Kipling's famous poem
12–75 An edible grain
15–107 Affected by visions
16–64 An element
17–133 Having feelings in common with another
37–70 Accomplished
49–74 Dread or veneration
55–135 Compliant
57–69 A Jewish month
64–183 To revive
89–125 A pledge
90–126 In the manner of (in music)
92–116 A spring of mineral water
94–118 Practical skill
109–195 Sensible to slight touches
110–196 Austerity
124–172 To obey
134–196 Truth
135–171 A colour
137–182 A pronoun of plural number
143–200 A full-grown person
144–187 To partake of food
146–189 An ancient native prince of Peru
148–191 A square measure
165–207 The back of the neck
166–208 Produced by the lachrymal gland
179–206 A card game

CROSSWORD No. 36

1	2	3	4	5	6	7	8	9	10	11	12	13	14	15	16	17
18	19	20	21	22	23	24				25	26	27	28	29	30	31
32	33	34	35	36	37					38	39	40	41	42	43
44	45	46		47	48			49	50			51	52	53
54	55	56		57	58	59			60	61	62		63	64	65
66	67	68		69	70	71	72		73	74	75	76		77	78	79
80	81	82											83	84	85
86	87	88	89	90	91				92	93	94	95	96	97
98	99	100	101	102	103			104	105	106	107	108	109
110	111	112	113	114	115			116	117	118	119	120	121
122	123	124	125	126	127			128	129	130	131	132	133
134	135	136									137	138	139
140	141	142		143	144	145	146	147	148	149	150	151		152	153	154
155	156	157		158	159	160	161	162	163	164	165	166		167	168	169
170	171	172		173	174	175	176	177	178	179	180	181		182	183	184
185				186	187	188	189	190	191	192	193	194				195
196	197	198	199	200	201	202	203	204	205	206	207	208	209	210	211	212

CROSSWORD No. 37

Crossword: I.—Feelers by Torquemada from the *Observer* (1926)

ACROSS

1 Point was
7 Crux of 'Wrong Box'
14 A poulpe
15 61 across was
16 Adamsonia digitata
17 Cape in Tripoli
18 Greek fire prefix
19 Allow
20 Preposition
22 British Dominion (init.)
24 Plaything
25 Poet of husbandry (init.)
27 Worth half heels
29 In reference to
31 Very, very hard
32 N.H.
36 Infinitive of 43
38 Right-hand (abbrev.)
39 Interjection
40 Jewish ruin
41 Frenzy
44 This in tongue of 5
46 Saves suitor expense
47 Little in 32
48 Wrote 'Bury fair' (init.)
49 My sons were sons of Belial
51 Depart
53 Before steamers
54 Sudden
56 Card game
59 We shatter sleep
61 Fabulous voyager (pop. spelling)
64 An Archbishop of York
65 Recovers
66 1578 Spanish book on drugs was this
67 Lie close . . . in tins

DOWN

1 Jemima's father
2 Higher than kings (anagram)
3 Halt
4 Tristram's uncle
5 Thin in Bordeaux
6 Best of three games
8 Should not indulge in 37s
9 Inquisitive
10 Vetch
11 Arab chief
12 Excludes some 20s
13 Stage paper
17 Livingstone and Stanley did
20 An invertebrate
21 Seville Nights
23 A constellation
25 Contains a window
26 I doubt it
28 Suited to anserine converse
30 63 is
33 Half a farewell
34 Citation makes me sale
35 Evening when good
36 Prefix of duality
37 Unready part of speech
42 Diary of 53
43 Part of 36 across
45 Downy Roman . . . female
49 Break out
50 Flows into Danube
52 Am olefiant
54 Island of Schlesing
55 Brothers of business
57 More than one one
58 With 37 on the way
59 Defeated Zerah
60 On London trams
61 Hundredth of yen
62 Kinds of money desirable
63 Dose without circle

CROSSWORD No. 37

CROSSWORD No. 38

'No Man can Serve Two Masters' from *The Sunday Companion* (1925)

ACROSS

1 One of the Apostles
6 Where Ahab went (I Kings xviii.)
12 Two
13 Conjunction
14 Of (Fr.)
15 Part of fish
17 Spoke to our Lord (Mark xii.)
19 A group of scientific rules
21 Recline
22 Males
23 Lieutenant (Abbrev.)
25 Wickedness
26 Took a chair
28 Point of the compass
29 Matchings
32 Cries of fear
34 Flying creature
35 The raising of taxes
37 Cover
39 The definite article
42 Supposing
44 Cowshed
45 Used by bricklayers
47 Royal Institute (Abbrev.)
48 To soil
50 Where Samson dwelt (Judg. xv.)
52 A wilderness (Gen. xxi.)
54 Town in Somerset [!]
55 Brought by Mary (Mark xvi.)
57 Thrown about
58 Bottom part of a ship
60 Small pocket case
61 Asset
63 Harm
66 Those who hone
67 Parentless boy or girl
68 In front of the door
69 Increase
71 Method of cooking
72 As well as

DOWN

1 Raincoat (Abbrev.)
2 Dries thoroughly
3 Prefix meaning three
4 Using certain garden tool
5 Irish
7 Enemy of Saul (I Sam. xiv.)
8 Wife of Haman (Esther v.)
9 Period
10 Ages
11 Nickname for lion
12 Religious song
16 Occasional winter occurrence
18 Without seeing
20 Twisted by age
24 Small label
25 Form of address
27 Do up
28 Above us
30 Small bird
31 Slope of hill or mountain
32 Father of Enos (Gen. v.)
33 First woman (Gen. iii.)
36 Small bits of straw
38 Rage
40 A mountain (Num. xx.)
41 The leper (Matt. xxvi.)
43 Move by breeze
44 Undergrowth
46 The scribe (2 Sam. viii.)
47 Unusual
49 Father of Bezaleel (Exod. xxxi.)
51 Town in Mesopotamia, besieged in the War (reversed)
53 Required
54 Heavy blows
56 Mount given to Esau (Deut. ii.)
57 Seen in the sky
59 Plural of 23 across (Abbrev.)
60 Poem (reversed)
61 Talk to
62 Method or rule
64 Cast out by Zebul (Judg. ix.)
65 Finish
68 Written folios (Abbrev.)
70 Perform

CROSSWORD No. 38

The filled-in letters spell: **NO MAN CAN SERVE TWO MASTERS**

CROSSWORD No. 39

Quick Crossword from *Daily Telegraph* (1985)

ACROSS	DOWN
1 Demolish	2 Happen again
4 Command	3 Place of higher education
10 Small shield	5 Smells strongly
11 Throw out	6 Precious stone
12 Poetry	7 Over
13 Forbear	8 Give medical attention
15 Entrance	9 Rock
17 Pilot	14 Small vegetable
19 Apart	16 Bend over
22 American coin	18 Farm vehicle
25 Rich	20 Broad-brimmed hat
27 Follow	21 Person in possession
29 Go in	23 Eagle's nest
30 Immediate	24 Moorland
31 Inexperienced	26 Curt
32 Trap	28 Step

CROSSWORD No. 39

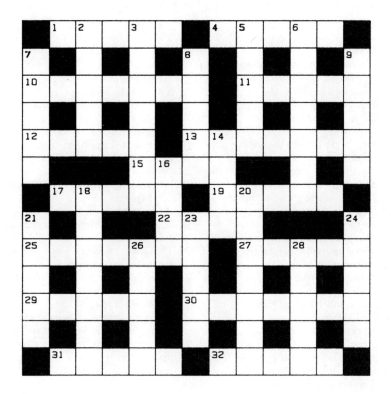

CROSSWORD No. 40

Daily Telegraph, 17 March 1928

ACROSS

1 International courtship repatched
10 In a bigger age colossal; the frozen tundra yields his fossil
11 However you take it this is stimulating
12 Confesses
13 With regard to this the nods usually precede the winks
14 These may suggest fun in the anagram of 12 across
17 Adoration travels with this cry
18 'Lip riot' (anag.)
19 As to manner, casual
22 May suggest 23 down, or an orator whose speciality is quantity rather than quality
24 A coming woman
25 A champion who did not burn his boats, but bartered them
26 Girl's name
29 Darkness and insulation characterise it
30 Use it before going to see that hair-raising play Dracula (hyphen)
31 These are inimical to continuity

DOWN

2 Nutritive seeds
3 A blind pilot
4 A lady from Shakespeare
5 An occasion when big ears are welcome
6 Made by those who favour a motion
7 A favourite in popular films
8 Descriptive of a plausible fellow (hyphen)
9 Whereat things of beauty are made up (hyphen)
15 What cooks need to do
16 Metallic adjective for a cheap loud-speaker
20 The sort of hope that seldom reaches a consummation
21 A useful thing to present to the importunate (two words)
22 'Show rip' (anag.)
23 A rising concern that presents many difficulties for the directors
27 More frequently leaves a church than enters it
28 Bird

CROSSWORD No. 40

CROSSWORD No. 41

Radio Times Crossword by D. F. Manley (1964)

ACROSS

1 Doctor refuses to work for TV series (10)
6 Writer distinctly lacking in warmth (4)
10 Animal in a most eerie context (5)
11 Comedian puts Scottish mountain before New York eminence (5,4)
12 What's my line? I must be absorbed by a measuring device (6)
13 Holidays for two opposites, Gilbert and Sullivan? (7)
15 Right back to 10 – putrid! (6)
16 It's on in wild parts of Canada: a gigantic reptile (8)
19 Lamb sees, oddly enough, how to start a meeting (8)
21 We should return to make a song about a household job (6)
24 Bird box leads to quarrel (7)
26 A trail suited to the Lone Ranger (6)
28 Notices by-product is unfit for TV or radio (9)
29 Livid singer with 5. (Tricky? Not altogether) (5)
30 Famous gallery in the States (4)
31 Lawyer gives drink to mother and child (5,5)

DOWN

1 Not associated with the Rolling Stones (4)
2 Poets rate these as dramatic musical performances (9)
3 Work for the home? (7)
4 & 20. Merry lot bore being tortured for actor (6,6)
5 Recognise Ron? He is moved to become a comedian (3,5)
7 Carmichael turns to the navy in Scotland (5)
8 Novelist has long way to travel for TV series (5,5)
9 Most of my rod has strange powers (6)
14 'My Word!' A really outstanding writer is needed for this (5,5)
17 Northern issue can lead to hindrances (9)
18 Note the soft whistle employed by a glass maker (8)
20 See 4
22 Listener who has read about drink (7)
23 Quiet hen in the field perhaps (6)
25 As before, radio is something well worth having (5)
27 Actor born in America is V.I.P. in Scotland (4)

151

CROSSWORD No. 41

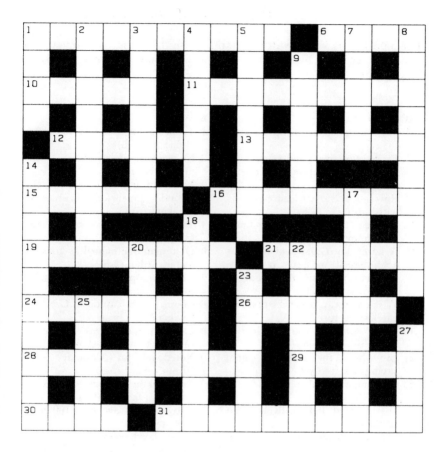

CROSSWORD No. 42

The Times Crossword Puzzle No 16,551

This puzzle was solved within 30 minutes by 15 of the 18 competitors in the 1984 national final of the Collins Dictionaries Times Crossword Championships.

ACROSS

1 Trick by gangster to capture king (8)
5 Penetration by a hundred toffs (6)
10 Bridge pair accepting one classic date (5)
11 Row about no enclosure of this with sardines? (3-6)
12 Strange airs shown by those chosen, or one of them (9)
13 A latter-day Galatea of no great achievement, we hear (5)
14 Aeneas's friend supplies headgear in the services (7)
16 Wise one recapturing the first fine careless rapture (6)
19 Many twists contrariwise in this urban development (6)
21 By which the message came, saying 'It's a boy'? (7)
23 A gunman turned on the man with a rod (5)
25 It's rammed awkwardly between banks (9)
27 Man of fashion joins informal party, I note (9)
28 Noise abroad sound description of some wines (5)
29 Regular boyfriend is by no means flighty (6)
30 What might well suit emulators of Shadrach & Co. (8)

DOWN

1 Trunks going ahead on his trans-alpine train (8)
2 No whisper of irregularity – the title proves it (9)
3 Make unprofitable use of the second dimension figuratively speaking (5)
4 Twins are crazy to take it in, the fools (7)
6 Olympian one named as alias for one in Arden (3-6)
7 Chaps in top form give a straight-sounding answer (5)
8 Country with capital in Czechoslovakia (6)
9 Lay out money in attempt to capture Troy for instance (6)
15 Noted job for Alexander – or Gilpin's men? (5-4)
17 Room on the quarterdeck in extra-terrestrial fashion (9)
18 A joy for the traveller at 100 miles perhaps (8)
20 Land's borders invaded by African warriors, it's clear (6)
21 Direct speech (7)
22 Jack's going over America from Paul's place (6)
24 Maybe Hercules dispenses with the French trimming (5)
26 Board highly amused by Yorick (5)

CROSSWORD No. 42

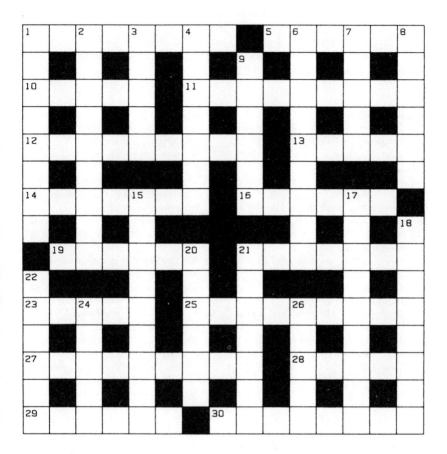

CROSSWORD No. 43

The Times Crossword Puzzle No 16,869

This puzzle was solved in the record time of 4½ minutes by Dr John Sykes, the 1985 champion, at the national final of the Collins Dictionaries Times Crossword Championship.

ACROSS

1 Producer of stage lighting for Pyramus and Thisbe (3,2,3,4)
9 High-flier having ended a brilliant career (9)
10 Stump from which some orators may speak (5)
11 Appoint as minister, or Hamlet as prince, say? (6)
12 Swimmer shows way to press forward (8)
13 Once called audibly the utmost degree (6)
15 Basil was over her Lorenzo's head (8)
18 Bird – that which is seen round Scotland's isle (8)
19 Wind instrument for communication commonly (6)
21 Ironclad might one surmise? Not this vessel (4-4)
23 Man, say, taken in by doctor is caused to go wrong (6)
26 Find out what's in the clear, naturally (5)
27 Putting a beer in it craftily could make him drunk (9)
28 But as its monarch Alexander went unrecorded (6,6)

DOWN

1 A short distance in light aircraft – prototype Jumbo (7)
2 No neo-Edwardian was so famous (5)
3 The age in which Kipling wrote (9)
4 The appearance, it's said, of one who may succeed (4)
5 Played majestically in Hollywood the West's also taking in the South (8)
6 Bid perhaps for grappling iron (5)
7 Salad's just what the old king (4-4)
8 Matchless poetess involved in 11 (6)
14 Muscovite in a one-goal result proves hostile (8)
16 Hazardous game for the serpent of old Nile (9)
17 Where fools are blissfully ignorant and the birds are gorgeous (8)
18 Street Browning visited going round in this headgear? (6)
20 Titian beauty number one in the Kremlin? (7)
22 Buddhist priest put together black continental cricket team (5)
24 A jungle climber's name inter alia perhaps (5)
25 Run fast or hide (4)

CROSSWORD No. 43

CROSSWORD No. 44

Guardian Crossword No. 15,000
Literal Transplants by Custos (20 February 1978)

The answer to each Across clue must have one of its letters removed before entry in the diagram. In each case the excised letter should be written instead alongside the word's clue. When this operation is completed the 26 transplanted letters, when read in clue order and added to 8 Down, will make an appropriate headline.

Definitions in these clues refer to the full, unmutilated answers (number of letters given in brackets); subsidiary parts lead to the mutilated forms to be entered in the diagrams. The first clue of each pair refers to diagram A, the second to diagram B.

Each of the Down clues is really two normal clues printed side by side, never overlapping, one leading to the answer in diagram A and the other to that in diagram B. The division is not necessarily marked by punctuation, and either A or B clue may come first.

ACROSS

5 Nobleman, top-drawer, I found among ruins (7)
Boring love I'd rejected in backward group (7)

6 Attendant, having pinched £2, gets sack (7)
Sends back mother after being captured by Communists (7)

9 Exams, including English, are severe trials (7)
Tolerated first of kids in family (7)

10 Fixer needs ceremony, one that conceals his true nature (9)
Unadulterated back-pedalling by heavyweights leads to outbursts (9)

11 Bankruptcy for the band (5)
A religious representation, a favourite one (5)

12 English clothing with a ring of dots around the edge (11)
What sounds like costly and better type of headgear (11)

13 At length in favour of having area left in backyard (12)
Plastic pressed so to become a diner's utensil (7-5)

18 Strait-laced in the end, blushing about it, given a sharp rebuke (11)
Why let a mob run riot? It's reprehensible (11)

21 A four-wheeled carriage that's cast in precious stone (5)
£100 is about right for the waiters' collection of tips (5)

22 Foreign girl has to write name when receiving a ring in one (9)
An undertaker, I'm in cart after a mix-up (9)

23 Servant, one who hurries about excitedly (7)
Doubles partners, perhaps, met running about court (7)

24 Putting things precisely? That's tremendous (7)
Live within confines of southern railway, in sedate fashion (7)

25 Separate company suffers setback in disreputable resort (7)
Felt hats, for when going about the East (7)

DOWN

1 Recommended getting a pleader to pass inside by means of a minister (8;8)

2 Laced stuff with which teachers' leader gets children drunk – see, dead drunk (6;6)

3 Long after the plane-trip makes frivolous petitions about having searches (8;8)

CROSSWORD No. 44 – Diagram A.

4 Fellow with skill made up a hymn tune, in the morning, after start of bardic festival (6;6)

5 Doctor, getting right on to a sovereign's deadly wound, carrying Edward round vessel (6;6)

7 Poem, produced by child with toil, still in existence, to be included in next anthology (6;6)

8 Being fuddled with claret, extolling a medium during a heat wave (11;3, 8)

14 Watched William's diving ducks – watches Thomas getting duck caught by the legs (3-5;8)

15 Our sot, tipsy, holding party in the open air, solemnly poured out wine, gaining freedom, losing 'er (8;8)

16 Smack during a quarrel is hardly the sound of a frolic among Civil Service office workers (6;6)

17 Refuse, causing a disturbance, to follow closely master's principles (6;6)

19 Right joint to be constantly annoying a girl who needs help when grabbed by chaps (6;6)

20 Brewing tea, try indefatigably to jabber rubbish that diverts brides (6;6)

CROSSWORD No. 44

Guardian Crossword No. 15,000
Literal Transplants by Custos (20 February 1978)

ACROSS

5 Nobleman, top-drawer, I found among ruins (7)
Boring love I'd rejected in backward group (7)

6 Attendant, having pinched £2, gets sack (7)
Sends back mother after being captured by Communists (7)

9 Exams, including English, are severe trials (7)
Tolerated first of kids in family (7)

10 Fixer needs ceremony, one that conceals his true nature (9)
Unadulterated back-pedalling by heavyweights leads to outbursts (9)

11 Bankruptcy for the band (5)
A religious representation, a favourite one (5)

12 English clothing with a ring of dots around the edge (11)
What sounds like costly and better type of headgear (11)

13 At length in favour of having area left in backyard (12)
Plastic pressed so to become a diner's utensil (7-5)

18 Strait-laced in the end, blushing about it, given a sharp rebuke (11)
Why let a mob run riot? It's reprehensible (11)

21 A four-wheeled carriage that's cast in precious stone (5)
£100 is about right for the waiters' collection of tips (5)

22 Foreign girl has to write name when receiving a ring in one (9)
An undertaker, I'm in cart after a mix-up (9)

23 Servant, one who hurries about excitedly (7)
Doubles partners, perhaps, met running about court (7)

24 Putting things precisely? That's tremendous (7)

Live within confines of southern railway, in sedate fashion (7)

25 Separate company suffers setback in disreputable resort (7)
Felt hats, for when going about the East (7)

DOWN

1 Recommended getting a pleader to pass inside by means of a minister (8;8)

2 Laced stuff with which teachers' leader gets children drunk – see, dead drunk (6;6)

3 Long after the plane-trip makes frivolous petitions about having searches (8;8)

4 Fellow with skill made up a hymn tune, in the morning, after start of bardic festival (6;6)

5 Doctor, getting right on to a sovereign's deadly wound, carrying Edward round vessel (6;6)

7 Poem, produced by child with toil, still in existence, to be included in next anthology (6;6)

8 Being fuddled with claret, extolling a medium during a heat wave (11;3, 8)

14 Watched William's diving ducks – watches Thomas getting duck caught by the legs (3-5;8)

15 Our sot, tipsy, holding party in the open air, solemnly poured out wine, gaining freedom, losing 'er (8;8)

16 Smack during a quarrel is hardly the sound of a frolic among Civil Service office workers (6;6)

17 Refuse, causing a disturbance, to follow closely master's principles (6;6)

19 Right joint to be constantly annoying a girl who needs help when grabbed by chaps (6;6)

20 Brewing tea, try indefatigably to jabber rubbish that diverts brides (6;6)

CROSSWORD No. 44 – Diagram B.

CROSSWORD No. 45

Observer Everyman

ACROSS

1 Was anxious about visitor's head getting cut (6)
5 Noisy fluter, out of sorts, peevish (7)
9 Holy man, a person to pelt with missiles (5)
10 Conspiracies made by ring in small patches of land (9)
11 People who are eager for alcohol? (6,7)
13 Kentish chaps, perhaps, in club's underground area (8)
14 A jewel in one constellation (6)
16 Disinter former Cardinal (6)
18 Tea-party in which there's rabbit, followed by a contest (3-5)
21 Nautical officer to give shelter to teacher (7-6)
23 I shall, joined by a tantaliser, become embarrassed (3,2,4)
24 Poke around Uruguay's capital, being arrogant (5)
25 Doctor's given the French girl wine (7)
26 Trimmer gets Diana in a row (6)

DOWN

2 Very ancient, all this, so held as mysterious (2,3,2,3,5)
3 Volcano captured by force in country of South-East Asia (7)
4 Ousting the editor, turning up before sitting (8)
5 Lord, if irritated, gets red-faced (6)
6 New net I twist and interweave (7)
7 Perfecting an oarsman's coup de grâce (9,6)
8 Secure with a rope left on a tree (4)
9 Quiet, strolls without a leader, making a mess (8)
12 Imagined ancient Briton, awfully rude (8)
15 Nourishing fruit I accepted in tenant's payment (8)
17 A husband's ruin – sex-appeal and a lot of beer (7)
19 Panicked and ran off, grabbing one very quietly (7)
20 Weed carrying periodical gains respect (6)
22 Section of auditorium lifted up for cinema show (4)

CROSSWORD No. 45

CROSSWORD No. 46

Financial Times Crossword Puzzle No. 4,882

ACROSS

1 They involve a shift in one's beliefs (6)
4 Insisted upon or abandoned? (4,4)
9 Penthouse let on a new arrangement (4-2)
10 Pretty useless object? (8)
11 Allow the Spanish poison to be brought back (6)
12 I'm off food and water (8)
13 This hat is out of date (3)
14 Put out in West winds (6)
17 One side of Glasgow (7)
21 Information a girl found in Switzerland (6)
25 The best-known surviving creature? (3)
26 Any crest may indicate it (8)
27 They grip and hold on in the last resort (6)
28 Ointment said to be used by the Royal Family (8)
29 He is or could be a shopkeeper (6)
30 Political favours? (8)
31 Stable companion? (6)

DOWN

1 It sounds highly unnatural (8)
2 Very frightened, I take a short rest before I can reorganise (2,1,5)
3 He expects people to put up with him (8)
5 Where you may find a sailor on the way (6)
6 Rising payment for the artist (6)
7 Key batsman? (6)
8 Growing anger? (6)
12 When people may collect in the streets (4-3)
15 The German uprising is serious (3)
16 A work unit (3)
18 Begin to fix a fight (3,5)
19 A lemon is strangely sweet (8)
20 TV's pop group? (4,4)
22 A bend in the road (6)
23 Climbs and balances (6)
24 Company guard (6)
25 First form (6)

CROSSWORD No. 46

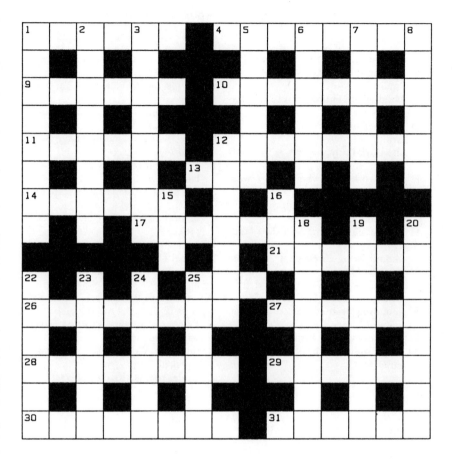

CROSSWORD No. 47

Alphabetical Jigsaw by Araucaria (*Guardian*)

A bell that rang elusively in part (7)

B ship on the wrong river gets more smart (7)

C bond where churchmen to a junction come (6)

D instrument left out of celli – drum? (8)

E the Dark Lady, topless, is way out (6)

F woodwork tool when worry was about (7)

G like an old tree sculptured by Legrand (7)

H first of all invading famished land (7)

I should bring interest at Mass as priests (11)

J girl – yes (Ger.) – catch terriers (men, not beasts) (7)

K sounding wanted, after may be rolled (7)

L in security, state bird of old (8)

M major route which City's fans (say) enter (4,4)

N false clue is innate – group round a centre (8)

O act too much: where's re-mi-fa in tune? (6)

P's only round about the rug too soon (11)

Q leave when obligations have been paid (4)

R music's ear returns without what's laid (6)

S dog or bitch? Dog's tailless, split in six (6)

T nethermost, ate piece the heat to fix (10)

U house with rows in sunset, not the Pope! (10)

V – by the left! – contains some drink or dope (4)

W vole: hence Watson's dad's docked slips (5-3)

X Persian king who punished waves with whips (6)

Y in Colne Valley, place he madly wrecked (7)

Z oxide, red, is citizen's effect (7)

CROSSWORD No. 47

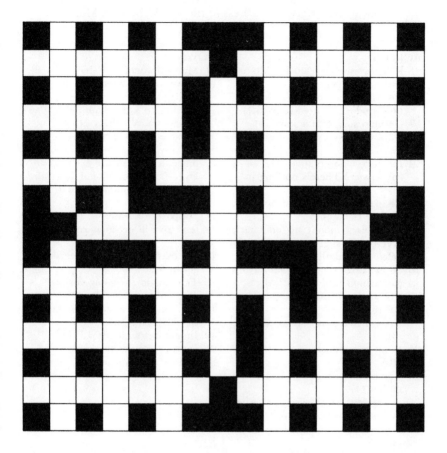

CROSSWORD No. 48

Birmingham Evening Mail 'Best of the Week' by Don Manley

ACROSS

1 Religious service featuring Mother and Saints? (4)
3 Instrument in country of Inquisition produces acute agony (5,4)
9 German song told a story (4)
10 Hobbyist's stuck into this book? (5,5)
12 Likened Conservative MP to a left-winger? There's nothing in it (8)
13 Chap for example with drop of asti in wine cellar (6)
14 Footballers mount up and hack everyone? It suggests a desperately defensive situation (5,2,3,4)
18 Supporting a newspaper having old-fashioned ideas? (6,3,5)
20 Not sharp, being somewhat over 90? (6)
22 Viewed man with dread, shaking (8)
24 What may knock you out – heat? (10)
25 The man leading some of Hitler's bullies (4)
26 Seven days with poverty, it's said, makes you irresolute (4-5)
27 College having fame, reactionary? (4)

DOWN

1 Married woman can show spite (6)
2 A way of cleaning best hat Ma spoilt (5,4)
4 Passionate kid, about 10 – one living in S.W. Africa (9)
5 Verse is heard (Frost) (4)
6 Op. 1 with a clarinet? That's out of place in this musical event (5,7)
7 Dye—I am Blue but not 'Lake' (5)
8 Feeling friendliness results in 'Can I?' (7)
11 Support for elderly? Legislation sent up will get monarch's assent (7,5)
15 For that reason the engineers must get in front (9)
16 Ten madmen going berserk – correction is called for (9)
17 You may get indigestion here – terribly bad sign (7)
19 Inventor noised abroad (6)
21 Journey east for food (5)
23 Painter not outside? It's wet (4)

CROSSWORD No. 48

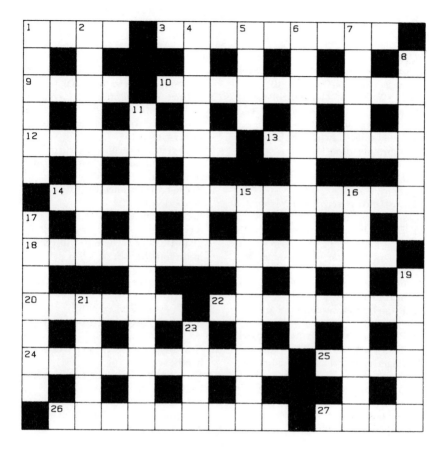

CROSSWORD No. 49

Birmingham Mail Special by Duck, 1 March 1982

ACROSS

1 One working out the taxes makes masses sore but not me (8)
6, 11, 24 Dn, 28: I have got jug at home – heed our rollicking. (Dai may sing this) (5,2,1,4,5,7)
10 Awful spite shown by the French in communication (7)
11 See 6 Across
12 Tooth? Not sweet rejecting bit of treacle (5)
13 Club having records on? Then it's sure tricky to talk! (9)
14 Timid chap, person pestered with kids? (3,5)
16 A witty saying about something very small (4)
20 One's 'green', vying? This may be in evidence (4)
21 Daniel's no wound leaving a - - - - - - - -! (5,3)
24 Pet has gone back to the street, girl! That's absolutely right! (4,5)
25 Lager would make this composer drunk (5)
27 Aged men tremble when mate is near (3-4)
28 See 6 Across
29 Appointed meeting to put good man to the test? (5)
30 Walk to Northern Territory? It's sounding harsh (8)

DOWN

2, 15 Dad's said 'Vanity!', spoiling this time of celebration (5,6,3)
3 Former wife, frightful rioter, creating a scene outside (8)
4 Sporting course – sea comes up – waver round (8)
5 Negligent concerning a girl (6)
6 Dwarf without foot on part of sundial (6)
7 Received from ancestors, it is put in abode (9)
8 Escape from eastern lord, end of servitude (5)
9 Oxford college where they'll celebrate tonight? (8)
15 See 2 Down
17 This country? My anchor is fixed here (8)
18 Bird's evening booze? (8)
19 Silly men, beginning to embrace, she had entangled (8)
22 Narrow passage of water without bends, we hear (6)
23 For a painter irritating experience has entity (6)
24 See 6 Across
26 Presented information about four in Ancient Rome (5)

CROSSWORD No. 49

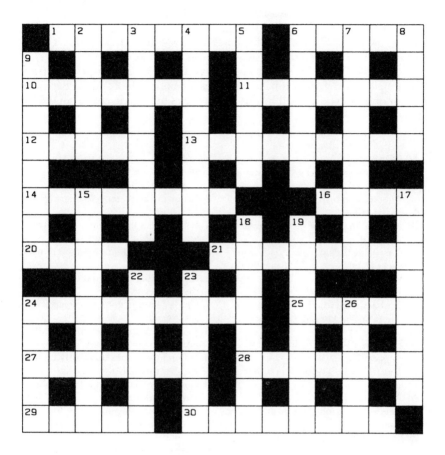

CROSSWORD No. 50

Sunday Express Skeleton

In the Skeleton Crossword the black squares and clue numbers have to be filled in as well as the words. Four black squares and four clue numbers have been inserted to give you a start. The black squares form a symmetrical pattern; the top half matches the bottom half and the two sides correspond. So you can fill in 12 more squares at once to correspond with those given.

ACROSS

1 Bible man with very little time to take a snack
4 Act oddly in providing food for one of the tribes
9 Money man able to achieve a flying turn
11 Last post dispatched by someone seeking business
12 Carry gently a short distance past Heathrow terminal
13 Embarrassed grandee in a passion
15 Means of making notes or backing a horse
16 Show it's wrong to be back in a depression
17 Your lot won't admit it's different inside
20 Nag a newcomer
22 Feeling it's a long way round Mile End
23 Real inciter of mischief going straight
24 Make further use of personal mobility
25 Islander organising a quiet upheaval beyond the city limits

DOWN

1 It might be longer if Tom got elevated on hot air
2 If not in the water one might give you sauce
3 It indicates the number approved for inclusion
5 The man who finds a way to move with difficulty
6 People afloat sounded pleased with themselves
7 Chalky having got it in the neck as a songster
8 Jack and Alan worried about trade union having eight members
9 When food comes up mostly fat he goes in for takeaways
10 Can it be right to find a thriller writer pedestrian?
13 It's the last thing one hopes to gain
14 Several light out when there's no drink
18 Praise what was formerly a different lot
19 Girl in a state looking after the kids
21 Being so taxing it's a departure from frivolity
22 Light-headed? Not a bad description

CROSSWORD No. 50

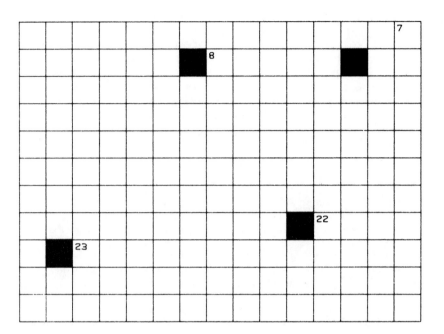

CROSSWORD No. 51

Misdirected Letters by Duck from *Quiz Digest*

A letter which should have appeared once in the answer to 5 across has turned up in the answer to 1 down (no other similar letter appears in 1 down). The same mistake has occurred in the answers to 7 across and 2 down, and so on. The subsidiary indications in the clues (*eg* anagrams) and the numbers in brackets refer to the mutilated forms to be entered in the grid; definitions are normal. When you have completed the crossword, you will find that the misdirected letters, taken in order, spell out an appropriate three-word message.

ACROSS

5 Clown, disgustingly idle beast (8)
7 Charm shown by backward-looking sultanate, primitive civilisation (6)
9 Russian exchange has leader of diplomats upset (7)
10 Marshal on far side of hill in old-style combat (6)
11 Bird with gloomy look evident around Early English church (6-3)
13 What makes crime soar disastrously (4)
14 Ugly woman's house somewhere in Surrey (6)
16 Piece of rag in wrong position (6)
18 Smooth beat (4)
19 Exceptional saint, inwardly so keen he is (9)
22 Enslave heart madly with hint of love (6)
23 Sheep with a twitch that's sudden (7)
25 One to expel a boy (6)
26 Fleet Street area rumour – leader in *Express* is obscure (8)

DOWN

1 Sounds of pain from gunners caught up in battle (6)
2 Something extra good in Paris to exploit (6)
3 B-brightened up – but not well (4)
4 Trade Union basis for action may undermine nation . . . (8)
6 . . . Give money perpetually to terminate dispute? (6)
7 Let Athens get adapted for Olympic contestants? (9)
8 Fabulous creature at sea intended to embrace marines (7)
12 Manager joining firm is chap who may get waxy (9)
14 In the country sit in bar getting drunk (8)
15 Racing vehicle with some pinking? OK. A retuning is needed (2-5)
17 Unusual herons somewhere near water (6)
20 Agitating Miss Proll's right let down (9)
21 Finally forgot a quote – must be unsaid (6)
24 Sound of animal in desolate area (4)

CROSSWORD No. 51

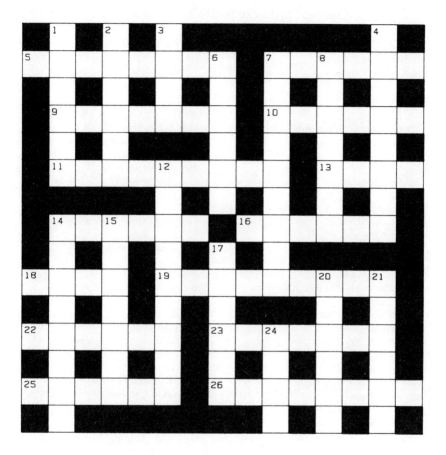

CROSSWORD No. 52

Numerical Sequence by Duck from *Quiz Digest*

Some of the answers are harder than others! *Chambers 20th Century Dictionary* could be useful.

ACROSS

1 3 (7)
5 Get big belly around with 'piggy' food that's on board (7)
9 Setter's gone wrong – tries again (7)
10 Sees the stars perhaps making visits (5,2)
11 Badly burnt, have become hazel-coloured (3-5)
12 7 (6)
14 Evilly influenced, a crude nurse needs to be reformed (5,1,5)
17 Smashing hotel (Hotel West) provides everything (3,5,3)
20 2 (6)
21 Bob not at home, having to go round supermarket – the way to get ice-cream in tubs? (5,3)
23 10 (7)
24 5 (7)
25 Oak, *eg*, chopped by a boy? It's criminal (7)
26 This mending makes Ming ever-lasting (7)

DOWN

1 9 (8)
2 Soft laxity like this is something that sounds commonplace (8)
3 Insecure, lacking heart – right? Pay me for security (7)
4 Unconstrained gate – it's favourable for progress (4,6)
5 1 (4)
6 Get no healing from an amateur? (7)
7 Insist upon having a bit of hair sticking up (6)
8 8 (5)
13 6 (10)
15 4 (8)
16 Good man speaks, speaks hesitatingly (8)
17 Germans munch a lot, we hear (7)
18 An older, decrepit man (7)
19 Start of university term, it seems, is to get modernised (6)
20 Travel to spot – see one expected to come? (5)
22 Some god, I (Norse) (4)

CROSSWORD No. 52

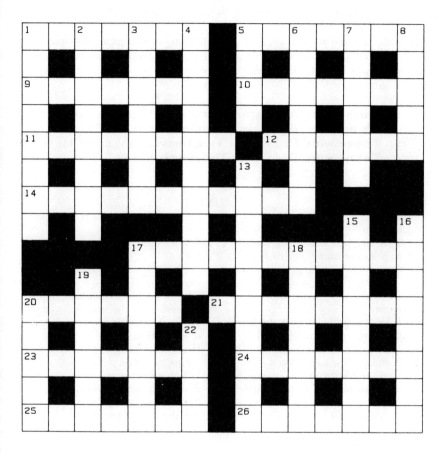

CROSSWORD No. 53

Theme and Variations by Duck from *Quiz Digest*

The four unclued theme words have something in common, and each has two variations. The four pairs of variations are related to their theme words in various ways, but both members of a pair are related to their theme word in the same way.

Theme word A: 27 across **Variations:** 12 across, 5 down
Theme word B: 3 down **Variations:** 19 down, 30 down
Theme word C: 13 across **Variations:** 20 across, 15 down
Theme word D: 16 down **Variations:** 26 across, 6 down

ACROSS
1 Greeting – it needs musical instrument (6)
4 Thrashes bat, slams spin (8)
9 Reprieve or annoy again? (7)
11 Can noisy? Then get lubricant, wrapping (7)
14 Shallow judgment only half formed (4)
17 Formal record touching the heart of the matter with hesitation (8)
18 Bit of wood to advance slowly? (5)
22 A sharp blow comes back, then a high ball comes back in a curve (8)
28 Wind in most of summer month (4)
31 Escaping number 1 rescue going west (7)
32 S American city has rest disturbed – by them? (7)
33 Road most messy? Use these coming home (8)
34 Fish Katharine's brought aboard (6)

DOWN
1 One making great effort – *eg* Peter on the water (7)
2 Left with a sharp pain, permanent (7)
7 Black substance the man had acted like a balm (7)
8 It's not heard to be golden (7)
10 One more for the team (6)
20 PS. Nudes are dreadful – keep out of office for a while (7)
21 Head of celery and eggs served up – a party hors d'oeuvre (7)
23 Let up on becoming rich (7)
24 Painters in dire straits (7)
25 Earth maybe putting energy initially into vegetable (6)
29 Business is steady (4)

CROSSWORD No. 53

CROSSWORD No. 54

Instruments by Duck from *Tough Puzzles*

Seven of the across clues are normal, but their answers must be transformed before entry in the grid. The remaining across clues have normal definitions, but their subsidiary indications refer to the form in which they are to be entered in the grid, that is, with one letter omitted. These letters, taken in order, give the name of the man desirous of the transformations to the other across answers. Solvers must decide to which type any particular clue refers. Down clues are normal.

ACROSS

1 Gravity to pitch into the trough of the sea one returning aboard
3 Being one of those called to decide damage?
9 After crash sends around box (black)
10 Bed – a bit of underwear needed by Virginia. A warm relaxing place? (2 words)
11 Instrument cut Italian flower first
12 Resolve but do show hesitation
14 A year's end, relaxing without energy, informal
16 Being without confidence should be praised somehow
17 Dignity of cardinal leading to bloody enmity
18 When most sent out various distributions
21 Infantry regiment – back half of it retreats
22 Brave appeal with exceptional pride
26 I supposedly get good results in the field or I sprint – versatile!
27 Uproarious noise – record by wiggling Rod
28 Artist steams angrily
29 Restrain river

DOWN

1 To produce drink mix two parts of lemon juice (no ice) with drop of port (5)
2 Thieves caught in country – egg-stealers? (5)
3 Ship's captain with father on the golf course (7)
4 She tells tales – cute senora, rambling (10)
5 German oil? (4)
6 Sailor's behind (5)
7 A little boy tucking into cereal like a cow? (8)
8 Dismisses bank workers (8)
13 Colleagues with zero assets, ruined – American agency brought in (10)
14 Telling your grandmother . . . ? (8)
15 Neighbourhood with endless sin and weapons (8)
19 Refuse to employ Marxist philosopher (7)
20 Rebel big just below the waist? (5)
23 Marks, singular cricketer (5)
24 Fine comic (5)
25 100 square metres – that's one (4)

CROSSWORD No. 54

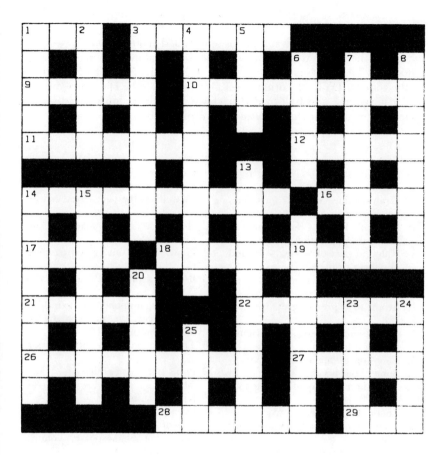

CROSSWORD No. 55

Next-door Neighbours by Duck from *Games and Puzzles*

Clues are normal but each solution is to be coded in one of two ways – either by taking the next letters in the alphabet or by taking the ones before (A follows Z). Thus FAG is entered as either GBH or EZF, and EZF could also be the code for DYE (the other possibility being CXD). Half the words are 'coded forwards' and half 'coded backwards'. Solvers must decide which code applies to each clue. *Chambers* is recommended.

ACROSS

1 Alloy in strange coin is all right (10)
9 Uranium in geological formation produces grin (5)
11 See Rolls-Royce – the ultimate in flashy transportation (5)
12 Ridge in part of Sussex – around Hassocks primarily (5)
13 Drags back for a pause? (5)
14 Missionary's old coin – catch (4)
15 Strain to express regret, we hear (3)
17 Brute issuing expression of disgust, getting a pair (5)
19 Poor house – one with a rodent (5)
22 Song about a valley (3)
23 Gin – homely way of getting Jock high (4)
24 Shoot chap in Devon? (5)
26 French vineyard and container for wine (5)
28 I'll have chanted about going to court (5)
29 Signal from British Prime Minister going West (5)
30 Salt – I'd eat it on bit of ham minced up (10)

DOWN

1 Laze around? One's immersed in rum and lemon, claret (10)
2 Go well together, get a local victory (5)
3 Hot old ale could make you spin round (4)
4 Plant, yellow one, given to child (5)
5 Brood of a nuthatch? No thank you (3)
6 Old backgammon? Wait to roll (5)
7 Gin, Alice? No, that's awful, it makes you numb (10)
8 Tribal woman with endless croak (5)
10 Bob's neck, something short and fat (5)
16 Kick old crank (5)
18 Everything's fine with a religious animal (5)
20 Part 1 of Shakespeare, volume given to relation (5)
21 See awful rot about an old city (5)
22 Batting? Illingworth's out – this weather doesn't help batsmen (5)
25 Tungsten embedded in another metal, something very similar (4)
27 Take for example Mr Maudling? (3)

CROSSWORD No. 55

CROSSWORD No. 56

Empty Pockets by Duck from *Games and Puzzles*

Each solution must have a word omitted before it is entered in the diagram. The missing words have something in common.

Both the definition *and* the subsidiary indication refer to the unmutilated solution.

ACROSS

1 O, a dunce will need it somehow! (9)
4 Jane? Inwardly English and very good, is outwardly not at all attractive (7)
7 Learner in art I must work – to become this? (10)
9 Heroic woman opposing subversive army activity (6)
10 Hampshire water, not fresh, provided by old spring (6)
11 Apparently I, bound by an ancient vow, will be most fortunate (8)
12 One lunatic somersaulting in a convulsive fit and going around naked? (8)
15 Crop to grind etc. when cut (6)
16 Marches past as red revolutionary (7)
18 Cooking apples out on the table as a matter of course (9)
19 Seemingly remove a barrier for protection (7)
20 Disparages exercises we hear (7)

DOWN

1 It's sensible having the top flat it seems (11)
2 Plain yellow record book with name entered in (8)
3 Ransack hotel's inside – in Scandinavia somewhere (7)
4 Condemned lover created by Continental writer – not half frightened (9)
5 Dazzlingly live deans e.g. gave gospel message (11)
6 Despatched about a hundred tree-trunks, dry through – sources of sweet smell (12)
8 Young member of family, girl gobbling short dinner, getting ill (10)
13 Commanding fairy in pain after initial application of iodine (8)
14 Harsh-sounding singer? Yes and no! (6)
17 Location with top class inside? (6)

CROSSWORD No. 56

CROSSWORD No. 57

Printer's Devilry by Afrit from *The Listener* 1937

The lights are complete words which were originally 'hidden' in the clues. It is to be presumed that the compositor, seeing that certain consecutive letters spelt a word or words, removed them and closed up the gap, sometimes taking a further liberty with the spacing and punctuation, but not altering the order of the letters. There is only one break in each clue, and the lights show the omitted letters in their original order.

ACROSS

(1) See 26D. **(4, 7D)** ' "Surely", said I, "surely that is something at my wine!" '
(7, 13D, 42D) Some numbers in Swinburne nest at Ely, kindly friend.
(11) ' "Pooh!" trilled a linnet, and each dew-note had a lilt'. **(12, 10)** An article of faith is not merely an opinion bet. **(16)** 'Ah, wasteful woman, she that may on her own self sown price!'
(18) 'The grey sea and the long band, the yellow half-moon large and low'.
(22, 14, 36D) 'Something . . . moved a poet to prophecies – a pinch o' guarded dust'. **(24, 39D)** In robore fasces. **(25)** Asters go out, cricket comes in. **(27)** 'Here tone is music's own, like those of morning birds. **(28)** 'My laver flags, and what are its wages?' **(30)** The party when parting had heard the curlew's knell. **(32, 21D)** The bad land is little but dear.
(34) In olden days two fat people on one leg called for no remark. **(38)** 'The cliffs of England stand glimmering, and vain the tranquil bay'. **(41)** How shall poet's soul stand rapt when 'throughout the music of the suns is in her soul at once!' **(43)** See 31D.
(44) Being a fashionable damozel, the stars in her hair were seven. **(45)** The concourse lulled to sudden silence awed my speech. **(47)** See 31D. **(48)** See 46D. **(49, 17D)** 'Shepherds feed their flocks by shallow river falls, melodious birds sing madrigals'.

DOWN

(1) 'Nor amid these triumphs dost thou scorn the humble glow-worms to adorn'. **(3, 35)** 'The dense hard passage is blind and stifled that crawls by a turn to climb'. **(4)** Errors oft in the stilly night break your slumbers. **(6, 2)** May the big never distinguish many merchantmen! **(7)** See 4A. **(8)** Some were here, some there, and the rest where? **(9, 19)** 'A good boy am I' makes Jack Horner's pie to *my* mind.
(13) See 7A. **(14)** 'Will there be children in their hall for ever and for ever?'
(15) 'Nor will occasion want nor shall wed with dangerous expedition to invade Heaven'. **(17)** See 49A. **(20)** Ascend we now, find foot-holds, cling to the rocks above. **(21)** See 32A. **(23, 29)** 'And that smile like sunshine (shall) dart into ma heart'. **(26, 1A, 5)** 'And not bows: only when daylight comes, comes in the light'. **(27, 33)** 'O the eternal sky, full of light and of dignity!' **(31, 47A, 43A)** 'Fatigued he sinks into some pleasant lair of wavy grass, an air and gentle tale of love'.
(36) See 22A. **(37)** A nod or a beck, a quip or youthful jollity – which do you prefer? **(39)** See 24A. **(40)** 'Let a Lord once own the happy lines, how it brightens!' **(42)** See 7A. **(46, 48A)** Aspirer 'with slow but stately pace kept on his course.'

CROSSWORD No. 57

CROSSWORD No. 58

Puns Asinorum by Afrit from *The Listener* 1948

AXIOMS

I. The distance traversed by a **9 30** is not the shortest distance between two fixed points.

II. No body, even after gin, can meet a body coming through the **20A**.

III. If one cyclic **26** be *C* and another *H*, then *H* is **26** to be *C*.

IV. If *T=d* feet (French) at *C*, then *T* **19** is in London.

V. If by a customs union more food is assured, then **4A** will be assured by a customs union with S. Africa.

THEOREMS

I. *If no* **7**=*good* **7**, *to prove the converse.* By nature all **7**=fast **7**, and by proverb **29 7**=fast **7**; therefore all **7**=**29 7**.

II. *Given that* **7** must be **28** *by S. African customs, to prove one* **30**=*any number of* **7**. Let any number of **7 28** by S.A. customs=*n*.**4A**; then, *n* being sufficiently great, *n*.**4A**=one **19 25**. Now one **30** is equal to one **19 25** any day of the week; therefore one **30**=one **19 25**=*n*.**4A**=any number of **7**.

III. *To prove that, if two* **9 30**-*s meet in a* **27** *so as to form a* **20A 13**, *then some of their* **19**-*s*=*the* **19** *of the* **3 41 7**. Given that **7 28** by **18**=a **32** of **7**, and **3 41 7**=un-**32** of **7**, let a **32** of **7** meet in *T* **19**; then, since *T* **19** is in London (*Ax. IV*), this is un-**32** of **7**, and by **3-41-22** *T* **19**=the **19** of the **3 41 7**. Again, if the two **9 30**-s form a **20A 13**, they may be involved to any required degree. Let them be involved till some of their **19**-s=the **19** of four **30**-s=*T* **19**=the **19** of the **3 41 7**.

ACROSS

1. Required a geometer (*G*) adjacent to *C* and supplementary to *T*, *C* being red, *T* black or green, and *G* black or white (5). 10. If *x*=Kingmaker, give one example of Exercises *f*(*x*) in which the answer contains a variable of **34** (7). 12, 13. Given that **13**=*GE*:*EL*, and the converse of **12**=*LE*:*EG*, then, if *LEG* be part of a figure, that figure is a sitter, and *LEG* has six positions in **12** (4,6). 15. If its upper surface=**3 27**, illustrate a frustum which shall be just the same if cyclic order be used (4). 16. Taking one bit=1/*n*, if **6**=the root of *H*, and *h*=the elevation of *H* by 50*q*/*n*, find a prime factor in *h* (6). 17. Where logs are used take soundings to make **31**=**17**, when **31** is the characteristic of **30** and **17**+**30** (3). 18. If a stress (*S*) have internal superficial limits (*L*), and *F*=the measurement in feet (*W* being indeterminate) of an arresting force, find *S* when *S*−*L* = *F*−*W*(10). 21. If a triangle *EAR* be part of a solid *FOX*, and *x* can support 1 stone, find *x*=*FOX*−*EAR* (4). 24. *N* being a considerable number, find by subdivision the differentiated aggregate of *N* cells (4). 28. Required the expanded equivalent of bread and mustard, assuming that after 4.68 miles the limiting point gave a false answer (10). 33. Describe a **31**, showing that if there be no arc the result may be equated to zero (6). 36. If $\frac{1}{2}x$=1 ordinary foot, and *y*= 1 diminutive yard, use descending powers of *x* to arrive at *y* (4). 37. If the back-answer to *RU.U*=*M*, and *ONION*='last words' of *M*, find an arrangement of *I*−*T* which shall be the same as using *AYZ* (6). 38. If a

CROSSWORD No. 58

1		2	3		4		5		6	7	8	9
10							11	12				
13	14				15							
16										17		
18			19						20			
21				22		23		24		25		
26	27		28									
29		30	31		32		33		34			35
		36				37						
38					39							
40							41					

decision be made by one man, what city will be made by ten men? (4). 39. Required a series 1234567 such that, if $b:c::123:321$, and $AB.D1$ is on the 27654, then Raleigh's tobacco-ash=1274653 1234567 (7). 40. If Porphyry's arrangement involves the Rule of Three, describe each one of six sets of books by Rule of Porphyry (8). 41. Solve x=Macgreegor's daud=converse of **6** (5).

DOWN

1. If the product of x and $y=x^8-z$, find y when x=**30**, and that which was to proved=$Q+z$ (4). 2. By conic sections and divided explosive find a volume which satisfies everybody (7). 4. Neglecting the old measurement, take newer measures to determine the **2** of Somerset (6). 5. Without determining how many beans make five, sift ten in the required order to make one (4). 6. First let Samuel Hugh, then integrate the pieces (4). 8. Solve x=**30**, given that out of the x came forth an arrangement of **1D** (5). 9. If U is old-fashioned

and V may be played up or down, show that **9** is without the prescribed limits when $9-U=V$ (7). 11. If a number of feet having been sat on be n (positive number), show n as minus power (6). 14. To find a series 1234=g such that, if 2314 may be drawn by G, and 234 given by G, then G may be grey=g (4). 15. Estimate the force required for thousands of old Italians to take into custody one Italian often drunk (7). 18. Required to make an indeterminate progression given the exchange for one piece of foreign currency (7). 20. Given ace=1 and putting F=factor, if $L+1$=the product of $F+y$ in x, find $(I+U)°=x$ in Bohemia (7). 23. Given m=Emma and b=a swift-running bird, find b when $b+m$=time for the early worm (6). 27. When c=coloured find a fourth proportional to $2d$, c, d (5). 34. If AB, CD are $x+ed$, and $AB=CD$=1 foot, show that AB, CD cannot be parallel if x=**34** (4). 35. If x=one like termination giving you no e's, find $2x$ to give you few e's (4).

CROSSWORD No. 59

From *Armchair Crosswords* by Afrit (1949)

ACROSS

1 Givest tips, from which the caddies receive what's coming to them (8)
10 You know your A.B.C.? Then the bet's off and you'll have to write this in as one letter (5)
11 A view which you may enjoy bareheaded, or in your hat (8)
12 Only a hundred left? It must be divided in two, then (5)
13 The telegram you send to your wife, perhaps, when she's away. Quite mad, of course! (4)
14 Describes what you will recognise in a twinkling, making the rest all look silly (9)
16 It's no good trying to make this more difficult. There's nothing to see except air (6)
18 You'll have to put back a lot more than a pound whether you pay it or not (4)
20 A bit more strenuous than golf: a course of it would straighten that slice (9)
22 You need this to get a bite with, though the fish won't be large (9)
24 No one can say it's a clear case even if they're up your sleeve (4)
26 He gives me pain, as Simple Simon might have said (6)
27 A. had something on, and it's all helped (7)
30 Keeps the home fires burning? Get that idea out of your head! (4)
32 Whoever gets slain won't find it as hard as these (5)
33 This is obstinately difficult, but then it's half Irish (8)
34 A fisherman might lose one if it were shorter, but it's a disgrace to lose it altogether (5)
35 The whole of it is only part of it, so there must be a bally contradiction in it (8)

DOWN

2 Tax-collectors do, and you can't say it isn't right (5)
3 A policewoman, no doubt; anyway, she takes a nine (5)
4 He did a lot of speaking in public, but Brother Aldous has caught him up and gone on longer (6)
5 When he's good he's very, very good; but it's the very devil holding a married man in Paris! (9)
6 What brings you to town? Oh, the market shows an upward trend (4)
7 Remember that it isn't only youth that may follow hounds, and you'll guess it, however well it's wrapped up (7)
8 If internal combustion must be taken on spec. as a particular remedy (8)
9 There's a tangle at first, but the hair is all right afterwards. If you can't guess it now, you'll be on to it before morning (8)
15 Since the money-box is broken, replace it with a cheerful air (4)
17 It has long been a popular form of collecting, but not altogether lately (9)
18 It's plain at half the price, but what don't you care about it? (8)
19 In the same way, you won't have to suffer fools gladly (8)
21 See which way the cat jumps, and then you can exercise it (4)
23 Glides away, making you turn pale (7)
25 If we anticipate evil, sure enough it's in the ship's biscuit (6)
28 The result of employing too many cooks. It brings your heart into your mouth (5)
29 If an artist ever wants a pound, he can raise it with ease (5)
31 Gives an imitation of split peas (4)

CROSSWORD No. 59

CROSSWORD No. 60

Justyn Print by Zander from *The Listener*, 1975

Each clue in italics is the imaginary title of a new book by an unknown author. Solvers are asked to deduce the authors' names from the broad hints given by their titles: e.g., if one such title were *The Broken Window* (3,5), the author's name might be EVA BRICK. Apart from several proper names, all words are in *Chambers 20th Century Dictionary*. The unchecked letters of the authors' names make up the following new book title: UP HILLS, BY AL PING.

ACROSS

1 See 50
5 Tax associated with square vessels (4)
9 It goes to a Scotswoman's head a great deal, we hear (5)
13, 36A *Drake's Hammock* (5,8)
15 Breath-sweetener offered by a child, round, swallowed by copper (6)
17 A drama out East, with one after a wild ox (4)
18 Source of a varnish that takes a heavy knife to impair (5)
19, 55 *The Sprawling Metropolis* (5,6)
20 A cake-decorator in a quick-service restaurant (4)
21, 37 *Left In Suspense* (5,6)
23 This act is wicked and spiteful (7)
25 See 28
28, 25 *News From De Southland* (6,2,5)
31 Fatty tumour caused by taking marijuana into the mouth (8)
34 Gift with built-in resistance element (5)
35 It's a day's work to check vessel coming into Strait (5)
36 See 13
37 See 21
39 Frontal surfaces appear to be reflected around the upper end (7)
41 One who's late can cross this river – or can he? That's questionable (7)
47 Suit having the tail in front is a bore (5)
50, 1A *Getting A Move On* (4,5)
52 Old-fashioned case from which to obtain quiet drink (5)
53 Quintet, having a crude violin, becomes indistinct (5)
54, 30 *De Bestest Band What Am* (4,9)
55 See 19
56 See 52D
57 Advance payment about right for a beastly home (5)

58 Earth dug out and thrown up reveals rejected English child (4)
59 Holy building at Mecca, a double one, attended by leaders of bedouin Arabs (5)

DOWN

1 Payment in old shillings and pence diminished in Milton's time (6)
2, 42 *Tudor Banquet* (9,5)
3 Bitter drug that forms oxygen in drinks (5)
4 Margaret rings one with a lasso (5)
5 See 47D
6 Type of fibre cloth, usually striped, laid on Mac's drive (5)
7 See 9D
8 Beetle caused endless panic, landing on a baby's head (6)
9, 7 *Stay Where You Are* (4,4)
10 Funny hat, one originating in an Asian country (4)
11 A Glaswegian buys, and —— up, by the sound of it? (5)
12 Hector achieving peaks of heroism under fiercest fighting (4)
14 Type of cereal that gives one endlessly passionate ardour (3)
16 Defensive apparatus fitted with spikes around battered portal (7)
22 See 38
23 Bond drops in for a cheering drink (3)
24 A month to live – start to tremble, getting het up about it (6)
26 Weel supplied wi' bawbees, I'll lodge in the better room (4)
27 Energy, having for basis a power emanating from the supreme deity (3)

CROSSWORD No. 60

29 Small flock of sheep you've to convey round river (4)
30 See 54A
32 Enraged, losing normal composure (7)
33 Stale cattle fodder, almost entirely (3)
36 A letter that's got lost without the end being lost (3)
38, 22 *Continental Breakfast* (6,6)
40 Find an easterner, used to the high life, with an unusual turn of phrase (6)
42 See 2
43 Malingerer is sullen, being without work ultimately (5)

44 Musical pipe accompanying English tale of yore (5)
45 Group of African peoples that has no beggars (5)
46 Mother in trouble looks up the serpent-witch (5)
47, 5D *Teenage Party* (4,5)
48 It's nitrogen in the Strait that makes the Scots yawn (4)
49 Frenzied shout given by woman embracing love (4)
51 Mixed fruit I lug all over the shop (4)
52, 56 *Incognito* (3,2,3)

CROSSWORD No. 61

Heart Transplants by Duck and Hen from *The Listener*

Each answer must be given a new heart: the word that would naturally belong at the heart of another answer. Each clue contains (in any order) a definition of the 'pre-transplant' answer, a subsidiary indication of the 'pre-transplant' answer and a one-word definition of the new heart. *Chambers 20th Century Dictionary* is recommended. Ignore one accent.

ACROSS

1 Cavalcade quite miserable round Scottish city boundary? (7)
6 Copper had news of explosive beside a road (5)
10 Bed one pal improvised, part of horse shelter (9)
12 One with pain curtailed thanks god (4)
13 Coin box, one in Italian city (5)
14 Whale? Money, we hear – no small amount – applaud! (8)
16 Corn, peel and suet cooked round plaice (12)
19 River tide that floods, swamping matter (limonite) (6)
21 Hard worker has not aged (4)
22 Vessel – note it by Channel Islands reversing (4)
23 Grandiloquent, reactionary judge imprisoning man shows excessive feeling (6)
24 Lu has my apron on, home protection (12)
28 Going round valley a little kid came to coin (3)
30 American place of massacre – in a short time, look – nothing! (5)
31 Site to be changed if this place is squalid (4)
32 Street in almost complete collapse, business centre before simplicity (9)
33 Spike sneering bitterly, blue about heartless exposure (5)
34 River with dye, see, spoiling fish, tree (7)

DOWN

1 Stay motionless? Old tablets set up twitch (5)
2 One at far post, waving to us, coming in vestment (9)
3 A foreign flower contest, old-womanish (5)
4 Ol' voter converted, a Conservative swinging round to the left course (12)
5 Party racket in bed-sitter or tenement (4)
6 Story-books – this chapter's all about joint rulers (12)
7 Evil Sarah harbouring anger when upset in a row (8)
8 English drinking cup's short gold letters (4)
9 Removes chemical product from animals, street being messed up with lead and sulphur (7)
11 Stain on one good man, judge maybe (6)
15 Court submission about to interrupt the accused's plea (9)
17 Superior trooper running wild – one driving out native fellow? (8)
18 Oxalis is sure to upset innards finally – they give out (7)
20 Engineers standing still begin to rest (6)
25 Look around – a learner beat man on his own territory (5)
26 In criticism revolutionary student hammers governor (5)
27 Chair, bottomless yielding one, exists (4)
29 Sloth? Get out of bed, rebel! (4)

CROSSWORD No. 61

CROSSWORD No. 62

Hydra by Duck from *The Listener*

The 11 unclued lights are words which have something in common and which have been processed in a similar way. *Chambers 20th Century Dictionary* is recommended.

ACROSS

11 People giving a refund for old collars? (8)
12 Strong chap sets one on edge (5)
13 Soon like a member of the Lords? (5)
15 A mostly sharp fruit (4)
16 We've some priceless oil! (4)
20 The EEC's confused about Germany's word to describe more than one German female (8)
23 Fails to justify unfilled tummies (6)
27 The man (lay worker) to get blunt (8)
29 Fillets, A1, eaten with excitement (7)
32 Onset of fever leads to a hospital note (3)
33 One-time flighty girl's engagement is fun (3)
38 Row about what's right? Judge required (5)
39 Simpletons, leaderless lot (6)
40 Bird hot with love? (8)
47 Wench shows desire bringing a touch of sexiness to the fore (4)
49 Swearword from the pastoral Henry (4)
50 To kick old copper's heartless crime (5)
51 Priest, a help for alcoholic chap (5)
52 One making a loan to leading character of Cowper? (8)

DOWN

1 Bird in California has sense to grab revenue (7)
2 Half peruse morning papers? (4)
3 Relation *not* 13, doddery (4)
4 Such primarily may have troughs (5)
5 Rough point in throat (4)
6 'Ellenic poet's dry measure (4)
7 Plant needing heat for brew (4)
8 Born in endless poverty (3)
9 Card game has fool taken in by wager (6)
14 Style of building, in short, is roguish (4)
17 To heal in oldentimes hand would conceal bit of old plant (8)
22 Cad's to hide as before (4)
23 Liz's letter to the Hebrews (4)
25 Socialist sets upset leaders of National Executive initially (6)
26 Discarded stakes – could be used around north for plants (4)
28 Rag sort of bandage triply wrapping one (4)
30 Indispositions caused by drinks we hear (4)
31 Instrument not half abused (4)
35 Plant with flower cracking a road up (7)
36 Australian beast in prison we hear (6)
37 Grass, rank when decomposed (4)
41 Worm wriggling round earth's surface may be seen on lawn (5)
42 More than one such guild could be gripping (4)
43 Cart may turn up here (4)
44 Goat-antelope – with head hung down it might appear to be a deer (4)
45 Boozy party for English after victory (4)
46 One wants the reverse of non-sweet sweets (4)
48 Kick and drag audibly (3)

CROSSWORD No. 62

CROSSWORD No. 63

Mixed Doubles by Virgilius from *The Listener*

Each clue has two possible solutions, thus each pair of clues yields four answers. Solvers must work out where these go – it is decided alphabetically where each one appears.

ACROSS

1 Usually nothing can be seen in this – but negro's in view/Transport flier from here – it gives harassed flier help, going round (8)

6 Sort of suit North or South might lead for this island?/Do some scratching in sporrans, perhaps – remove quarters outside and it's left over (4)

9 Give clear bit of encouragement –. you might have it on horse/As done in Scotland, produce a bit of witch-craft, parking in sea-tangle (4)

10 Not concluded yet, and put into view – without use of crook?/Dancing walk produced by one who's staggered (4)

11 Completed – a bit of paper work (it precedes the start of tippling)/One attracted by male swan, almost kept under control (3)

12 Rum else Madeira or Curacao is, left at end of bottle/Name for girl, is this? Look back in Biblical legend for answer (4)

15 Eel's first (and second) in Italian fishing-place – it's little use as wages these days/I display vacancy, with an extreme of eccentricity – mouth's opening here (4)

16 Article with a point – are women left this?/A result of manipulating enough of electorate? That might shock you (3)

18 Rod may be used for me, or Kipling's master/Mature, at end of life, moved to one side in Cumbernauld (4)

20 River in which Oxford college's dumped last of hock? Just the opposite/I'm true royal chap – prince for a Russian community (4)

21 Used for observations rarely (third letter made plural)/Inert material – use this, also, as lights' contents, perhaps (4)

22 Faults in red items uncommonly required/Walter wanting fifth part upset, it's clear – I go into sea near Dover (8)

DOWN

1 Sort of neat, to shape course for fish/Spot an edge, last put inside in a fairly bad condition (8)

2 Small part of old language, literally a vowel/River making appearance at centre of Firenze (4)

3 Female I watched (out West) and I associated with sexiness?/Up country in S.A., dispatch first letter in practice (3)

4 Girl's married name to a certain extent/What rivers may come from, though poet's lost source of brook (4)

5 I uphold what's been laid down – e.g. it's all in order/Tapered wood holding pole when in action – got from wine casks? (8)

7 It's associated with an unusual girl/Result of instinctive impulses in South-East part? (4)

8 Easy, in a way, for party after end of debating/Device for catching side in piece at end of boot (4)

13 Behaves amorously – see a bit of England (South)/Ultimate of sites originally, soon inaccessible since in Scottified environment (4)

14 Not working with energy, one takes set without last letter/Seen in noble regalia, in different version of 'Lear' (4)

CROSSWORD No. 63

15 Not favourable weather required to start producing ore under regulations/Musical female (4)

17 Designed to give sharpness in argument – you'll observe only second to change/Don's last English North-East river (4)

19 Bit of food we passed up? Not a great amount in proportion/Some suitable region to plough (in accepted English long given up) (3)

CROSSWORD No. 64

Plain by Ximenes from the *Observer*

ACROSS

1 They're commoner in a plane in bad weather – and, indeed, always (5)
5 One's fare may be about April – April 1999? (7)
10 Bad Queen lets Ian oust ours – was most uncivil (9)
12 Engraft a cutting of Poinsettia (5)
13 Used to being tortured and turned out (6)
14 Ham derivative, for use in hot pie (6)
16 The tangle a lot of Scotch wool gets into (4)
17 Sunday suit (not one that is hanging up—) (6)
18 Fern – needs water, in stalk, when it's hot (11)
20 God made Pharaoh still harden, and not this alternative possibility (11)
24 Note – almost complete idiot with a bob backs it (6)
26 Type you can easily see demanding wrong fare (4)
28 Matter you wouldn't expect to see causing a row (6)
29 A bit of ring gossip kept under people's hats (6)
30 Transport a flock of birds (5)
31 Bird showing abnormal growth in a rubber-tree (9)
32 *Neer-do-weel*, a film running into a lot of money (7)
33 Bores describing more than half the classic races (5)

DOWN

1 Like silks, in panties? (7)
2 What paves the way is being classy in one of the Societies: (don't, in the end, forget E for ego) (9)
3 His man's sure to break this old law (6)
4 (2 words) I, being in liquor, don't dance (6)
5 Old style of football – Orient trains after changes in the field (11)
6 Little box that's turned up with vital note in (4)
7 Inside of a yard – something over a foot – something well over two feet (6) . . .
8 . . . Will people give you these if they're *that* long? Green young men might do (5)
9 And 'er . . . (to be amended) was sticking out (5)
11 Ancient kangaroo in same south part of vivarium (11)
15 Old parson gets more peevish about curtailed, reversed part of crossword (9)
19 Dates – a problem arising for a great scholar (7)
21 Arrange a round dance, following the measure (6)
22 A cluer twisty, harsh – one of those Scots words (6)
23 Something to make fathers lean all round? (6)
24 Men without women are shadows (5)
25 This old darky'd be lewd with one (5)
27 I'm almost hag-like: dark dye wanted (4)

CROSSWORD No. 64

CROSSWORD No. 65

On The Wagon by Ximenes from the *Observer*

Ximenes (in Lent) invites solvers to join him in substituting soft drinks for hard in the answers to the ten italicised clues; thus *ransacked* might appear as RANCOCOAED, *lauwine* as LAUWATER, *Martinique* as VICHYQUE. The definition parts of these clues, and the bracketed numbers at the end of them, refer to the original words; but subsidiary portions, such as anagrams, reference to parts of words, etc., refer to their 'softened' forms which are to be entered in the diagram.

ACROSS

2 *Buttercup: see same among a tangle of vegetation, pale, about beginnings of Oct. and May* (7,5)

9 Badly off, without a start – that's dreary in Glasgow (5)

10 Total battle produces a call to surrender (7)

13 Products of the soil, mixed, are stored here (4)

15 Sweat goes through it, to make a careful study (4)

16 *Very good reversed Indian pillar, all of a piece – a memorial* (10)

17 That hurts! Stop! That hurts just the same (That's like what may come out at the dentist's) (8)

18 Ill-founded pleas will do (5)

19 *It's a marauder: fight back in the confusion* (8)

20 *Ingenuous and a novice? Quite the reverse: I wake people up* (5)

24 Small vehicle, in a restrictive space, may sting you (5)

28 Revolutionary gripped by Irishman or marauder (8)

29 *Ten injured – keeping cool – makes car move on* (6)

31 Tear open one bank of the Tiber of old (4)

32 The old port must be made to go round (4)

33 Opposing Territorials between Genoa and Milan (7)

34 A few drams helpful for forgetting fevah when full of the warm south? (5)

35 *M.D. wanted: you'll find M.D. alone here, harassed* (6)

DOWN

1 *Rolly couple here, rocking wildly – I'll sell tracts* (10)

2 *'U' old ruffian, ancient bird, with grasp of the turf* (6)

3 Stuffs the last of the infantrymen in trenches (6)

4 Take a quick look up and down in Princes St (4)

5 Having a bend – here's a thing to drink out of (6)

6 In Latin you and I have grasped the reverse of badly Cicero & Co. (6)

7 Leaves that could well be moist (5)

8 A mere number, a corporal: his name's not given (6)

11 *Secretary's job – the pay-rate's absolutely rotten* (11)

12 To make a searching enquiry about a fuddled toper is an employer's right (8)

14 Let's have an aid to calculating – I almost get bogged in sexagesimal arithmetic (8)

21 She's one to relax – she often spoils children (6)

22 A 'U' Frenchman is seen in skill over love (6)

23 Matthew Arnold's watery husband of a human bride has to flirt with one (6)

25 Deserved attention and study – get it up (6)

26 *To choose, in brief, glorification of principle* (6)

27 Unjustifiable delays keep one in longer (5)

30 Label bag, inside, last stop before Waterloo (4)

CROSSWORD No. 65

CROSSWORD No. 66

Letters Latent by Ximenes (No. 1000)

Someone somewhere claims (as Ximenes couldn't dare to when this series started) to know of '—— . . . . ——'. Each of the two blanks represents 4 words (18 letters); the dots represent 4 other words in the middle of the quotation which are disregarded here as irrelevant. The 36 relevant letters in turn should really occur (in some cases more than once) in the 36 answers to be entered in the diagram, the first in **1 ac.**, the second in **6 ac.**, and so on successively in the right order up to the last letter, which should occur in **30 dn.** But these letters must all be omitted, wherever they should occur, when the answers are entered. Definitions in the clues refer to the full, unmutilated words; subsidiary indications, e.g. anagrams, references to parts, etc., refer to the mutilated forms to be entered in the diagram. Numbers in brackets show the full lengths of unmutilated words.

17 is a compound word in Webster, not in Chambers; **20** is the Greek form, given in Chambers as a derivation, of a Latinised word; one answer is a prefix.

ACROSS

1 Rough-tongued red revolutionary about in Feb. (8)
6 Expand old railway – augment, perhaps, as before (7)
10 Sid got wild, gripping club, stubborn as before (13)
12 Greek money down – a quid short: the unit system (8)
13 Groans, tetchy, losing heart, inclined to grumble (7)
14 Returning east likewise was sweet (5)
15 Pop singer – wrong transactions curtailed (7)
16 Snakes like consuming a satisfying finish (9)
17 Ties can, when broken, make a law void (8)
23 They cause variations: choosed – that's wrong (9)
24 Ornamental vessel, incorrectly centred (8)
26 Premier returning in state, waterlogged (6)
28 Squabbles shortly following in certain conditions (5)
29 Concentrated, with a distinct aroma, we hear (7)
31 Beauty queens? They always get left (8)
32 It helps the crystal-gazer to see heroics, love, gold in a cache returned (12)
33 Eskimo conjurer in strange occultism (8)
34 Bird gets half dose of the cat with severity (7)

DOWN

1 Clasps in grief – O, O, O, O, O . . . . (6)
2 A bribe – dollars, apparently (9)
3 Officer gets commendation, derived from calculus? (6)
4 Relay high spot – hare all over the place (9)
5 Salt – it's multiplied by one pinch of Jock's (8)
6 I'm hippy: off with constable's headpiece (7)
7 Ruddy Scots dove up a tree – or Scots cuckoo (7)
8 (2 words) We're in slapstick – dress up, act madly (11)
9 The man overcomes trouble without any guidance (8)
11 Filmy green plant – fibres rent all to pieces (11)
18 Heere's the best of luck, little birds (8)

CROSSWORD No. 66

19 Unmechanized cultivator, pipe with prominent ridge (8)

20 With no S.A. wild youth, uppish, harbours mites (8)

21 Powerful car – girl unwell inside (8)

22 Something orthorhombic, even including a monkey (9)

25 This introduces something hairy, waving a torch (6)

27 Big city wise, one hears, about rising purpose (6)

30 Sharp rebuff – certainly not, little sir (5)

CROSSWORD No. 67

Legsin Cricotas by Ximenes (No. 1200 in the *Observer*, 1972)

Today's puzzle, the last to be composed by Ximenes before his death, marks the end of an era. The brilliance of its diagram composition and the ingenuity of its clues combine to show the compiler at his most inspired.

The 21 initial letters of the words ACROSS, when correctly shuffled, form a 3-word Single Acrostic appropriate to the number of today's puzzle. Every word is in *Chambers 20th Century Dictionary*.

ACROSS

1,23 (3 words) HQ makes dolt err, scoring duck (18)

5 Jovial chap – tipsy veteran by end of bar (8)

11 Is one, a sticker, sent back? That's divine (7)

12 Bill O'Reilly's last two: he has to sweat (5)

13 Club has last of tail in, and there's a spot (5)

15 A player catches Hill – it's the Guv'nor (6)

16 No-ball? Accuse then – hand over for penalty (9)

17 Old province puts one in the air, wildly (7)

18 Eat away part of the wicket, chaps (4)

22 One in a tour shows Mac in a good light (7)

23 See 1 across (13)

25 Overseas hero, X, produces a screamer (7)

29 A Surrey batsman back: once went in first (4)

31 Opening, stumped in Fifty club's reverse (7)

33 Ray going after club's feminine supporter (9)

34 Ere a collapse, returning, might miss stump (6)

35 Am run out, take off pads (5)

37 Gil—— bowled fast: observe wreckage (5)

38 Rest bat here very badly (7)

39 We look fine in the middle – pegs ne'er upset (8)

40 Ray's batting – it's sticky (5)

DOWN

1 We amuse – a lot of cricket among the trees (9)

2 Flighty opener's caught in gully, 50 (6)

3 Youngster put up in order – pulse noticeable (3)

4 Made a test 100 – was worth weight in gold? (6)

5 Slow – encourage to go for low catch? (7)

6 Tourist gets six – one right over the hill (6)

7 Spinning – rubbish: a century about one (8)

8 See 'im in a knock that's uppish – it's usual (5)

9 Boundary up – batting when he's round's fast (8)

10 Hendry out – he's out – it's under a ton (4)

14 With a brilliant pair set up, playin' in (9)

19 These diggers are tidy craftily led players (9)

20 Old game trio on a tour (8)

21 I am what's wanted in a bad spot, a cutter (8)

24 More than one third man at Perth? Without hesitation, that's stupid (7)

26 Men from overseas: slip in silly miss (6)

27 He who gets out is down on maker of appeal.

28 Ray taken in by shooters – long, hard test (6)

30 Saw an Indian cutter in maturity (5)

32 Lure towards short leg (4)

36 Dinna rin – bear up as before (3)

CROSSWORD No. 67

CROSSWORD No. 68

Noah's Ark by Azed from the *Observer*

The 26 Across lights are all creatures (20 animals, 5 birds and a fish), each beginning with a different letter of the alphabet. They are clued two by two, each double clue being an anagram of the two creatures to be entered in the relevant row. Down clues are normal, but the answers are to be entered in jumbled form (in one case reversed). The three unchecked letters in the down lights, from bottom left to top right, spell, as befits, another animal. *Chambers 20th Century Dictionary* is recommended.

ACROSS

1 and 7   Jays clench bun (7,6)
12 and 13 Rush up our axis (4,9)
15 and 16 Octoroon pact (5,7)
17 and 20 A warm R.A. cobalt (10,3)
21 and 24 Make ale as well (8,5)
27 and 30 Half an ugly fey (6,7)
32 and 33 Our Welsh ogre (6,6)
35 and 38 O, million merge (7,6)
40 and 42 Ah! Vice scandal (5,8)
45 and 47 Zebra-hide oven (3,10)
49 and 51 Aliquot delta (7,5)
53 and 54 No foreign chum (9,4)
55 and 56 Always disable (6,7)

DOWN

1 Stays in bounds (5)
2 Middle of the boat on the river? Could be (3)
3 Give up including Latin in worship (4)
4 Views expressed by the church in organized fast (6)
5 Wild and woolly one inhabiting mountain range (5)
6 Dance is almost over (3)
8 Lack nothing needed to manufacture this disguise (9)
9 Refined corporal, say, a remarkable thing in Edinburgh (4)
10 North French cable-bar (6)
11 Moves unsteadily – it's a tropical disease (4)
14 Old clothes, inclined to sag (5)
18 Battle-axes pound twice, cleaving twice (5)
19 Expert Aussie shearers, going like the clappers? (7)

22 Endless stretch of land? No, precisely measured (3)
23 Sunday's this even when Ida comes in (4)
25 Almost everything in moderation – the sign of a saint (4)
26 It may form part of manure agriculturally (4)
27 Squint? Put head in this – it's used for tests (4)
28 The attraction of beer and of getting up before noon (4)
29 Glacial snow still rises (4)
31 Freeman of old King Cole possibly (5)
34 Internal goddess in Swedish Elysium (3)
36 It shelters some skiers caught holding drag (6)
37 Delicious food for good behaviour, we hear (5)
39 M. Antony's wife, 56, embraced by rising changeling (6)
41 Was patient – same where patients should be (5)
43 Contemptible types, sly Scotsmen, take one in (5)
44 Silver, a length of worsted? That's cock-eyed (5)
45 Mexican ruler, dead, one superior to leaders of Aztecs (4)
46 To frighten away, fire guns endlessly (4)
48 A flooded dale – that's pleasant to the ear (4)
50 Gull, making old belly rise (3)
52 Bewitch upset Nigerian (3)

CROSSWORD No. 68

1	2	3	4		5	6	7	8		9	10	11
12				13					14			
15					16							
17				18		19				20		
21	22						23	24		25		26
27		28		29	30		31				
32						33			34		
35	36		37			38		39			
40			41	42		43					44
45		46	47						48		
	49				50		51			52	
53								54			
55					56						

CROSSWORD No. 69

Plain by Azed from the *Observer*

ACROSS

1 Government ails badly imprisoning the Queen and King (7)
7 Unco plenty in all quarters? Well, all but one (5)
12 I brightened, admitted by flower of the clan (11)
13 Fuel for fire – take one back, get another (5)
14 Utter obsolete coin? Jock's counted (5)
15 Kids' name for beak, perhaps, crusty, old (7)
17 Notice endlessly fertile round ait battered in sea (8)
18 Transferor of property, I, having organised reloan outside (7)
20 Sun's brought about unusually large flowers (4)
22 Doubly like the Scots, from England's point of view (4)
23 Seaman lost in one race (7)
25 Cackling birds love to whisper hoarsely, interrupting talk (8)
30 Restricting l-long story's excellent – it *must* have a point (7)
31 In winter, I shiver, a mere writer of verses (5)
32 Briefly fashioned Mrs Sharples in stage setting (5)
33 Great Trekkers, say, ransacked rondavels without hesitation (11)
34 Chill, the noo, ducks? That's touching – I'd come in (5)
35 French composer composed 'Cinquante Sœurs' (7)

DOWN

2 Bird gets to be sorry for appearing topless (5)
3 Fancy dress, what Churchill was often seen with (7)
4 I raise hands, clean nose up holding front of kerchief (9)
5 Look, I propose, enthralled – by this? (6)
6 What fatal disease, perhaps, makes you after its start, progressively (5)
7 Like a bird I nest fluttering round tree (7)
8 Bank's home to me because of lifting plenty (5)
9 Heat's terribly expensive (4)
10 In heart and core belied the face (11)
11 Sun above, sailor holds water-jug, oo! – I've a pouch down under (11)
16 Shells quickly penetrating airship parts (9)
19 Having raced uphill on tottery leg I – I get puffed (7)
21 Tipsy old fogeys? They bray wildly (7)
24 You'll see one having avarice, say, in company here (6)
26 Lower rate curtailed in pub (5)
27 Bishop capturing first man almost anticipates attack on . . . (5)
28 . . . His base? That'll require subtle means (5)
29 Lively in Israeli city, love – no one let up (4)

CROSSWORD No. 69

CROSSWORD No. 70

Spoonerisms by Azed from the *Observer*

Half the across and half the down clues lead in their definition parts to Spoonerisms of the correct answers to be entered. Subsidiary indications in these clues lead to the correct answers themselves. In the remaining clues the definition parts have been distorted by one Spoonerism per clue. Subsidiary indications in these clues likewise lead to the correct answers.

NB: Spoonerisms may be either consonantal (e.g. MENHADEN/HEN MAIDEN) or vocalic (e.g. BUNTING/BIN TONGUE), and may be accompanied by changes in punctuation.

*Every word is in Chambers 20th Century Dictionary, except **8** (in O.E.D.) and one archaism.*

ACROSS

1 Tetchy king – what you might call 'sticky' round about (5)
5 Pigs from the fast, head following bottom (7)
11 'Here Priam perished' – with which chorus-leader harmed cheerers? (9)
12 Crown king one held in palm (5)
13 Almost give up, concealed inside straw (a tip-off) (6)
14 Sparing backchat, left workers to go to bed (8)
16 Nail to turn round gorse bark (8)
17 Belt a Scot? Confront one rudely (6)
18 Wave out breast, perhaps; I'll turn holding it (5)
20 Scrambled egg or bright produce (5)
23 Desert food – it's wallop one imbibed (6)
25 Sounds like best crew get to meal faster of old (8)
27 Fighting bout – it's great getting hand in (8)
29 Medley gets a toe twinkling round – not the thing for one wanting slow number (6)
30 Maud Barker married Eric, Conservative turned Liberal (5)
31 Hide head: hides once in difficulties (9)
32 World out as haste set edge spinning (7)
33 Deflector of signs at me, more lustful losing head (5)

DOWN

1 Genuine ice-cream lingers – count nuts (12)
2 Plan in main a way to row initially (7)
3 J.B.'s sound of distress when beheaded (4)
4 Winging steed first in National on purpose (6)
5 Dog tail appendage (tree family) (6)
6 Paddy cut Enrico in pieces (6)
7 Lop parts of teg, long hung in street upside-down (6)
8 Bottom raised, tidy round pillowcase (8)
9 Ne'er rice irrigation rears (5)
10 Spaded roughly, long engrossed, not well – a sovereign spade money (12)
15 Peeps excitedly round stroke of luck – period property location (8)
19 Issue perverse fit assurance with formality (7)
21 Call 'Smash' for Jews first in Golan, climbing division (6)
22 It's torn to make sables, maybe, happiness with a soft inside (6)
23 Ate a little? Quite full round end of Lent (6)
24 Stop English river from right to left on map (6)
26 Take what has been let off wine, one rustic drink (5)
28 In dormer phase rest out (4)

CROSSWORD No. 70

CROSSWORD No. 71

Here is Wisdom (Azed No. 666 in the *Observer*)

To mark the number of the puzzle (see *Revelation* xiii, 18), Azed this week offers a beastly competition. Each of the 23 asterisked clues leads to an answer which contains in consecutive letters the name of or word for an animal. On entry in the diagram the animals are to be omitted. In an asterisked clue the definition refers to the full answer, whose length is shown by the number in brackets; subsidiary indications refer to the answer entered in the diagram (rarely a real word). The clue also contains a consecutive jumble or reversal of the letters of the omitted animal. Remaining clues are normal. All full answers and animals are in *Chambers 20th Century Dictionary*, 1983 Edition, except two geographical names (one of them appearing in the definition for its derivative), and the adjectival form at 2 (in *Collins English Dictionary*).

ACROSS

*1 Power of mesmerist, one in amalgamation of items (15, 2 words)

*8 Who often has named entrances, cunning turns? (9)

*11 Brood of pheasants, not old, twelve (8)

*12 Family of trees, and apparently bushes: name one fringing river (11)

13 Divine spear brandished in rituals (7)

*14 Coat for walking (double-breasted), intricate weave (9)

16 Certain whitefish die, netted by nippers in US (8)

*17 Start of reading must be in simple story (9)

*20 Unfinished gloss, what one in cast goes by? (9)

21 Pope, one in American city (6)

22 Tomboy (och aye!) at home fairly made to swallow loose lip (6)

*25 What's dead, murdered, gone, curtailed, gathered? (8)

27 Soak, dry inside, cut off (6)

29 I crash badly: as before cuts, bangs, etc (8)

*32 Frenzied shout, call to rise (7)

33 Hydrocarbon responsible for a fair amount of interpenetration (7)

*34 Remove tail of bear: task anticipated (11)

*35 Vital asset that idiot's left mostly frozen (6)

*36 Dismal backward cranial sutures (7)

37 Actor struggling with task – what to stand round in? (9)

DOWN

*1 Purple, old, suffering harm at inn (9)

2 I take lead in batting after knocking up 100, blissful (8)

*3 They're meant to encourage laying – get the point? (8)

*4 One sneaking AB receiving shelter? (10)

*5 Maintains existence having grabbed privy watch-towers (9)

*6 Society caps duck, creature with more leg than body (9)

7 Samba dancing round band circling percussion instruments (8)

8 Cow having to stagger round was hobbled (8)

*9 Vagrant fixed course on Bangalore finally (8)

10 Non-verbal mode of expression, one lemans contrived (7)

CROSSWORD No. 71

*15 Right wing splitting out is oddly traditional (12)

*18 Passing name in temper I misspelt (11)

19 See in one such as Heraclitus what's loosely symbolic (8)

20 Superbrain? Mine endured round middle of Dec. (7)

23 Coin, one going quickly in gambling game (6)

*24 Those responsible for grouping roster disastrously (9)

26 Papilionaceous trees, bushy, not lacking leaves? (5)

28 Concern following the Northern migration (5)

*30 Jakarta brew, narcotic, I swallowed (7)

*31 Mangle's replacement raised cloth in ridges (9)

CROSSWORD No. 72

Plain by Mephisto from the *Sunday Times*

ACROSS

1 Boss of ring caught this year with large amount (6)
6 Leader of men required in international football (4)
11 Scots choose a drop of whisky with beer chaser (4)
12 Contrarily, one about to be taken in by trick's a fighter (8)
14 Hair going white? Perm it in case! (8) . . .
15 . . . no hair repels – find restoration of this capable of taking hold (12)
16 Unique shell sailor's abandoned (5)
19 I'm nearly defunct with much to invest – banks give me livelihood (6)
20 One in the grip of recurrent experiences on drugs and drink (6)
21 Carbohydrate long consumed by nearly all Eskimos to the North (6)
23 In overhaul to strip it is out (6)
26 Note delicate fabric here like lustrous silk (5)
27 Stuff's little short of nothing on me – on terrace I may seek tan (12)
29 Neat liquor consumed by worker (8)
30 You'll have bearing to take off on this (8)
31 Make sure percolator starts and filter slowly (4)
32 Scots steep in still before first bit of Scotch runs back (4)
33 Century call when runs are restricted by new ball (6)

DOWN

2 Thinly striped cloth, old type supplied to order (8)
3 I'd be against taking old fashioned gamble in every American depression (8)
4 In school get trained with time as an applied scientist (12)
5 Slight difference universal in unmanly fellow (6)
6 In gathering of statistics result's not fully revealed in Civil Service (6)
7 Champion's flung from racing car out of control (5)
8 Distance you need on each side of track to avail yourself of machine-gun (12)
9 A dwarf growing up as a circus performer (4)
10 When covered in greasy substance it's illuminated (6)
13 Fresh team of oxen went swiftly as before (4)
17 Spell of exercise for swimmer about to plunge in (8)
18 Joiner's work – not antique restoration initially (8)
21 Internal transactions always will reach my desk here (6)
22 Play, not one, some say, based on the Muses? (6)
23 It's a struggle with one on first of colours having no angle (6)
24 Sit upright in the manner of king (4)
25 Coloured crayon for roughly cobbled note (5)
28 Bankruptcy of one caught in rush for payment (4)

CROSSWORD No. 72

CROSSWORD No. 73

Book-ends I by Duck from *The Azed Book of Crosswords*

ACROSS

1 Put in exalted position after you've got foremost of clues (3)

3 Loud 'oliday resort, a low down place (5)

5 I've a long day – little kid's swallowed acids (7)

11 See 48 across

12 Beat me and lump will appear terribly (6)

13 A sling specially prepared, did David wait for this? (6)

16 What you may have found in some rye-bags (4)

17 Start of snoring by inconsiderate person? Give a jolt (4)

19, 22 down. Author's output gets purely nominal reward – worth £3.50 at most (4,5)

20 Have a little look round part of fortification (4)

23 A definite amount obtained by collector of money in street (5)

24 A planet without radioactive material. There's some vegetation (5)

29 Hitherto could include head of ale, bit of spume (5)

32 Fur is more exciting for 'Arry (5)

33 Prince, one beset by wickedness, is to succeed (7)

34 An old poem to repeat (5)

36 After year's end gives extra, cares as of old (5)

37 Exceptionally odd Sabbath craze – being gripped by it you'll have uttered defiant noises endlessly (4,9)

38 Almost the only one to be a greedy type? (5)

41 Withered dean organised – could you call it 'evensong'? . . . (8)

42 . . . Inquire about strange rites and symbol mentioned in the rubric (8)

45 Refuse malt – it's sharp and deadly (6)

46 Old fashions – square hats (6)

48, 11, 49. Frenzied soul (canon) is anti-porn – zeal produces rewards (6,11,6)

49 See 48

50 Queen conveniently beheaded – an Elizabethan slaying (5)

51 Society has anguish; it used to glitter (5)

DOWN

1 I gather in material from the seam, having taken up short dress (4)

2 My position produces ill-feeling we hear (4)

3 Old deceiver very much in evidence around London college (6)

4 What *was* wooden and used for defence in field – or what *is* . . . ? (6)

6 Flower cut for love (3)

7 See 25 down

8 Improper international gathering? (6)

9 See 25 down

10 Fabulous contender gets record score broken (9)

12 Inconsistent rubbish in lyric (7)

14 Player of Derby Co. team in unexposed position (7)

15 We serve refreshments – spirits but not gin initially (5)

18 Beastly homes constructed by e.g. sober men of Kent (5)

19 What nasty tribes may turn out to be? (6)

21 Father almost 2 metres? That's not English, common speech is required (6)

22 See 19 across

24 In brief very old and devious (4)

25, 9 down and 7 down. To a great extent, my cover being tatty must get repaired on the outside – oddly enough a nice, appropriate description for Azed's book (4,6,9)

CROSSWORD No. 73

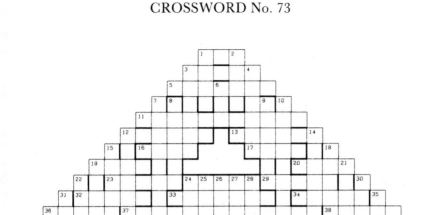

26 Stag night? Get a round in – and whoopee! (4)

27 Name remains – in Bath especially (4)

28 Jock's to stop fellow without hesitation (4)

30 I scored with unusually long shot (5)

31 You want to get to the heart? Meal is to be cooked (6)

35 Risk a bit of fun? That would be unusual for them (6)

39 Lottery selector misses one out. Pine as before (4)

40 One who used to persecute Jock's very being (4)

43 Solver's error e.g. may be noted hereon (4)

44 Compiler's taken up my name – see me on his stickers (4)

45 Inmate of zoo, I and my kin are sung about (3)

47 Tiny sum of money for a qualified nurse (3)

CROSSWORD No. 74

Book-ends II by Merlin from *The Azed Book of Crosswords*

The three theme-words form a group. The variations on each theme-word are related to their theme-word in the same way but this way is different for each theme-word. The variations on A are two pairs of words. The eleven remaining across clues each contain a definition (of one or more words) and a mixture of the letters, either beginning at the start of a word or ending at the end of a word. The down clues are normal. All words are in *Chambers* except for a scientist (given under his Christian name) and a familiar geographical name.

THEME-WORDS
A 34 across; variations 15 and 16, 25 and 28 across
B 6 across; variations 1, 12 across
C 2 down; variations 18 down, 22 across

ACROSS

13 Played without care, being leg before wicket (7)
14 Run out trying to back up, not grounding the bat (4)
17 Retired hurt after a battery of three bouncers (4)
18 Caught off a ball moving away, not keeping the bat straight (5)
19 Bowled: this bowler, if erratic, is a really fast one (5)
21 Hit wicket! Don't be hard on him – I observed many stars do that (5)
23 Obstruction! A brazen act! I hold no truck with it (4)
32 Handled the ball! Must offer the skipper an olive branch – an ale or two (4)
33 Hit the ball twice – run to the pavilion in shame (7)
35 Stumped – what you get anticipating a delivery that may yet alter course (7)
36 Not out – this youngster is an example to the others (4)

DOWN

1 Prince and the class he might join if bewitched (4)
3 Age makes a chap do as Old Father William (4)
4 Sound made by washing-machine? Put a pair of tee-shirts in this and see what they become (4)
5 Vessel contains mostly gas (4)
7 One with funny lumps? I have rash (9)
8 Old mounds containing iron show some volcanic activity (8)
9 Heartless con-man is more impressive (6)
10 Polish comedian (5)
11 Radio with a cat's whisker, maybe (4)
19 Bean, see, in pile rising, with Jack on top (9)
20 Two things put on trifle may be put in crackers (8)
22 Take in output of quarry on railway – clockwork model (6)
23 'Ey! What 'ave we 'ere? Close to a Dollar (5)
24 Corrupt pound has uncertain weight (4)
26 The Times shows English-ness? (4)
27 Bird, small breed swallowing bit of daddy-long-legs (4)
29 Like the sea in Sunderland (4)
30 Decrees followed by Romans (4)
31 It's handy for pottery with middle bit missing (4)

CROSSWORD No. 74

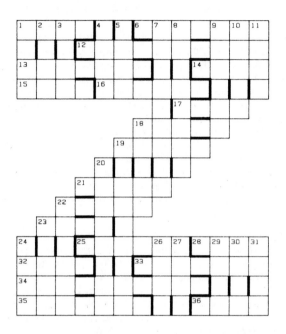

CROSSWORD No. 75

University Challenge by Apex from *Games and Puzzles*

Clues are either Definition and Letter Mixture or Printer's Devilry. Solvers must discover which is which. DLM clues each contain a definition (one word or more) and a mixture of the letters (beginning with the beginning or ending with the end of a word in the clue) of the required word. Example: 'Why has the sea-going captain upset the Question-master?'; Answer: GASCOIGNE (SEA-GOING C . . .). Printer's Devilry (PD), each clue is a passage from which the printer has removed a hidden answer, closing the gap, taking liberties sometimes with punctuation and spacing, but not disturbing the order of the remaining letters. Example: 'Is the question "Mice?" asked the Principal of Somerville.' Answer: ASTERN ('Is the Question-master nice?' asked the Principal of Somerville.) Each passage when complete makes sense. At the end of an exciting contest the Chairman, who had asked all the questions without batting an eyelid, added up the scores (two points each PD, one point each DLM) and announced that a replay would be necessary.

ACROSSBRIDGE

1 How does Euripides encourage the writer of tragedies? (9)
10 Why does a bride have tows after a wedding? (7)
11 Why is the poem a goer in the front row? (5)
12 Who relinquished the kilt to teach Scots a lesson? (4)
14 Which racehorse always bolted when the stabs were opened? (6)
15 How often did Lely visit the buxom beauties of Hampton Court? (6)
18 When did the kangaroo get a footing in Australia? (7)
19 Why did the malignant sprite keep ill-treating the Water Babies? (6)
20 Do all footballers report swear in contrasting colours? (6)
21 Why shouldn't the Cobble rub standard rubbers on? (6)
23 Which dramatic critic said 'This wreath is best!'? (6)
25 In which month were the seven veils chosen for dancing? (7)
28 Which Indian asked if he could have the chapter because he was full up? (6)
29 Who swam out every morning to collect alms in Scotland? (6)
30 What will all the idle hands do in a dispute? (4)

31 Which gambler always entered for a set never won? (5)
32 Why did the kind-hearted wardress lather dinner? (7)
33 Which dramatist in Eire is updating the plays of George Bernard Shaw? (9)

DOWNBRIDGE

1 Why has poet most of the tories against him? (5)
2 Who outwitted the Red Villain in Lear's Book of Nonsense? (6)
3 Which TV Publicity Agent said 'Tow or tar wood below you!'? (9)
4 Which of the beneficiaries of a will said 'Is the Mall yours?'? (6)
5 Who was the most threatening of all Guy Fawkes' confederates? (4)
6 Who accused the strange Mr. Otis of poisoning his daughter? (8)
7 Why did the reputable firm give the biggest raise? (6)
8 Which well-known flirt gazed and winked at the poet laureate? (10)
9 Would Ophelia have loved ads like Hamlet? (6)
13 Which General gave his brave horse wine after every battle? (10)

CROSSWORD No. 75

16 Why does inferior cheese put some rats off? (9)
17 Why are the top pieces of a lantern light always obscured? (8)
21 What should one use to prevent worming over a garden? (6)
22 Why is the bruiser at fun facing everyone? (6)

23 Do you know that ass trying his luck on Mastermind? (6)
24 How does a revolving index help one to read a dial? (6)
26 Who relaxes with Margery on the see-saw? (5)
27 At what time did the mound own the clock? (4)

CROSSWORD No. 76

Murder Mystery by Stephen Sondheim from the *New York Magazine*

'I **40A**(3) we're **39D**(3) here,' said the Inspector. He was standing in the jungle-like **1D**(12) of the **6D**(9) of the late Sir Leonard Feisthill, **19A**(4) while adviser to the Secret Service Department of **11D**(12) and setter of the weekly crosswords in its house organ, *The Secret Service* **3D**(6). He was speaking to Lucius I. Feisthill, the deceased's nephew, Dr. Nathanael Parmenter, his medical adviser, and **37A**(3) LaFollette, his secretary: 'Last week we had a **18A**(3) that Sir Leonard was about to denounce someone close to him for selling state secrets to the **33D**(5). His **35A**(6) was to publish the traitor's name – in **21A**(4), perhaps – as a warning to the betrayer to cease his nefarious activities. But it looks as if he was **13A**(6) at his own game, for here he lies, **2D**(4) in the back. I suggest we step into the study, where the victim's flight from the murderer began, to **40A**(3) if his desk will **44A**(5) us further clues.' None of the suspects dared **5D**(4) the suggestion and they **39D**(3) followed him, walking carefully around Sir Leonard's **1A**(7).

The walls of the study were lined with books on classical antiquities, Sir Leonard's only reading **7D**(6). (Hidden behind some of them was his famous collection of pornographic one-**20D**(7).) Among the **38A**(6) furnishings (Sir Leonard was a devotee of the decorative **37D**(4) and **25D**(7) on nothing) was a large African desk, acquired in the **26A**(5). On it were a glass of **30A**(3), his well-thumbed copy of the **45A**(7), his rusty typewriter, a thin **16A**(7) of ferric **12A**(5) all over it, and the crossword reprinted on this page, which was to be published the following week. The only other **8D**(4) was an unfinished pencilled work-sheet of Clues for it, as follows:

Gun Bogart might have used in 'Born to Say No'
Stare and see parts of the mosaic!
Alternative finish for a Biblical witch? Quite the reverse!
Call for help gets nothing for fair.
Plan in retrospect to help if you put on weight.

'A four-letter, five-letter, six-letter, seven-letter and an eight-letter word,' murmured the Inspector, no **29D**(6) at puzzles himself. 'Odd . . . well, no **7D**(6).' In the **42A**(6) room, **39D**(3) that could be heard was a ladylike **22D**(4) from **37A**(3) and the rasp of a **43A**(5). The Inspector lit his pipe and suddenly turned.

'Miss LaFollette, Sir Leonard had a reputation for being quite a **41A**(3). How well did you know him?'

'Quite well,' the **32D**(5) replied. 'We first met **34A**(3) years ago at one of those literary **36D**(4). **10D**(6) summer it was, I remember, the trees all gold – '

'Her favorite color,' sneered Lucius, trying to **7A**(5) her innocent tone.

'In your **23A**(3), you **9D**(8)!' she screamed – inaccurately, for Lucius was by no means stupid.

CROSSWORD No. 76

1	2	3	4	5		6	7	8	9	10	11
12					13						
14					15						
	16				17				18		
19	20			21				22	23		
		24		25							
26		27					28			29	
30			31		32		33				
34			35					36	37		
38			39			40			41		
	42						43				
44					45						

'**15A**(6) on,' the Inspector cautioned.

'**37A**(3) is right,' the Doctor put in with his characteristic Vermont **28A**(5). 'I was treating **27D**(6) for a ruptured **31A**(4) at the time – he had chronic trouble with his back.'

'But not with his head,' mused the Inspector. 'Sir Leonard was a man who **4D**(7) himself quickly to any situation and I'm convinced that somewhere in this puzzle is an indication of the murderer's identity, made perhaps even in his presence but too subtle for him to **40A**(3) and therefore destroy.' He gave the puzzle and Clues a moment's study, then whistled softly in realization. 'Now I **40A**(3),' he said, and promptly arrested one of the people in the room.

Whom did he arrest, and what was Sir Leonard's method of accusation?

CROSSWORD No. 77

Automania by Salamanca from *New Statesman*

Three types of clue are encountered: i) Who For; punning or definitive hints are given as to suitable owners – e.g. dog-lover (ROVER): ii) Used Cars; clues treat answers in their subsidiary forms as though they are locked inside a car (total length indicated) while defining the real answer only: iii) Scrap; each clue contains a definition of one or more words and a hidden jumble of the answer, the answer in each case being entered with an extra letter to make another real word, the extra letter being the 'bonnet' of one of the cars used in ii, the remains of that car also to be found as a hidden jumble in the clue.

WHO FOR

1Ac A boulevardier (8)
1D The DIY golfer? (8)
3 An astronomer (4)
5 A Covenanter (7)
7Ac A glutton? (4)
9 A Caribbean? (6)
10 A grass (4)
22 A geologist (8)
23 The forgetful (5)
24Ac The drinker/driver (6)
24D A simpleton (2 words, 7)
31Ac A circus performer (6)
32Ac The drinker/driver (6)
32D An old-fashioned girl (4)
33 A sportsman (4)
39 A fighter ace (8)

USED CARS

7D Ghostly old English learner drivers with big bird in road smash (12)
8 Flying one got cut, ovine perhaps, of deer (15)
12 Author to live secure mostly (8)
14 Well-built small dog's brown, a wild hound, see? (14)
16 Devil grasped by head lama after gold deer (10)
17 Girl showing pain mostly is aged, decrepit (11)
18 Fail to hold what's threadlike one time (8)
19 Praise specially huge lump of wood, i.e., as I chopped (12)
21 Lord in court has game in hand perhaps (8)
25Ac Bird season for turning coalman out (11)

26Ac Tree: one's to spot one in mud (9)
27 Burgundy eleven study (7)
31D Pal flew in patterned flight (8)
35 Learner to choose one different role (8)
38 Have an advantage, being gowned in e.g. dress (9)

SCRAP

2 Driving made pleasant at this school (3)
4 Going to pass, I'd use signal correctly (3)
6 Drove excitedly and once gave a yell (4)
11 Pressed, pedal would go down to the bottom without a hindrance (4)
13 Local man that carries blood to save noble (4)
15 Tool vital for measurement of axle load (3)
20 Driver, one going over six acres (3)
25D Made engine rods go smoothly inside lorry (5)
26D Good drivers are ones that listen and look (4)
28 Tangle caused by the Rolls crashing initially (3)
29 Birds fare badly on these roads (4)
30 Avoid bad language, do! (3)
34 Employ lorries up in Bolton (3)
36 Many chaps taking the final test now (4)
37 A battered Beetle stuck in a trench (4)

CROSSWORD No. 77

CROSSWORD No. 78

I-Spy by Mass from the *The Listener*

Twenty-four letters of the alphabet occur round the outer circle, each one being diametrically opposite itself (e.g. R at 3 and 27; or Q at 15 and 39; etc.). In one case, the letter is initial to a radial answer entered normally from rim to pupil; in the opposing case it is the first letter of a jumble of an answer, e.g. QEVIUR from *QUIVER* (or QCITAU from *ACQUIT*). Two radials are proper names and one a Latin plural not in *Chambers*.

The second circle from the rim contains eight thematic words of six letters each, reading clockwise.

The fourth circle from the rim, reading clockwise, contains five words of an expression continued by those letters which have been *misprinted* in the twenty-four clues leading to *normal* entries. In half these clues the misprint affects the definition part; in the others it affects the subsidiary indications. The remaining clues for answers to be jumbled are conventional.

RADIALS (6)

1 Try sex for a change: it'll grate on Jones
2 Monastic place for cats: Father divided by cost
3 Woolly gelding, sow and most of stock
4 Double German craving?
5 Extract from ballad in old, old Castalian tongue
6 Like a swine dropping new penny in a phenol
7 Toothy construction mounted above round cote
8 Caught US General consuming endless oil
9 Who once deceived is ardent, we hear, with the Queen
10 Sword and plates are kept here, it's said
11 One unformed barrow for Jock getting right
12 Scottish king's evil pointless yarn
13 Worker chiselled on the inside, tilted antique
14 Guess old type's making a will
15 Wood man in distance in drizzle
16 Greet return of copper packing-ring
17 Deity has power with horrific clipped head

18 Spine of arch is forked elaborately
19 A smile *can* be seen in a visor
20 Turning dotty about me with pithy sayings
21 Greek priest swallows heartless lay humour rarely
22 One who stands in record breaking attendance
23 Domes of antiquity quite round in appearance – almost
24 Coax lo'ed one into kinky lace
25 Annoying losing face to an unknown, belching
26 Personal likeness for eastern t-trifle with bit of yoghurt
27 Like Panama, dry as pea-stalks
28 Bruce up first, to sustain
29 One hard at it, (and, for Spooner, what he's unlikely to do!)
30 A Red header in play – or back-heeling
31 Look, register's backed and bound clumsily!
32 Roil, ring and shake
33 Wild zebra crushing Eastern farrier against wild beasts
34 She's out of breath (after blasting a lot?)
35 Arabic bird, shapely in manner of chest

CROSSWORD No. 78

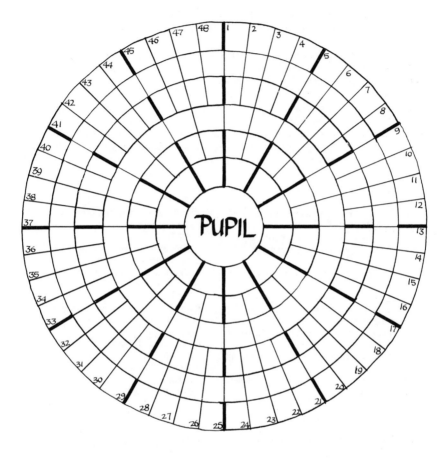

36 Gets to register end of dyspepsia
37 A metallic monoxide counter unknown with tantalum
38 Deity, in wood, burned as tray exploded
39 Injure, snare recoiling like weasel
40 Goddess, with a palm, king suits
41 Cope with American notable Centaur
42 Kicks and struts around North

43 They're ruts: one limps round one
44 Spirits must have gravity, landlords
45 Dissembler returns concession whole
46 Luke has disorderly rooms with entrance to tombs
47 Rectifiers for features of shells
48 More than one rubs e.g. glass boss, edge of lens

CROSSWORD No. 79

A double harness by Leiruza
All the Queen's horses from *The Listener*, 1977

The diagram represents an opened-out cube around which two knights, starting at 1–1, make independent closed tours, each knight visiting each square once only, conveniently missing the date. The moves of each knight give 180 degree symmetry to the halves of each side of the cube, and an identical pattern to each pair of *opposite* sides, consecutively spelling its respective clue answers, stopping one move from the start. The five 3-letter words in each circuit are to be entered as written. Thirty letters and eight moves common to each tour have been entered, further to assist the solver. *Chambers 20th Century Dictionary* is recommended, except for two proper names, viz clues 23– & –21.

CLUES

1– Hawk's rein attached to Eastern church candlestick (5)
2– Scot scratches back in prison (4)
3– Wind socks as told, using separate threads (7)
4– Rarely rode up North to attack, we hear (4)
5– Nothing taken from native bottle returned for medicine (4)
6– Rash firm (4)
7– Type of ringworm caught in the forest in Eastern parts (5)
8– A shark to rub the wrong way, Noel! (5)
9– GET
10– What the accoutred knight did, when late? (6)
11– Trap some tame shrew (4)
12– AGE
13– DEY
14– Viewer takes in first newsletter with old-fashioned grin (5)
15– Local food supplied by meat shops (4)
16– ERR
17– To be inconstant can stir up anger (5)
18– French sketch is ruined without first and last numbers (7)
19– One day's work, in Scotland, to get a saint's mausoleum? (5)
20– Spenser's temper is a hindrance (5)
21– Cheater comes back a month short over bet! (5)
22– Tidy kine (4)
23– A portrait painter solely, but not very good (4)
24– It is pure shame to cover with wax (7)
25– Malay boat comes to different end from a Dutch one (4)
26– SUE

–1 In France I deliver a blunt javelin (5)
–2 Fixes the price of brandies and soda (4)
–3 RED
–4 The brat to catch one in (4)
–5 Spenser's hair was hearsay! (5)
–6 Sporting combination of brass and wood, of course (4)
–7 EAU
–8 Even if stale, beer gets no soaks back (5)
–9 Stable to a degree, was fitted with drains (5)
–10 This vessel has speed when there's nothing in it (4)
–11 Some transient Shakespearian offspring (4)
–12 Meaningless kink (4)
–13 Short violent blow naturally causes traumas (7)
–14 DEE
–15 High note or *not* – a note! (4)
–16 An abyss has no sun going over to truly speak of (4)
–17 Reckon the term of life from tree (4)
–18 Without song, French zany son shows over-excitement (6)
–19 Sandarac tree around about here? Or a little behind? (6)
–20 Take in, for example, Solomon's common NCO (5)
–21 It's hard to be in this German district (5)
–22 Was this impudent person once very clever? (4)
–23 The Bard's carrion eater in an earthy environment (4)
–24 Sallow skin (4)
–25 Head back and double in Paris (4)
–26 Artists' frame pointed South towards the East (6)

CROSSWORD No. 79

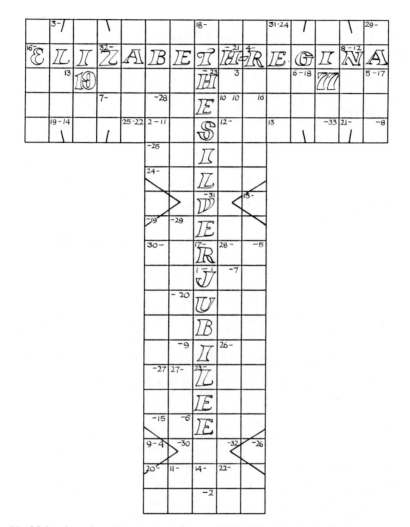

27– Malay boat has new prow getting lakeside salt (4)

28– Sounds like the bunny-girl part of the joint! (6)

29– On the sheltered side although the heart's not in it (4)

30– Get the vinegar on the way back, otherwise I must go in (5)

31– Foot's last product is said to scare! (4)

32– Perhaps the zip required to trap a Turkish bobby (7)

–27 Loki's daughter freezes screw-propellers (7)

–28 GAS

–29 Tangles with Swedish money (4)

–30 For blackcurrants and the like, car is best thrown away (5)

–31 With no returned sale, evaluates old cellar (5)

–32 I *must* be absorbed by Dane to condescend to take in Shakespeare (5)

–33 GAY

CROSSWORD No. 80

Tribute by Duck from *Crossword*

The clues are of two types: **1 Letters Latent** (L). From the answer to each clue one letter must be omitted wherever it occurs in the word before entry in the diagram. Definitions in the clues refer to full, unmutilated answers; subsidiary indications refer to the mutilated forms to be entered in the diagram. Numbers in brackets show the full lengths of unmutilated words. **2 Misprints** (M). Half of these clues contain a misprint of one letter only in each, occurring always in the definition part of the clue: their answers are to appear in the diagram correctly spelt. The remaining clues are correctly spelt: all their answers are to appear in the diagram with a misprint of one letter only in each. No unchecked letter in the diagram is to be misprinted; each letter appearing where two words cross is to appear as required by the correct form of at least one of the words to which it belongs. All indications, such as anagrams, etc, in clues lead to the correct forms of words required, not to misprinted forms.

The diagonals 1–37 and 10–36 spell an appropriate message.

ACROSS

L 3 He engraves lines around about piece of wood and ridge (11)

M 11 Diplomat's concluding words (5)

M 13 Caste once, to cease without god (6)

M 14 Bit of overstrain has mother closing exhausted eye (8)

L 16 Observe number – put it in! (7)

M 17 Secluded old offices set back (6)

L 19 Returning to look for tall plants (5)

L 20 Lent goes out with ultimate in jollity immediately after (6)

M 21 Filthy spectacle taking man aback initially (7)

M 23 Butler taking care over connection on drain? (7)

M 25 Hands cut off – is severe reproof putting disciple off? (5)

L 28 Fine, dry (5)

L 31 Most Excellent name that is recollected by solvers primarily? (7)

M 32 Jock's building-site shows his building material perhaps round about (6)

M 33 Geller? Trick has endlessly mysterious power (8)

M 34 A holy Frenchman, it seems, rare as before (6)

M 35 Suppress not completely novel idea (5)

M 36 Being sure offer a prominent position (10)

DOWN

M 1 Dan-Air is company flying a particular class of planes (10)

M 2 The old wonder at the present-day morass? (6)

M 4 Scientist's answer to 'What'll make the world go round?' perhaps! (6)

M 5 Song about e.g. sergeant in place of massacre (7)

M 6 Find new cork for liqueur half gone (5)

M 7 Resin in a source of gold (6)

M 8 Words from blown up cads? (8)

M 9 Volume discharged from Severn exceptional in eagres (5)

L 12 Woody tissue – what could be 'elmy'? (5)

CROSSWORD No. 80

L 15 Unusual screen around this French church, grotesque projection (11)

M 18 See this A1 performer producing rats? (8)

M 22 It's odd getting upset over a shower? Pestilence as before (7)

M 24 Succeed in getting pike fried (outside Scotland) (6)

M 26 Become wearisome aboard ships (6)

M 27 English snipe to get away safely (6)

M 28 Show excess feeding in the motel (5)

L 29 One scrapes – yen to get endlessly austere? (6)

L 30 Fibre, one sow turned up (5)

Solutions and Notes

Solutions are provided in diagrammatic form. This makes reference to any particular solution relatively easy and facilitates the separate provision of notes. For most of the early puzzles complete notes are provided, but not all the clues are explained for some of the harder puzzles already published. In such cases the solution notes are usually those already published. The provision of notes on all clues would be extremely space-consuming and for a solver tackling (say) puzzle No. 79 understanding the clues is likely to be the least of his worries!

There are alternative ways of providing crossword notes—e.g. (car + pet)/(car-pet) and (1 in man)/(ma-1-n). No attempt has been made to enforce a complete editorial consistency, but the meaning in each note should be evident.

In addition to the notes I have taken the opportunity to comment on aspects of some of the puzzles.

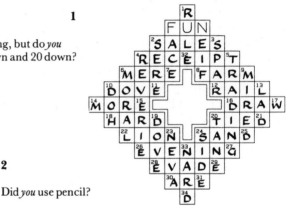

Don Lemon's Puzzle No. 200

Don Lemon's Puzzle No. 541

COWSLIP

1

Not too demanding, but do *you* understand 9 down and 20 down? *I* don't!

2

Did *you* use pencil?

3

4

Note how this diagram has the same pattern when given a 90° (quarter) turn as well as when given a half turn. This is an optional extra that can give a diagram a particularly pleasing appearance.

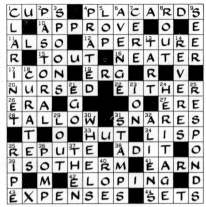

5

Are you getting bored with EGO, EGG and ERG?

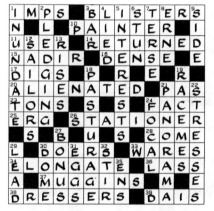

6

Not for the first time we meet SET. Unlike EGO, though, this word has many meanings—in fact, more meanings than any other three-lettered word in the English language.

7

The setter of this puzzle used the *Reader's Digest Encyclopedic Dictionary* and the *Dell Crossword Dictionary*

8

9

Across: 6. cryptic definition; 12. cryptic definition (an 'er word').

Down: 2. cryptic definition; 4. cryptic definition; 5. reference to sugar (Tate and Lyle); 7. flower=river (a common 'er word'); 9. upright type used in printing; 14. not really!

10

Anagram indicators:

Across: 1. newly; 5. form of; 6. it could be; 8. translated into; 10. to upset; 12. destroyed; 13. redeveloped.

Down: 1. unruly; 2. may become; 3. possibly; 4. diverted; 7. swinging; 9. weird; 11. odd.

11

Across: 8. reference to rugby; 19. I will=I'll; 21. out is a common AI.

Down: 1. AI: get excited; 4. AI: could deviate; 7. cryptic definition; 22. pro=professional.

12

Across: 1. lad in May; 4. side in as; 8. 2 meanings; 9. anagram; 10. red actors; 14. gran+den (verb in the straight reading, but noun in the cryptic reading)+trance; 16. range in Oman; 20. The ban; 21. drawer reversed; 22. anagram; 23. anagram.

Down: 1. 2 meanings; 2. tool reversed; 3. sir in deed; 5. anagram; 6. Di's+count (adjective in the straight reading, but noun in the cryptic reading); 7. desserts reversed; 11. mined reversed; 12. anagram; 13. cad avers; 15. 2 meanings (note double meaning of doubles, which may mislead); 17. 2 meanings; 18. Edam reversed; 19. anagram.

13

Across: 1. sounds like heart; 3. lisped sound of sinkers; 8. hidden; 9. anagram; 10. anagram; 14. glanced decapitated (i.e. losing g)=lanced; 15. anagram; 17. a+bun+dance; 20. rep+rises; 21. drop h from hedge; 22. lit+1+gate; 23. tasks minus t.

Down: 1. nest in holy; 2. rum in ant (Were you looking for a word meaning 'booze' inside a word meaning 'worker'? Bad luck!); 4. heroine minus final e; 5. anagram of 'and gave it'; 6. hidden; 7. wets reversed; 11. anagram; 12. anagram; 13. ever in lets; 16. hidden; 18. pastoral minus past; 19. Sprat when heartless (i.e. without r)=spat.

14

Across: 1. f+east; 4. t+rifle; 9. ten in Anna; 10. pie in SS; 11. RA+RE; 13. s+ketch+ER; 14. Dr+agony minus y; 17. be+a+St.+s (first letter of slay); 21. V+era; 25. W in sing; 26. anagram; 27. hidden; 28. even+t (last letter of August).

Down: 1. l in fair; 2. a+C+tor; 3. tend (10d in old money); 5. anagram; 6. L in fights; 7. censures without head (first letter)=ensures; 8. M(=2×500)+Ark; 12. AI+R; 13. NUS (National Union of Students) reversed; 14. EP (extended play record) in dosed; 15. sail in a SS; 16. range in OS (outsize); 17. bus is almost bust; 18. hidden; 20. 2 meanings (Sir Anthony Eden); 22. I in Eyre (Jane); 23. AB+out; 24. hidden.

15

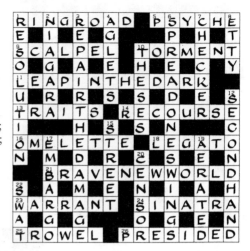

Across: 1. ring+sound of rode; 5. hidden; 9. anag. of collapse minus O; 10. men in tort; 11. e+a+pint+he'd in lark; 13. anag.; 14. RE course (religious education); 15. 'ome+let+te(a); 18. legat(e)+o; 21. brave+New World; 23. war+rant; 24. rev. of art+an+is; 25. hidden, rev.; 26. p+resided.

Down: 1. re+solution (message to solvers!); 2. again, rev.+RA; 3. anag. of 'hate made rip' in rage; 4. Ag+lets; 6. spread+one+swings; 7. Chubby C.; 8. 'etty; 10. the ses(sion); 12. 2 mngs.; 15. s+tree+t; 17. hidden, rev.; 19. a+era+Ted; 20. anag.; 22. taws (rev.).

16

Across: 1. 2 mngs.; 5. az in hard; 9. anag.; 10. cat's+pa+w; 11. anag.; 12. hidden; 13. 2 mngs./cryptic defn.; 16. right+r+ever+end & lit.; 20. share; 21. anag. in Oaks; 23. dud+anag.; 24. May+Pole; 25. err in shy; 26. L in (in Kings).

Down: 1. spa in car; 2. Ava+I+led; 3. rings+up+there in bar; 4. times, rev.; 6. anag. & lit.; 7. A+p-plies; 8. do+wagers; 10. C+oracle; 14. lied+own; 15. (ed+1) rev. in press; 17. anag.; 18. O in dragon; 19. ass-ess; 22. Tim+on.

17

Across: 1. 2 mngs.; 3. ado in barbs;
9. c+hatter; 11. lean in cup;
12. shaw+L; 13. otter in lies;
14. anag.; 16. 2 mngs.; 19. anag.;
21. neat+H; 23. out+cast; 24. anag.
in dose; 25. d+eluding; 26. bet+a.

Down: 1. ref. Gregory Peck;
2. tr(y)+avail; 4. a+p+ril(l);
5. cryptic defn.; 6. anag.; 7. sun (sound
of son)+laid (rev.); 8. EP+is+odes;
10. anag. (find: imperative instruction
to solver); 14. a keg in mood; 15.
a+f+flic(k)+Ted; 17. anag.; 18.
ana+to+le (semi & lit?); 20. el+don;
22. yen in ha.

18

Across: 1. la+MB; 4. init. letters;
10. (do+later) in is; 11. hidden;
12. anag. in cake+a+way;
13. sal(t)+via; 14. (a+son) in reed;
16. anag.; 18. O in baths; 21. anag.
(semi & lit.); 23. L in bind;
24. concern+ed; 25. res(t) in digs;
26. L+Ely.

Down: 2. a Ken in (a+wing);
3. br.+ewer; 4. anag.; 5. sound of
cast; 6. (win(dow)+anag.) in Strand;
7. anag.; 8. discus(s); 9. social+
standing; 15. anag.; 16. (r)ich+a+bod;
17. AB+ducts; 19. trad in SS; 20. NN
in feel; 22. G in ride.

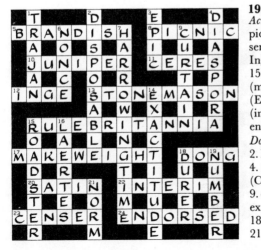

19

Across: 5. bran+dish; 8. sound of
pick+nick; 10. J+anag.; 11. rev. of
sere+C & lit.; 12. hidden (W. R.
Inge); 13. St.+one+Mason (Perry);
15. n in anag. & lit.; 17. Kew in
(ma+eight); 18. n in dog & lit.
(E. Lear); 20. SA+tin; 22. I in
(in+term); 23. anag.; 24.
end+'orse+D.

Down: 1. raja in t(raditio)n;
2. Di's+po(or)+sable; 3. E+pic;
4. (I+asp) in anag.; 6. non-CE
(Church of England); 7. cryptic defn.;
9. curt+a+in; 14. (act+it) in
exude; 15. anag. in roar; 16. anag.;
18. (en)durer; 19. cryptic defn.;
21. N or M (*Book of Common Prayer*).

20

Across: 7. anag.; 10. 'amper+sand; 11. anag.; 12. MA+con; 13. anag.+t; 14. RAF+fle(w); 16. pun+c.+Hy; 17. 2 mngs.; 19. S+camp; 21. 2 mngs. (Oliver T.); 22. Poe+taster; 23. 2 mngs.

Down: 1. EC in balm; 2. hidden; 3. anag.; 4. ad in show; 5. pa+anag. of 'inn got'; 6. ER (East Riding), rev.+vert (ER now fading from use); 8. anag.; 9. 2 mngs.; 15. fals(e)+Taff; 16. P+recedes; 17. SE+toff; 18. imp+TU(rev.)+e; 19. scar+AB; 20. 2 mngs.

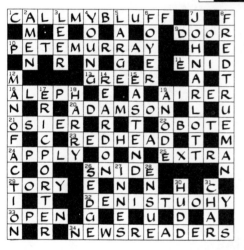

21

Across: 1. anag. (semi & lit?); 10. pet+emu+R-Ray; 11. E+din (rev.) (cricketer); 13. hidden; 16. anag.; 19. a+ire+r; 20. a+dam's+on; 21. 'osier; 22. o+anag.; 23. red head; 24. anag.; 25. hidden; 26. anag. of Denis; 29. to+R+y (semi & lit.); 32. Ed(rev.)+anag.; 33. 2 mngs; 34. anag.

Down: 2. amen(d); 3. le+ER; 4. 2 mngs.; 5. 2 mngs.; 6. ye in for & lit.; 7. anag.; 8. f+red+true+man; 12. anag.+faction; 14. rear+don; 15. (a+sten) in (T)ed; 17. Eric (alternative to Victorian title)+porter; 18. 2 mngs.; 19. a+node; 26. S+edge; 27. e in inns; 28. e+n+Sue; 30. (Trevor) Hudd(lestone); 31. 2 mngs.

22

Across: 1. 2 mngs.; 9. anag.; 10. Rita in pun; 11. anag.; 14, 33. anag. (semi & lit.); 17. c+'andles; 19. d-din in pug; 21. init. letters; 24. anag. incl. two O's; 28. RE+eve; 29. anag.; 30. anag. (101=CI).

Down: 1. sigh+t; 2. a+p+Ron; 3. anag.; 4. sub, rev.; 5. hidden; 6. (b)lu(e)+red; 7. hot+el; 8. n in much; 12. I+rate; 13. anag. of (m)elody; 15. (b)older; 16. pant+O; 18. hidden; 20. hidden; 22. pier+rot; 23. verse in OE; 25. aver+age; 26. out(verb)+do(n)or; 27. Mark's; 31. hidden, rev.; 32. sound of Sun.

23

Across: 1. a-r-gem-one; 7. nu'll;
8. As-ar; 10. h in anag. & lit. (1st prize
in Crossword Club comp. for author);
12. e-I-ld; 13. pom-E; 16. hidden;
17. s-one & lit.; 18. gei(s)t; 19. i.e. ten
dance.

Down: 1. anag. minus U; 2. hidden,
rev.; 3. anag. incl. E & lit. (1st prize in
Azed comp. for author); 4. MA-ser.;
5. n-a-il; 6. anag.; 9. s-MIT-ten;
11. men-ed; 14. ob-O-e; 15. init.
letters.

24

Across: 1. anag. incl. MM;
7. bo(rev.)-late; 8. 2 mngs.; 9. stic(k),
rev.; 11. ut-is; 12. sound of Thames
(Jumblies – E. Lear); 15. 'ared;
16. sound of barred; 17. g-H-AZ-al
(36 clues in normal AZ puzzle);
18. ent-end-er.

Down: 1. anag.; 2. tale(rev.)-ER;
3. ro(b)in; 4. I-blis(s) (semi & lit.);
5. t-a-it; 6. mes-s-Ido-R; 10. tit-ree;
11. ur-ban; 13. m-eat & lit.; 14. L in
dab, rev.

25

Across: 1. comp. anag. & lit.;
5. (r)asp(ing); 8. move s of sort;
10. f for p in painting; 11. alt. letters;
12. move d of drape; 17. at for IV in
oblivion; 18. interchange n and w of
nowt; 19. comp. anag. & lit.; 20. move
s of sting.

Down: 1. alt. letters; 2. comp. anag. &
lit.; 3. move s of tipples; 4. alt. letters;
6. interchange t and s of tens; 7. ag for o
in Poe; 9. i.e. Miss Ion if positively
charged; 12. interchange o and r of
orcs; 13. a but; 14. comp. anag. & lit.;
15. comp. anag. & lit.; 16. comp. anag.
& lit.

26

¹L	²A	³C	⁴C	⁵O	L	⁶I	T	H	M	⁷M⁸O	⁹A
¹⁰A	L	U	M	M	O	O	R	B	A	N	D
B	S	L	M	A	N	D	I	O	C	C	A
¹³L	O	V	A	G	E	O	¹⁴B	O	R	E	R
A	R	E	T	H	¹⁵S	¹⁶F	E	¹⁸D	O	R	A
¹⁹B	A	R	R	I	C	O	S	²⁰O	B	O	²¹L
²²A	N	T	E	²³B	²⁴A	R	M	O	I	R	²⁵E
²⁶A	²⁷B	A	T	O	R	M	²⁸M	K	O	V	N
²⁹B	E	I	N	G	I	³⁰M	A	N	T	I	S
³¹A	L	L	E	N	D	I	N	G	I	E	E
³²I	C	E	B	O	A	T	S	³³A	C	T	A
L	H	D	³⁴P	R	E	H	E	N	S	O	R

Across: 1. la-c.-col-it-H; 10. a-lum;
11. moor-band; 12. anag. minus OK;
13. lov-a-g-e; 14. b-ore-r; 17. f-E-Dora;
19. bar-rico(chet); 20. hidden;
22. (D)ante; 24. RA(rev.)-moire;
26. a bat or; 29. be(gg)ing; 30. anag.;
31. a-L-lending; 32. O in anag. incl. C;
33. ac-TA; 34. p-re-hen-sor(t).

Down: 1. lab×2; 2. anag. of a l an
'ors(e) & lit.; 3. culvert-ailed; 4. hidden;
5. 10 do form; 6. T-rib-ES;
7. ma-C-rob-1-otics; 8. 2 mngs;
9. RADA, rev.; 15. alt. letters;
16. scar-I'd-a-e; 18. do-OK;
21. or-vieto (anag.);
23. B-ogno(anag.)-R & lit. (ref.
George V); 25. hidden; 27. bel-ch;
28. m-a-n-S-e & lit.; 29. 2 mngs.

---

¹S	²T	³A	⁴R
⁵T	A	L	E
⁶I	R	O	N
⁷R	E	E	D

27

Across: 1. be/t (... best art); 5. Tes/s
(... test, a lesson ...); 6. G/ot (Giro
not ...); 7. t/own (... tree down).

Down: 1. 'er/e (... players tire?);
2. street-bu/s (... street, but a rest is
impossible ...); 3. Cat/s (Cataloes ...);
4. T/ies (Trendies dress ...).

28

¹S	²D	³P	⁴P	⁵E	⁶T
⁷T	E	L	E	G	A
⁸I	N	C	O	M	L
⁹V	O	R	D	O	O
¹⁰E	T	A	L	O	N
¹¹R	E	L	E	T	S

Misprinted words and notes:

Across: 1. sippet (sip-pet); 7. wagon
(te-leg-a); 8. income (2 mngs);
9. voodoo (v-oo-do-o); 10. light
(anag.); 11. leases (anag. minus SS).

Down: 1. Coin (St.-Iver); 2. Mean
(den-OT-e); 3. plural (p-l-Ural);
4. people (Pe-Op-le); 5. Egmont
(e.g.-Mon(E)t); 6. claws (t-a-L-ons).

R	A	G	M	A	N	F	C	I	G	A	R
E	L	A	S	C	R	U	M	M	A	G	E
N	E	R	V	A	T	E	T	P	L	I	M
E	M	B	A	C	E	L	B	O	L	C	U
W	B	N	S	I	A	L	U	S	I	A	D
P	R	E	F	A	C	E	D	T	S	U	A
O	O	R	P	E	A	R	S	H	E	L	L
S	T	R	A	N	D	S	P	D	I	D	H
W	H	H	S	N	E	G	A	L	O	R	E
A	L	I	T	H	M	O	R	A	V	I	A
L	E	N	I	N	I	S	T	S	U	F	L
D	W	E	L	L	C	H	A	R	M	E	D

Z A N T H
O X Y L U
M B C D E
F G I K P
Q R S V W

29

The code word was
ZANTHOXYLUM

Across: 1. 2 mngs.; 6. rev. minus t;
10. sc.-RU-m-mage (anag.);
11. (E)nervate; 12. plim(soll);
13. anag.; 15. RESIGN (2 mngs.:
re-sign); 17. anag.; 18. p-re-face-d;
22. ear's-hell; 24. 2 mngs.;
25. WICKET (2 mngs.); 27. gal-ore
(2)*; 29. al-1-t.; 30. mora-via; 31. nine,
rev. in lists & lit.; 32. l-lewd, rev.;
33. H-armed.

Down: 1. re-ne-w; 2. ale-m.-broth;
3. garb(oil), of=made from (usually
disliked by Ximeneans as redundant
word?); 4. AC×2-1-a; 5. fu-elle-rs;
6. BEADLE (be-adle, anag.);
7. interchange t and s of impots;
8. gall-is-e; 9. mud in anag.; 14. anag.
in cafe; 16. a-cade-Mic(key), ref. Mary
had a little lamb; 19. ER-rhine;
20. rev. of (law in do); 21. past IL
(=49, supposedly); 22. CHATTY
(c-H-atty); 23. S-part-A; 26. hea-l-d;
28. (n)ovum.

*This denotes the second word spelt ORE
listed in Chambers, a standard convention
in notes. An alternative would be ore², also
commonly used.

30

S	R	A	P
A	L	L	E
R	N	D	N
E	T	E	D

Full words and notes:

Across: 1. SCRAP (s-rap); 5. HALLE
(all-E); 6. RANDAN (RN'd-n.);
7. METED (hidden).

Down: 1. SABRE (eras, rev.);
2. RELENT (R-L-n-t); 3. ALDER
(anag.); 4. SPEND (2 mngs.)

The word made from the latent letters:
CHAMBERS.

31

The unclued lights are the names of Astronomers Royal, 'given a start' by Galileo (24A).

Across: 9. 2 mngs.; 14. M.Ali (ali(t)); 16. land-au; 18. hidden; 20. sear-is-k; 22. et al.-on-s; 25. twits with last 2 letters twisted; 26. coom-B; 28. O in anag.; 31. 3 mngs.; 33. Theta-sk(y); 37. d.-rape; 39. e-is-el-l; 40. 'arm; 41. anag.; 42. b-y(e)w-ays; 43. Earp(rev.)-tors.

Down: 1. anag.; 2. re-a-st (without=outside); 3. sting-O; 4. (m)alari(a), rev.; 6. Aga can't; 7. l-add(anag.)-ie; 8. hidden & lit.; 10. anag. & lit.; 11. un-crow-de-d; 12. anag. incl. S(=Society); 13. eye-toot-H; 15. bon-nil-y; 21. S-US-pens-E; 29. As-Kant; 30. l-eas-ow; 32. e-MB-ase; 34. anag. incl. p (soft); 35. 2 mngs.

The original puzzle omitted 'unconsciously' at 31A, and I am still slightly worried about the fairness of 4D.

32

Across: 1. anag.+t'+ant; 11. a-n-ur-ous; 12. hidden; 13. s-tr-ong; 14. SP-here; 17. Ure-ter(race); 18. ee in anag.; 19. U-rar(e)-l; 21. rev. of Silas-an (*Acts of the Apostles*); 24. SA-tana-S; 25. cen. in SA; 28. comp. anag. & lit.; 30. car-lo-t; 32. anag.; 33. rev. of red-e'er; 34. 2 mngs.; 25. c-l-trine; 36. anag. in site.

Down: 1. u in spy-sad, rev.; 2. anag. of animal, tre(e),R; 4. comp. anag. & lit.; 5. (c)rone (wanting=lacking; c=common time, p. 1563*); 6. anag. in ea; 7. I'm press; 8. t-e-hee; 9. anag.; 10. sound of tears; 15. p for f in refinement; 16. seat-Ur-tle; 20. anag. of O is not+H; 22. aspirin'; 23. SA-tires; 26. S-cup-S; 27. 2 mngs.; 29. (C)overt; 31. yet-I.

*p. 1563 refers to the page in *Chambers* (1983 edn.).

33

The notes below are those supplied by X himself. From this point on we shall not necessarily provide an analysis of every clue.

Across: 6. R. go by; 7. ul(na);
8. L. Delian:R.B-Ra-g-ly; 10. L.B.
(road); 12. L.ela(n)-net; 16. L.clam-be;
17. L.a-l-B.-ion & lit.

Down: 1. L.W.R.-link-E. & 2 mngs., by
J. H. Grummitt, 1st prize; 3. R.sail;
11. L.été; 15. L. ob.-oes.

```
W H O R T L E B E R R Y
R A S U R E G O B I E S
I N U L I N G U I N E A
N A I L E D B R A G L Y
K P A I R S I N S T E E
L O B O S E R E T A R D
E L A N E T D E R I D E
S O T S O I B G I L L A
C L A M B E L E G I O N
A L B I O N A R O U S E
P O L L E N K I P P E R
A P E R S E E A S I L Y
```

```
P U L S I D G E S H A M
A B I N N E R S P A C E
R E G A I N O A I R E R
T R A N S U M E G A N S
S M N S L D E G E S T A
P E E W E E T O L S E L
O N W A R D P R I O R Y
U S A N C E E E A F P L
T C R M C A S H M E R E
I H R A M C H E R E I N
N E E R D O W E L L S D
G I N K A N A L Y S E S
```

34

35

Definition-word first, then no. of word clued, then note if needed.

Across: 1. body: (25); 5. coach:
(32) (anag. & lit.); 11. bird: (18);
12. flounder: (31); 13. state: (30);
14. together: (19) (no=far from);
15. slough: (6) (E.-Lt.-Chi-N.-A.);
18. bit: (24); 21. mineral: (17)
(p-a-tin-ate-d.); 22. intrigue: (16);
24. awful: (33); 28. hollow: (7);
29. bird-fancier: (2); 30. vases: (26);
31. view: (3); 32. pony: (5)
(pony=crib); 33. stuck: (11);
34. flower: (1ac.) (3 mngs.).

Down: 1. cross: (20) (guy=flight);
2. fly-by-night: (14) (go-there-d): by
J. H. Eyre, 1st prize; 3. spray: (34)
(da-is-y & lit.); 4. measures: (22ac.)
(mate, tea); 6. envoy: (28) (envoy,
envoi=last part); 7. split: (23);

```
F L E S H T E A C H E R
R E D P O L L F L U K E
A V E R G A T H E R E D
M A R I S H C P A R D D
P N A G H S H A V I N G
O T T R E L I T E C O U
L E H M A C H I N A T E
D R E A D E D N U N O R
K A R L S R C A V E R N
A V I A R I S T U R N S
V I S T A S H E L T I E
A D H E R E D D A I S Y
```

8. storm: (21) (anag. & Te);
9. supplemented: (27); 10. rubbish:
(13); 16. fairly: (8) (hurr-y);
17. filmed: (4) (hog=arch, vb.: ads.);
19. bird: (29); 20. garment: (1dn.)
(f-ramp-old); 22. salt: (15)
(salt-marsh); 23. red: (22dn.); 25.
lobe: (12) (3 mngs.); 26. drink: (10);
27. keen: (9).

Romp Answers

36

37

Across. 1. Yeomen of the Guard;
7. Stevenson and Osborne;
22. South Africa; 25. Thomas
Tusser; 27. cribbage; 31. pencil;
40. Hebrew; 44. French;
48. Thomas Shadwell; 66. C. de
Acosta.

Down. 2. ace; 4. Tristram Shandy;
5. French; 21. Spanish; 25. J. M.
Barrie; 33. tata; 34. licitation;
35. 'Give you good den' (Shak.);
45. Latin; 58. obiter; 63. d(o)se.

38

Truro (54 across) is of course in *Cornwall*!

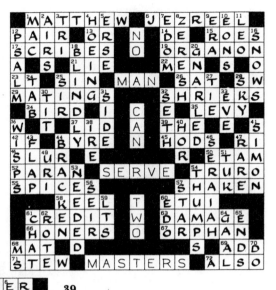

39

The first pair of words in the Quick Crossword always make a pun when read together (WRECK ORDER= RECORDER).

40

Some nice attempts at cryptic definition (esp. 5 down). 3 down is outrageous: ('blind' is supposed to suggest 'without eye' and hence 'without i'; hence 'i-less' pilot =plot!). The unhelpful checking is infuriating at 25 across (if you did not understand the reference might you not guess 'Harry'?).

41

By Ximenean standards this is not a great puzzle, but I was (and remain!) proud of the charades at 1 across, 31 across and 8 down. RICKY (29 across) was Ricky Livid, the pop panellist in 'Round the Horne' presided over by 5 down (surely better known as Kenneth Horne).

42

Some leader dots between 'enclosure' and 'of' in 11 across would have been welcome. For thoughts on many=L (19 across) see pp. 65–6, the clue at 8 down see p. 61 and the use of 'perhaps' at 18 down see p. 60. What a delightful vocal clue at 21 across ('heir male')!

43

A puzzle with some entertaining features but does it depend too much on the solver being well read? I confess to having guessed the answer to 8 down (correctly as it happened).

44

The transplanted letters spell out QUINDECIMILLENARY CROSSWORD. A model of soundness with clues that paint interesting pictures. The meanings of some of the double clues are bound to be a bit stretched though because of the constraints imposed.

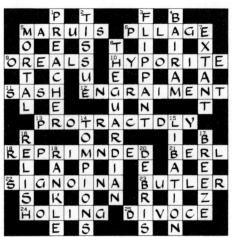

Diagram A

Diagram B

45

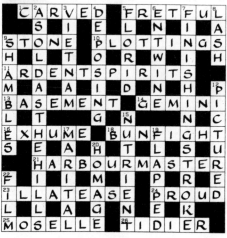

A complete set of notes for this one will show the variety of clues in a typical puzzle by Alec Robins.

Across. 1. v in cared; 5. f+anag.; 9. St.+one; 10. ting in plots; 11. 2 mngs; 13. S.E. men in bat (note how 'club' misleads); 14. gem+in+1; 16. ex+Hume; 18. bun+fight; 21. harbour+master; 23. I'll+a+tease; 24. U in prod; 25. M.O.'s+elle; 26. Di in tier.

Down. 2. anag.; 3. Etna in vim; 4. ed (rev.)+posing; 5. anag.; 6. anag.; 7. finishing+stroke; 8. 1+ash; 9. sh+(r)ambles; 12. Pict+anag.; 15. nut+1 in rent; 17. mar+it+al(e); 19. (a+pp) in fled; 20. mag in hoe; 22. hidden, rev.

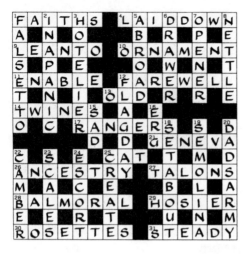

46

Quite a different flavour from the previous puzzle as the full notes show:

Across. 1. anag.; 4. 2 mngs; 9. anag.;
10. cryptic defn; 11. el bane (rev.);
12. fare+well; 13. cryptic defn; 14. anag.;
17. cryptic defn; 21. gen+Eva; 25. cryptic defn; 26. anag. & lit.; 27. on in anag.;
28. balm+oral; 29. anag.; 30. cryptic defn;
31. cryptic defn.

Down. 1. cryptic defn; 2. 1 nap+anag.;
3. cryptic defn; 5. A.B.+road; 6. reward (rev.); 7. 2 mngs; 8. 2 mngs; 12. cryptic defn; 15 das (rev.); 16. (cryptic?) defn;
18. 2 mngs; 19. anag.; 20. cryptic defn;
22. cryptic defn; 23. 2 mngs; 24. 2 mngs(?);
25. cryptic defn.

Some of the cryptic definitions are superb, but perhaps there are too many. Anagram indication is dubious in places and the definition not always adequate (e.g. at 28 across). Nevertheless this puzzle has much to commend it.

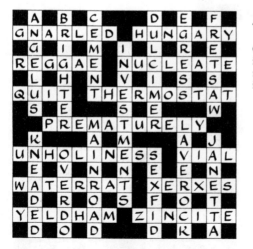

47

Clues not entirely Ximenean (e.g. innate=in nate: see pp. 64 and 130) and rather weak on meaning in places. An interesting challenge, though.

48

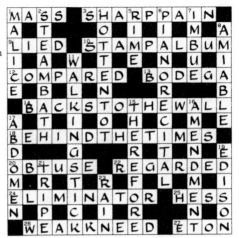

Across. 1. Ma=SS (semi & lit.); 3. harp in Spain; 9. 2 mngs; 10. cryptic defn; 12. O in C+MP+a+red; 13. bod+e.g. +a; 14. backs+tot+hew+all; 18. 2 mngs; 20. 2 mngs (90 degrees); 22. Reg+anag.; 24. cryptic defn; 25. he+SS & lit.; 26. vocal (week+need); 27. note, rev.

Down. 1. m.+Alice; 2. anag.; 4. ten in (hot+tot); 5. vocal (rhyme); 6. anag. & lit.; 7. I'm+b(L)ue; 8. am I able?; 11. law (rev.)+king's tick; 15. the+R.E.+ fore; 16. anag.; 17. bad+anag.; 19. anag.; 21. trip+E; 23. RA+in.

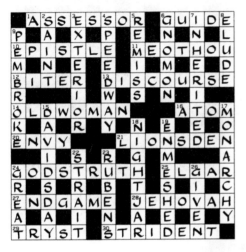

49

An example of how many clues can be linked by a common theme.

50

An entertaining puzzle but there are difficulties with parts of speech (see pp. 61–2). In particular note the clueing of 17 across, DESTINY. The words 'won't admit' could denote 'denies' but not 'deny'.

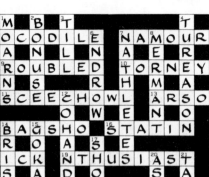

51

The message is RETURN TO SENDER. In 26 across rumour=on-dit. 20 down refers to Astrid Proll, whose 'r' is moved.

52

The answers to the numerical clues are the ten numerals, in ascending order of hardness, used in Moh's scale of hardness—hence the hint in the preamble. They are listed under the entry for 'hard' in *Chambers*.

53

The themewords are from Churchill's wartime speech: BLOOD (variations: VEIN and ARTERY, blood vessels), TOIL (variations: LABOUR and WORK, synonyms), TEARS (variations: STARE and ASTER, anagrams), SWEAT (variations: SHOP and BAND, words to which it can be added).

Note the anagram indicator at 4 across (spin, an intransitive verb, not a noun). The less than helpful checking at 13 and 27 across, 15 and 16 down can be justified by the close linking of the themewords and their variations, and by the need to fit in a lot of short words.

54

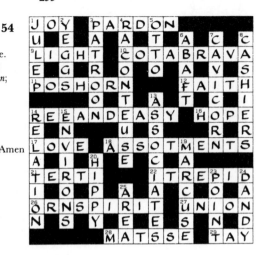

Lord, make us *instruments* of your peace.
Where there is *hatred*, let there be love;
Where there is *injury*, let there be *pardon*;
Where there is *discord, union*;
Where there is *doubt, faith*;
Where there is *despair, hope*;
Where there is *darkness, light*;
Where there is *sadness, joy*;
for your mercy and your truth's sake. Amen
St Francis (of Assisi)

55

Across: 1. NICROSILAL; 9. RISUS;
11. LORRY; 12. RAPHE; 13. SELAH;
14. PAUL; 15. SYE; 17. YAHOO (O+O=
pair of ducks in cricket); 19. HUTIA;
22. RIA; 23. TRAP; 26. CRUET;
28. SUING; 29. BLEEP;
30. DITHIONATE.

Down: 1. LOLLSHRAUB; 2. AGREE;
3. PURL; 4. ORACH; 5. SITTA (sitta
minus ta); 6. LURCH; 7. LIGNO CAINE;
8. SQUAW; 10. SCRAG; 16. WINCE;
18. OKAPI; 20. VAUNT; 21. TRURO;
22. RAINY; 25. TWIN; 27. REG.

56

Missing words are all sums of money, in
this order: ducat, ore, mina, rag (farthing),
sol, pie, dam, mil, para, sou, fen, sen, lev,
dinar, fin, franc, angel, cent, rand, rial, as,
lac

Across: 4. Jane Eyre

Down: 4. Francesca da Rimini: France
(Anatole)+sca(red)

```
S T E R N D O W L A R E T
T E N A C I N I U T A R Y
A O S C S E E N E T H E R
L A C K L A N D F I O N E
L F U N A M E L I C S O Y
V E R Y U B O U R N E W E
E D D A G E O N E A N N A
R E R S H R A L S T O U T
M T E N T E R E B O N N H
E N A T E L E S I R E N E
S A D G R I D S N S T O W
```

57

Original report in *The Listener*: The only mistake was ALIBI at 11A, but TESTER at 41A and IT ARID at 46D, 48A were offered in a few cases. All three clues were quotations—TORE at 9D ('it makes J.H.'s pie *to* recur to one's mind') is rather awkward, but is accepted.

Across: (4,7D) Poe, Raven. (7) To a Cat. (11) Humbert Wolfe, The Lilac. (16) Patmore, Angel in the House. (18) R. Browning, Meeting at Night. (22) Hardy, Shelley's Sky-lark. (27) E. C. Pinkney, A Health. (28) Hood, S. of Shirt. (38) M. Arnold, Dover Beach. (49) Marlowe, Pass. Shepherd.

Down: (1) Marvell, Hymn to Light. (3) Swinburne, Forsaken Garden. (14) Tenn., Aylmer's Field. (15) Paradise Lost. II.340. (23) Longfellow, Maidenhead. (26) Clough, 'Say not the struggle'. (27) Emerson, Each and All. (31) Keats, To one long in City. (40) Pope, Criticism. (46) Richard II, v.2.

```
M O C H A S A U S A G E S
A N O I N T S L A G N A T
T A N G L E M E S A U T R
E S T H E R I X L G S E A
T H E M S E L V E S W R Y
R Y N D Q S I S E D E M E
A P T M U L T I P L I E D
I L L M A H I C R I N A L
P A I A R E A S A N E L Y
S I O N E R W A S T R E L
E N N E A D I C P O T T Y
```

58

Across: (1)=geometrid moth. (*Century*) = geometer (*Webster*); Red Sea. (12, 13) tan G, tan GLE, since LEG is a rt angle. (15) Cyclic *same*. (16) H. the Agagite; 50 cubits, *Esther* iii.I, v.14, vii.10. (18) Police Force; *Twelves* when *w=hems*. (21) Reynard *minus* ear. (33) Arc, nil. (37) Are you ewe? No, I'm ram=rev. *Marmion*: S(t)anley, using a wise head. (38)=10 times deci-sion. (39) Be, see; was, saw; a beady eye. (40) Shorter O.E.D.; Ch. Biog. Dict. (41) *Wee Macgreegor*.

Down: (1) Lion cub. (2) Con-e, T.N.T. (5) Lue X. (6) *I Sam*. xv. 33. (8) *Judges* xiv, 14, 18. (14) One-horse *shay*. (15) Milia, It. (18) Piastre. (20) We, inert; *we* to the power nought. (23) Six ask emma. (27) Penny plain, etc. (34) Intoed. (35) *Euphues*.

WEINERT was a misprint in *Pears' Cyclopedia* for WEIPERT. Afrit apologised.

59

Few of the clues are less than 10 words long; 7 down has 20 words. Despite this prolixity Afrit often only provided a subsidiary indication for part of the answer (see e.g. 33 across—PERVERSE indeed!).

60

Across: 5. VAT-s 9. sound of much 15. a-ch.-O in Cu 31. tea (=marijuana) in stoma 34. bo-R-on 35. tin in St. and two mngs 39. rev. of seem around top 47. agree (=suit) with last letter first 53. V+a gue 58. rev. of E.-kid 59. ka-a-b(edouin)-A(rabs) *Down*: 4. Ri-a-ta 6. aba-ca' 8. scar(e)-a-b(aby) 11. sound of coughs (up) 12. initial letters 14. zea(l). 16. c. + anag 23. cha(in) 24. be-t(remble) in rev. of het 27. E-on. 29. t-R-ip 32. anag. and literally 33. fee(d) 36. san(s) 43. s-(wor)k-ulk 46. rev. of ai-ma-l.

61

Pre-transplant answers (heart in parentheses):

Across: 1. so(war)ry; 6. h(ear)d; 10. ped(alb)one; 12. i(do)l; 13. p(ais)a; 14. ca(chal)ot; 16. pleu(rone)ctes; 19. bo(go)re; 21. h(an)t; 22. s(ai)c; 23. e(mote)s; 24. orph(anas)ylum; 28. to(tall)ed; 30. A(lam)o; 31. s(ti)e; 32. rus(tic)ity; 33. s(ark)y; 34. re(dey)es.

Down: 1. s(lee)p; 2. out(sen)try; 3. a(nil)e; 4. levo(rota)tory; 5. r(an)t; 6. hept(arch)ists; 7. se(rial)ly; 8. e(ta)s; 9. de(sal)ts; 11. l(egis)t; 15. def(ere)nce; 17. up(root)er; 18. is(sue)rs; 20. re(po)se; 25. l(oca)l; 26. m(all)s; 27. s(of)a; 29. r(is)e.

62

The uncllued answers are place-names in Thomas Hardy's novels entered with remaining letters after the first in reverse order, viz.:

Across: 1. Wintoncester; 18. Marygreen; 24. Ivell; 34. Idmouth; 36. Knollsea; 42. Tivworthy; 53. Casterbridge.

Down: 10. Shaston; 19. Trufal; 21. Dundagel; 33. Glaston.

Other notes: 52 across. ref. John Gilpin, 3 down. indirect anag.: anag. of late (naughty? see pp. 60–1).

63

Note: Allocation to the four squares is on the basis of the letters—A, B, C, D—in the top left-hand square (*where each one appears—see preamble*).

64

Across: 1. bu-M.P.-s; 5. che-Ap.-er; 10. G-E.R.-trude, Hamlet; 18. stalk=hunt, n.; 20. anag. & lit.; 24. re-mut(t)s & lit.; 29. arc-ana; 31. ule; 32. kell; 33. (St. L)egers.

Down: 2. U-in-Tahit(i),e: Society Is.; 6. i.-ut-e; 8. putt=greenhorn & lit.; 15. clu(e); 23. li-pas-e, & lit.; 24. shadows, vb.; 26. uncle(an); 27. anil(e).

65

Grid:

```
C M I L K A T W O M A N
O O R I E S U M M O N S
L S P N E T L S I L O T
P O R E K O L A T O N E
O D O N T O I D S G Y T
L A P S E P I L L I M E
L A E V I A N V E S P A
Y U R M P R E D A T O R
E N T O N I C E R I P A
U T Y R E S K L N C T P
R I V A L T A B E K A H
H E L E M O N A D E R Y
```

Across: 2. bumbo-at woman (*H.M.S. Pinafore*): m-ilk-at, w-o-m-an; 9. (p)oor; 13. anag. & lit.; 16. Graves-tone: O.K.rev.-lat-one; 17. O-don't-O-id.; 18. anag. & lit.; 19. pil-lager: pi-llim-e; 20. la-rum: naive-a-L.; 29. en-gin-e: ent-on-ice; 34. beaker, Keats; 35. he-ale-r: anag.

Down: 1. col-port-eur: anag.; 2. mo-hock: mo-sod-a; 6. tu-lli-I; 8. Nym, *Merry Wives*; 11. ste-nog-raphy: anag.; 14. stic(k); 23. ballad. *The N.*; 26. ava-tar: p-opt-ar, par=brief, noun.

Grid:

```
R D U L T E X S R E C H
I A S T O M A C E D U E
N B M H R M N A D I S M
G R O C H Y T T O O T E
S I N T R A A C O D A S
I S E N A C T H D B R S
A T Y E E H E O C O D S
D E C N T E R S A M P Y
I F F S R E C E N T E D
L E G A C E S H O I S N
L R B I H R O O S O P E
A N G E O S T E R N L Y
```

66

Quotation: 'A thousand raw tricks ... which I will practise': *Merch. of V.* iii.4.end.

Across: 1. radulate: ult.; 6. stretch: S.R.-ech; 10. high-stomached: mace; 12. monadism: mna-dism (a − £), down=dismal; 13. grouchy; 14. soote; 15. Sinatra: tr.; 16. anacondas; 17. disenact; 23. rheocords; 24. decanter; 26. swampy; 28. tiffs: f.; 29. centred; 31. legacies: leg-aces; 32. dichrooscope: epos-o-or-hid rev.; 23. angekkok; 34. sternly: ly(nx).

Down: 1. wrings; 2. hush-money; 3. lithic; 4. torch-race; 5. xanthate: x-an-tate; 6. sciatic: scat; 7. redwood: doo; 8. custard pies; 9. helmless; 11. bristle-fern; 18. cheepers; 19. horse-hoe; 20. domation: domatium: no-it-mod rev.; 21. Cadillac; 22. enstatite; ene.sai; 25. tricho-; 27. Sydney; 30. noser: sr.

67

L	O	R	D	S	T	A	V	E	R	N	E	R
I	S	I	A	C	A	L	I	C	O	O	L	Y
M	A	C	L	E	R	D	A	M	T	M	A	N
E	X	T	R	A	D	I	T	E	A	I	P	D
R	H	A	E	T	I	A	O	E	T	C	H	R
I	T	L	S	T	V	C	R	U	I	S	I	E
C	R	I	C	K	E	T	G	R	O	U	N	D
K	A	M	I	C	H	I	R	I	N	G	E	D
S	Y	A	M	A	E	N	O	S	T	R	I	L
T	T	D	I	B	R	A	S	S	I	E	R	E
O	R	A	T	O	R	L	E	U	N	A	R	M
L	I	G	A	N	E	B	R	E	A	T	H	E
E	P	E	R	G	N	E	S	R	E	S	I	N

1200=MCC=Marylebone Cricket Club

Across: 25. X=chi; 33. ray=re; 37. A.E.R. Gilligan.

68

Down: 1. jumps; 2. oar; 3. cult; 4. la-CE-ts; 5. urial; 6. pas(t); 8. cloak; 9. unco; 10. norman; 11. yaws; 14. togas; 18. bills; 19. ringers; 22. are(a); 23. holy; 25. halo; 26. urea; 27. (Headin)gley, cricket ground; 28. loam; 29. névé; 31. ceorl; 34. Hel; 36. chalet; 37. manna; 39. Fulvia; 41. bided; 43. toads; 44. agley; 45. (Porfirio) Diaz; 46. shoo; 48. aria; 50. mew; 52. obi.

J	A	C	C	H	U	S	B	L	E	N	N	Y
U	R	U	S	X	I	P	H	O	S	U	R	A
P	O	T	T	O	R	A	C	C	O	O	N	S
M	A	L	A	B	A	R	R	A	T	C	O	W
S	E	W	E	L	L	E	L	K	A	A	M	A
Y	A	F	F	L	E	N	Y	L	G	H	A	U
G	R	O	U	S	E	S	H	O	W	L	E	R
L	E	M	M	I	N	G	O	R	I	O	L	E
E	L	A	N	D	V	I	S	C	A	C	H	A
Z	H	O	A	B	E	R	D	E	V	I	N	E
A	T	O	A	D	L	E	T	Q	U	A	I	L
I	C	H	N	E	U	M	O	N	F	R	O	G
D	A	S	S	I	E	W	A	L	L	A	B	Y

69

S	E	R	K	A	L	I	S	O	N	S	E
R	G	E	N	T	I	L	I	T	I	A	N
A	R	G	O	L	B	L	T	E	L	L	D
T	E	A	C	H	I	E	T	C	O	T	O
K	T	L	K	A	D	R	I	A	T	I	C
A	L	I	E	N	O	R	N	R	O	S	A
N	E	A	R	A	O	C	E	A	N	E	R
G	O	B	U	R	R	A	S	P	A	M	D
A	V	A	P	G	A	S	S	A	G	A	I
R	I	S	H	I	D	I	S	C	E	N	A
O	V	E	R	L	A	N	D	E	R	S	L
O	O	R	I	E	R	O	U	S	S	E	L

Across: 7. so-N.S.E.; 12. I lit in gentian; 13. log-r-a (rev.); 17. anag. in ad-ric(h); 30. s-saga in A1; 32. sc-Ena (*Coronation St.*); 35. anag.+L.

Down: 2. (r)egret; 3. big cigar; 4. k in pure conk (rev.); 5. I bid in lo; 6. (k)iller, fatal disease; 7. ti in anag.; 10. anag.+dial; 11. Ra+kang in tar+oo; 21. i.e. on agers; 24. a sin in co., & lit.; 26. se(t) in bar; 27. Ada(m) in RR; 29. Tel-Aviv-O less a let (rev.).

Azed's fiancée: Alison Sergent (see first two rows).

70

```
C A R N Y F O O T R A S
U V O E P I R R H E M A
R I A T A R C H I D E D
L A N T S K I P G B N D
I T P L P I N W H E E L
N O S E A N E O S A G E
G R E G O S S A T R A P
S U P E R A T E O D L I
T N H R S P A W W E L L
O P I A T E T M E R I L
N E T H E L E S S S C A
E G E S T E D O T T E R
```

Across: 1. narky, R in cany; 12. tiara, R+a in ita; 14. scant lip; 16. whin peel; 17. zone Inn; 18. SA in ego (rev.); 20. gay grow; 23. rat sap, a in strap; 27. war spell; 30. board marker (1st prize by R. A. Mostyn); 31. leather ness.

Down: 1. sterling cone, nuts=mad; 3. bay gee (g)roan; 5. cur fin; 6. ire sawn; 8. bed reared; 9. enema (rev.); 10. paddle siller, l in anag.+ill a R; 15. fee site; 19. sally gee; 23. tasted; 24. wo Test; 28. anag.

```
A N I N E T I S M T R A
N I D E N A C E A E U M
T R I S U L A I R E T E
I V T S V E N D I S E S
N A R I V E S E M W A L
E N A M E R U R B A N A
G I L P E Y O L A T I N
G C A E S B R E S E C T
H A I R C U T S S R O R
E V O E U T E R P E N E
A I U N D E R G E T I C
D A S T O A S T R A C K
```

71

Across: 1. animal magnetism; 8. tradesman('s entrance); 11. noontide; 12. Pandanaceae; 14. redingote; 17. narrative; 20. stage-name; 22. anag. in gey; 25. dog-Latin; lat(e) in; 32. evocate; 34. undertaking; 35. zoetic; (ass)et ic(y); 36. lambdas.

Down: 1. amarantin; 2. 1 r van in in (rev.)+C; 3. nest-eggs; 4. tale-bearers; 5. barbicans; 6. sea-spider; 9. runagate; 15. tralatitious; r ala in anag.; 18. impermanent; 20. egg+e in had. ref. Observer OUP comp.; 24. assorters; 26. bu(shy)+tea; 30. Batavia; 31. spin-drier.

72

```
C H A T O N C A M P F G
W A L E G U E R I L L A
S I V C C A N I T I E S
P R E H E N S O R I A L
A L O N E C U T A B P I
N I L O T E S P I R I T
I N U L I N A S L E E P
N E S O C O G L A C E
T R I G O N O M E T E R
R U M I N A N T U H N R
A I R S T R I P S E E P
Y N S T E Y C H E R R Y
```

Across: 16. (A.B)alone; 21. Inu-l-i(t)-n.

Down: 3. Al-v.-EO-l-U.S.

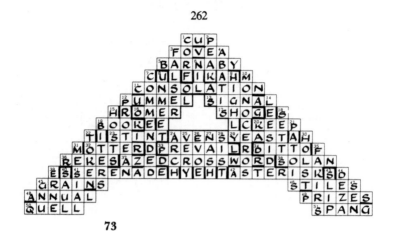

73

Across: 1. c-up & lit., ref. Azed comp.; 5.
RNA; 16. hidden & lit.; 19,22. ref. Azed
comp. 24. U (abbr.); 24. ye-as-t & lit.; 32.
'otter; 37. swor(e) in anag. & lit.; 42. ref:
Azed comp.; 45. 2 mngs; 48,11,49. ref. Azed
comp.

Down: 1. froc(k) rev.; 3. LSE; 6. Nil(e); 10.
Lion & Unicorn; 14. Francis Lee; 19. anag.
& lit.; 21. pa-tois(E); 24. abbr.; 25,9,7.
highly in anag. & mended; ref. Azed comp.;
27. Beau Nash; 30. Gustav Holst; 35. anag.
& lit.; 39. erne(2) (Ernie); 43. def. & lit. ref.
Azed comp.; 47. sen(SEN).

74

Themeword A: Torquemada
(variations: Adam, roquet;
amoret, quad—
anagrams)

Themeword B: Ximenes (variations:
rays, chromosome—
words prefaced by X–)

Themeword C: Azed (variations:
alpha, omega—Greek
equivalents of A and Z)

Across: 21. Tycho Brahe, astronomer.

Down: 3. a guy (rev.—i.e. standing on its
head); 4. whi(te)r; 5. argo(n); 7. I+anag. of
lumps+I've; 8. Fe in mottes; 9. nob(b)ler;
11. set+a; 19. flag+(lo in tee) rev.; 22. r.
in ore+ry; 23. (h)alloa (near Dollar in
Scotland); 26. E.ras; 27. d in toy; 31. de(l)ft.

75

263

```
W O D E H O U S E S F A
E A R R I N G O R C I N
L E I R L E L E G A T E
L I V E L Y Y M O L Z L
S S E E B R O O T A G E
K E L P I E Q U I R E S
S N A I L S A S S A R T
C H I S L E V E M L A E
R O R C Y U A T T I L A
A W M O U S N R O D D S
W E E P Y E T A L A G E
L R N E U R I P I D E S
```

Clue types with word breaks for PD

Across: 1. DLM; 2. PD, tow/s; 11. PD, po/em; 12. DLM; 14. PD, stab/s; 15. DLM; 18. DLM; 19. DLM; 20. PD, re/port; 21. PD, r/ub; 23. PD, w/reath; 25. DLM; 28. PD, chap/ter; 29. DLM; 30. DLM; 31. PD, s/et; 32. PD, l/ather; 33. DLM.

Down: 1. PD, po/et; 2. DLM; 3. PD, t/ar (Mike Yarwood, Harry Worth); 4. PD, M/all; 5. DLM; 6. DLM; 7. PD, ra/ise; 8. DLM; 9. PD, ad/s; 13. DLM; 16. DLM; 17. DLM; 21. PD, worm/ing; 22. PD, f/acing; 23. PD, as/s; 24. DLM; 26. DLM; 27. PD, mo/und.

76

```
C A D A V E R M I M I C
O X I D E B E A T E N R
N E G A T E S T E A D Y
S D E P O S I T M T I P
E R S T C O D E Y H A T
R E T E S S E R A E N O
V E L D T O N T W A N G
A L E D I S C E N D O R
T E N I N T E N T A V A
O R N A T E S E E R I P
R S I L E N T M A T C H
Y I E L D O D Y S S E Y
```

The first four clues written by Sir Leonard led to negate (ne-gat-e), tesserae (anag.), Endor (end+or) and so-so (S.O.S.+O) and the fifth was the devious indication of where to look for the murderer. It led to the word 'diagram' (aid(rev.)+gram), which told the Inspector to look not at the puzzle, but at the bars which separated the words. These bars are in the shape of Lucius I. Festhill, whom he promptly and correctly arrested.

77

```
C O R N I C H E L A D A
A G L O W O I V E N A L
D A U V E L L H M T T F
I M P A L A L O U I S A
L O S E L O M E R L U B
L O T U S S A L O O N O
A F A L C O N P I P A L
C O N R F E E D I D O
M I D G E T M A G N U M
A L I I D T I R O E S I
T E N S E O N S L E E T
E D G E S P I T F I R E
```

Used cars:
7D. Elan; 8. Volvo; 12. Daf; 14. Polo; 16. Audi; 17. Dodge; 18. Fiat; 19. Ghia; 21. Honda; 25Ac. Llama; 26Ac. Saab; 27. Maxi; 31D. Ford; 35. Opel; 38. Robin.

78

Title/4th circuit/corrected misprints = I-SPY/
WITH MY LITTLE EYE SOMETHING/
BEGINNING WITH ALL BUT Q AND
Y.

Corrected misprints/JUMBLES: 1. *b*ones;
2. *e*ats; 3. *s*og; 4. HUNGER; 5. Cast*i*lian;
6. ORCINE; 7. *n*ote; 8. GOTTEN;
9. GLOZER; 10. *p*lanes; 11. *i*nformed;
12. CREWEL; 13. *t*inted; 14. DEVISE;
15. *g*ood; 16. SALUTE; 17. VISHNU;
18. *w*orked; 19. MESAIL; 20. *d*itty;
21. *t*umour; 22. DEPUTY; 23. *h*omes;
24. CAJOLE; 25. YEXING; 26. EFFIGY;
27. STRAWY; 28. *b*race; 29. TOILER;
30. *l*eader; 31. LOLLOP; 32. *r*oll;
33. *b*arrier; 34. BERTHA; 35. ARKITE;
36. *g*uts; 37. BARYTA; 38. *t*urned;
39. MARTEN; 40. *q*uits; 41. *c*ape;
42. SPURNS; 43. *n*uts; 44. GHOSTS;
45. POSSUM; 46. *d*uke; 47. VALVES;
48. rub*y*.

79

Word chain 1–
JESSE; STIR;
SLEAVES;
RADE;
DRUG; FAST;
TINEA;
NURSE; get;
BELTED;
MESH; age;
dey; SNEER;
EATS; err;
RANGE;
EBAUCHE;
DARGA;
DELAY;
REVIE;
NEAT; LELY;
SINCERE;
PRAU; sue;
URAO;
RABBET;
ALEE;
ESILE;
SHOE;
ZAPTIEH.

Word chain –1
JERID;
PEGS; red;
GEIT;
HEARE;
CLUB; eau;
ALBEE;
SURED;
BOAT; SIEN;
NULL;
SUMATRA;
dee; NETE;
AVER; DATE;
FRENZY;
ARREAR;
SARGE;
HESSE;
PERT;
HYEN; SEAL;
TETE;
EASSEL;
HELICES;
gas; ORES;
RIBES;
VAUTE;
DAINE; gay.

80

The puzzle was published ten (X and no. of
letters latent clues that omitted X) years
after the death of Ximenes (X). Hence the
X-shaped message: In Memoriam Derrick
Macnutt. The clue types are those invented
by X.

Appendices

266

Appendix 1

Some common indicators for one, two and three letters

This list is by no means comprehensive, and is designed for the solver to browse through rather than refer to for specific answers. Ideally we should provide another appendix where the solver can look up 'doctor' to find DR, GP, MP, MD, MO etc., but it is beyond the scope of this book to provide a crossword dictionary. Such dictionaries do, however, exist (see Appendix 2).

| * = | used mostly in advanced cryptics |
| + = | unsound/not liked by all Ximeneans |

A	one* [not used by all setters of everyday cryptics, more common in Azed etc]; adult [as once used to denote certain films]; note + ; key +
AB	able-bodied seaman *(sailor, tar)*
ABE	Lincoln [Abraham]
AC	alternating current; account *(bill)*
ACC	account *(bill)*
ACE	card; champion; expert; one; pilot; service (tennis)
ACT	decree; performance
AD	In the year of our Lord *(in the modern age)*; advertisement *(notice, promotion* etc.)
ADD	sum; tot
ADO	fuss
AG	silver
AGE	(long) time, mature, period
AI	first class [the letter I and the number 1 are mutually transposable in crosswords]
AIR	appearance; display
AL	Aluminium; Alan; Albert; Capone
ALE	beer
ALL	completely; everybody; everything
ALP	mountain, peak
AM	in the morning; American
AN	one* [see A above]
ANT	worker [working insect]
APE	copy; primate
ARC	curve
ARM	limb; member
ART	contrivance; craft; cunning; painting; skill
AS	when

ATE	(goddess of) mischief
AU	gold, to the French
AY	yes
AZ	Azed* [most frequently in his puzzles]
B	British; black; born; bowled; book*; note + ; key +
BA	Bachelor of Arts (bachelor, scholar, graduate etc.)
BAN	curse, outlaw, prohibition
BAR	Inn; prevent; pub; save
BE	exist; live
BEE	worker [working insect]
BIT	chewed; piece
BR	British Rail (railways); branch; brown*
BRA	female support(er); undergarment
C	100; carbon; conservative; circa (about, around, roughly etc.); caught; cold; note + ; key +
CA	accountant; circa (about)
CAN	is able to (able to +); vessel etc.
CC	two hundred
CE	Church of England (church)
CH	church; child; Companion of Honour (companion)
CHA	tea
CHE	revolutionary; guerrilla [Guevara]
CI	Channel Islands; 101
CIA	spies
CL	chlorine; 150
CO	care of; commanding officer (commander); company
COL	pass, neck
CON	study, trick
COT	bed
CR	credit
CS	Civil Service
CU	copper
D	500 (many +); (old) penny; dead; died; note + ; key +
DA	District Attorney (American lawyer); dagger*
DAM	barrier; restrain
DD	doctor of divinity (doctor, theologian)
DE	of French
DEE	river
DEN	study; retreat
DI	Diana (Princess); 501
DIS	Pluto; hell; underworld etc.
DO	act; cheat; cook; ditto (the same); note; party; work
DON	fellow; nobleman; put on; university teacher
DR	doctor [also clued by MB, MO]
DU	of the French
E	East; Eastern; energy + ; English; note + ; key +
EA	each; river*
EAR	listener; organ; spike*
EC	London district
ED	editor (journalist); Edward
EER	always
EG	for example, for instance

EGG	bomb; cocktail; encourage
EL	the Spanish
ELI	priest
ELL	measure;length
ELY	see
EM	printer's measure *(measure)*; them
EN	printer's measure *(measure)*
EON	age
EP	extended play *(disc, record)*; epistle *(letter* or *short letter,* short denoting abbreviation)
ER	hesitation; (the) Queen
ERA	time, age
ERE	always
ERR	blunder; sin; wander
ET	and French
EX	former, one-time
EXE	river
F	female; feminine; foot; forte *(loud)*; note + ; key +
FA	note
FE	iron
FF	fortissimo *(very loud)*
FO	Foreign Office
FR	Father; French
FT	feet; foot
G	gramme; note + ; key +
GAL	girl
GEL	jelly
GEN	low down; information
GG	Gee-gee [i.e. a horse]
GI	American soldier *(soldier, doughboy* etc.)
GO	bargain; energy: in good condition; ready; success; work
GR	King George
H	hard; hospital; hot; hydrogen
HA	laugh
HAM	(poor) actor
HAS	bears
HE	His Excellency *(ambassador)*; (high) explosive; the man
HER	the woman('s)
HI	hello
HM	His or Her Majesty
HO	house
HP	hire purchase *(never-never)*
HR	hour
HT	high tension
I	one
IC	in charge
ICE	diamonds
ID	fish; I had; I would
IDE	fish
IE	that is (that's)
IF	provided
II	eleven

IL	the Italian
ILL	badly; unwell etc. [these words are also used as anagram indicators]
IM	I am
IMP	little devil; mischievous child etc.
IN	at home; batting; in fashion; not out; wearing
IO	ten
IRE	anger; rage etc.
IS	exists; island
ISM	theory
IT	Italian; sex-appeal *(SA)*; the thing
IV	four
IX	nine
JE	In Paris, I; I, being French etc
JO	little woman
K	constant; thousand; King
KA	double*; genius*
KM	kilometre
KO	kick off, knock out *(decisive blow)*
L	50 (many +); lake, Liberal, learner *(inexperienced driver, novice* etc.); left; pound; *(sovereign)*
LA	the French; Los Angeles; note; look*
LAB	Labour
LAM	beat, pound
LB	pound
LE	the French
LEG	limb; member
LEI	wreath*
LES	the French
LET	allow(ed); hindrance; permit(ted)
LI	51
LIT	drunk; loaded; settled
LO	look, see
LOG	record
LOT	large amount
LP	long playing *(record)*
LT	Lieutenant
M	1000 (many +); married, male; masculine; maiden over *(maiden)*
MA	Master of Arts *(master, scholar, graduate* etc.); mother
MB	doctor
MC	master of ceremonies
MD	1500; doctor
MI	motorway; note
MO	doctor; short time *(second* etc)
MP	member of parliament *(member, politician, representative* etc.); mounted police; military police *(mountie(s))*
MR	mister
MS	manuscript *(handwriting, writing)*
MU	Greek character
MUM	mother; quiet
MY	gracious me etc.
N	nitrogen; North; Northern; pole +

NB	nota bene *(note)*
NE	north-east
NET	capture etc.; fabric etc.
NI	Northern Ireland *(Ulster)*
NIL	love; nothing
NO	refusal; number
NT	New Testament *(part of Bible, book(s) etc.)*
NU	Greek character
NW	north-west
NY	New York
O	zero *(duck, love, nil, ring, round* etc.); oxygen
OC	Officer Commanding *(commander)*
OK	okay *(all right)*
ON	about; being broadcast; leg[cricket]; on the menu etc.
OP	opus *(work)*; operation
OR	alternatively; before*; gold, yellow
OS	Ordinary Seaman *(sailor)*; outsize *(very large)*
OT	Old Testament *(part of Bible, book(s)* etc)
OX	bull
OZ	ounce; wizard place
P	page; parking; *penny;* piano *(softly)*; power; president
PA	father
PAR	standard
PAS	dance; step
PC	policeman *(copper)*
PE	physical education; gym
PEN	author; writer; enclosure; prison
PER	by, for each
PET	favourite; cherished
PI	confusion*; Greek character; religious
PM	Prime Minister; in the afternoon
PO	Post Office; river *(Italian flower)*
PP	pianissimo *(very softly)*
PR	prince; price; public relations
PRO	for; public relations officer
PS	postscript *(second thoughts* etc)
PT	physical training
Q	Queen
R	King; Queen; right; river; take*
RA	Royal Academy, Royal Academician *(artist)*; Royal Artillery *(gunner(s))*; sun (god)
RAB	Butler [R. A. Butler]
RAM	butter; sheep
RAT	desert(er); scab
RC	Roman Catholic
RD	road
RE	about (concerning, touching etc.); Royal Engineer(s) *(engineer(s), sapper(s))*; religious education; note etc.
RED	bloody; cent*; communist; revolutionary
REP	agent; traveller
RET	soak
REV	vicar etc.

RM	Royal Marine(s) *(jolly)*
RN	(Royal) Navy
ROT	corruption; decay; rubbish etc.
RR	Right Reverend *(bishop)*; Rolls Royce
RT	right
RU	rugby
RUN	manage
RY	railway *(rail, line(s))*
S	South, Southern; pole + ; Saint
SA	South Africa; South America; sex appeal *(it)*
SE	south-east
SEA	main
SET	put; group etc.
SH	quiet [interjection]
SHE	the woman, novel [Rider Haggard]
SIN	err; evil; wrong etc.
SO	therefore; well; note
SP	starting price *(odds)*
SPA	spring
SPY	agent
SS	steamship *(ship)* [*on board* or *on board ship* denotes that something is to be placed inside the letters SS]; saints; Sunday School
ST	saint *(good man* etc.); street *(thoroughfare* etc.); stone
STY	filthy place
SUB	substitute; stand-in etc.
SW	south-west
T	model + [old Ford car, favoured by Araucaria in the *Guardian*]; time
TA	Territorial Army *(army, terriers, volunteers)*; thank you, thanks
TAN	beat; brown
TAR	sailor
TE	Lawrence; note
TED	Edward; Heath
TEE	peg
THE	article
TIC	spasm; twitching etc.; note
TIN	money; cash; vessel
TIT	bird
TOM	big bell; cat
TON	hundred; weight; large amount
TOR	hell
TRY	attempt; essay etc.
TT	thank you, teetotal, teetotaller *(abstaining, dry, on the wagon* etc.); race [bikes on Isle of Man]
U	Universal (film certificate) *(for all to see, on view to all, suitable for children* etc.); upper class *(uppish, socially acceptable, posh, superior* etc.)
UK	United Kingdom
UN	United Nations
UP	in court; excited
UR	old city [from whence came Abraham]
US	America; American; you and me

USE	application; custom; employ(ment); practice; practise
V	five; verse; versus (*against, opposing* etc.)
VI	six
VOL	volume
W	West; Western
WE	you and I
WI	West Indies
X	cross (*kiss, sign of love* etc.); ten
XI	eleven (*team* etc.)
Y	yard; year
YE	you [old]
YR	year, your
ZO	cross*
ZZ	(sound of) snoring

Appendix 2: Bibliography

Further reading and further solving

Other Books on Crossword Theory

Afrit's book (*Armchair Crosswords*, Warne, 1949) has long been out of print (and it is not held by either the Bodleian Library or the British Library). The preface is short and the most significant section is reproduced in this book on p.59. The main books known to the author are:

Anatomy of the Crossword by D. St. P. Barnard (Bell, 1963)
Ximenes on the Art of the Crossword by D. S. Macnutt (Methuen, 1966)
Crosswords by Alec Robins (Teach Yourself Books, Hodder and Stoughton, 1975): subsequently revised as *The ABC of Crosswords* (Corgi, 1981).

These three are also (alas) out of print. In print are:

How to do Crosswords Better by May Abbott (Collins, 1975): an entertaining book by the *Daily Telegraph* crossword editor with many illustrations on how to clue the word TRAIN, also a glossary. Sadly it is non-Ximenean.
Crossword Solving by Don Putnam (EP Publishing, Know the Game Series, 1975): crisp and to the point, by the former crossword editor of *Games and Puzzles*.

Books on Crossword History

The books by Barnard, Macnutt and Robins have interesting historical components. For further reading consult:
The Strange World of the Crossword by Roger Millington (Hobbs/Joseph, 1974; Coronet, 1976)
A History of the Crossword Puzzle by Michelle Arnot (Random House, 1981; Macmillan Papermac (1982).

Both are strong on early US history and contain many interesting puzzles including the 'leadergram' or 'double-crostic', a close relation to the crossword.

Solvers' and Setters' Aids

The Complete Cruciverbalist by Stan Kurzban and Mel Rosen (Van Nostrand Reinhold, 1981) offers advice on how to solve and how to compose puzzles for the American market, giving a very good insight into the different forms of plain puzzle. It also offers advice on cryptic puzzles, and Chapter 1 provides a 'history of cruciverbalism'.

Chambers 20th Century Dictionary (W & R Chambers, latest edn. 1983) must be the crossworder's ('cruciverbalist's'?) 'bible', but *Collins English Dictionary* also has its merits (with the inclusion of proper nouns), and the whole range of Oxford Dictionaries from the *Concise* to the full *Oxford English Dictionary* can be useful. For American words and meanings it is desirable to have *Webster's Third International Dictionary* accessible, especially for advanced puzzles.

Access to the *Encyclopaedia Britannica* is useful, but it is cheaper to possess a one-volume encyclopedia (two or three on the market at £15-£20—no obvious preference). An atlas is handy, and *The Times Concise Atlas of the World* is adequate for most purposes. For useful lists there are a number of books including *The Hamlyn Crossword Dictionary* (first published by C. Arthur Pearson in 1932 and now retitled *The Newnes Crossword Dictionary*). The best thesaurus for definitions is probably the Harper & Row edition of *Roget's Thesaurus*, though you must make allowances for American spelling.

OUP produces many fine reference books. The most useful for the crossword enthusiasts is probably *The Oxford Dictionary of Quotations*. This is much used by setters for literary references, as are *Brewer's Dictionary of Phrase and Fable* (published by Cassell) and *Everyman's Dictionary of Fictional Characters* (published by Dent). Make sure you buy the latest UK edition of *Brewer's* published by Cassell and not the facsimile edition (published in the US on cheap paper and sold in the UK at a 'bargain price').

The list of possible reference books could be endless, but mention should be made of a set of three American books discoverable in larger public libraries: *The New Century Cyclopedia of Names*. For proper nouns it is magnificent.

Solvers and setters who want a particular word with particular letters can use *Chambers Words* (words listed alphabetically under length) and *Chambers Anagrams*, and there are other anagram dictionaries on the market.

For help starting at the end of a word *Walker's Rhyming Dictionary* published by Routledge & Kegan Paul is useful. Also recommended are *The Crossword Completion Dictionary* compiled by R. J. Edwards, one of a number of crossword reference books published by Stanley Paul, *Cassell's Crossword Finisher* by John Griffiths (1985 paperback), and *Chambers Back-Words for Crosswords* (compiled by J. C. P. Schwarz, 1986). *The Modern Crossword Dictionary* (Pan) contains lists of useful phrases as well as words.

A number of books offer an 'inverse' to my Appendix 1, so that you can look up SAILOR to discover AB, RATING, SALT and TAR. Some are excessive, taking the opportunity to list almost every conceivable battle, for instance. I would, however, recommend Adrian Room's *Dictionary of Cryptic Crossword Clues,* a fairly recent (1983) publication for Routledge & Kegan Paul, which offers a 'crib' followed by 'illustrative clues'. Afrit is misquoted and many of the clues are lamentably non-Ximenean. The book does, however, give a fair picture of modern practice. Also available is *The*

Complete Crossword Companion by Jeremy Howard-Williams (Panther, 1985) which has a bizarre entry under 'Hidden word'.

Further Solving

Crosswords abound, in papers, magazines and books, as never before. You should be able to find your level of 'extension material' in the shops. For those who want to advance beyond the daily 15 × 15 cryptic I recommend *Tough Puzzles* (available monthly on subscription only: Details from BEAP Ltd., Glenthorne House, Hammersmith Grove, London, W6 0LG). This contains a novelty puzzle each month that offers a foretaste of the more advanced cryptics. Azed, Mephisto, Salamanca *(New Statesman)* and *The Listener* are all easily obtainable, but joining the Crossword Club is also recommended. In their magazine *Crossword* you will find very hard puzzles along with clue competitions, discussions, articles and the occasional gossip column from your author. For details write to The Editor, Hilberry Farm, Awbridge Hill, Romsey, Hants, SO5 0HE.

By now you have more than enough to get started—but don't get on the train without a pencil!